Center for Basque Studies
Conference Papers Series, No. 6

Knowledge Communities

EDITED BY

Javier Echeverría, Andoni Alonso, and Pedro J. Oiarzabal

Conference Papers Series
Center for Basque Studies
University of Nevada, Reno

This book was published with generous financial support from the Basque Government.

Center for Basque Studies
Conference Papers Series, No. 6
Series Editor: Joseba Zulaika

Center for Basque Studies
University of Nevada, Reno
Reno, Nevada 89557
http://basque.unr.edu

Cover and Series design © 2011 Jose Luis Agote.
Cover illustration: Juan Azpeitia.

Library of Congress Cataloging-in-Publication Data

Knowledge communities / edited by Javier Echeverria, Andoni Alonso, and Pedro
    J. Oiarzabal. -- 1st ed.
     p. cm. -- (Conference papers series ; no. 6)
Includes index.
Conference proceedings.
Summary: "Collection of articles from the Knowledge Communities Conference on
    information cultures and communities"--Provided by publisher.
ISBN 978-1-877802-97-3 (hardcover)
1. Information technology--Social aspects--Congresses. 2. Information society--
    Congresses. 3. Communities of practice--Congresses. 4. Knowledge management--
    Congresses. 5. Community life--Congresses. 6. Computers and civilization--
    Congresses. I. Echeverr?a, Javier. II. Alonso, Andoni, 1966- III. Oiarzabal, Pedro J.
    IV. Title. V. Series.

HM851.K596 2010
303.48'33--dc22

2010045337

CONTENTS

Part 3—Arts

Part 4—Online

Introduction—From Communities of Practice to Knowledge Communities

JAVIER ECHEVERRÍA, ANDONI ALONSO, and PEDRO J. OIARZABAL

The communities of practice concept has been used since the 1990s by those specialized in knowledge management, with the purpose of analyzing and promoting the transfer of knowledge within a business or other institution type. However, two cognitive anthropologists, Jean Lave and Etienne Wenger, were the first ones to use such a concept to refer to a group of people who share a particular interest, activity, and occupation, and were able to generate a learning process, which in turn created knowledge at both individual and collective levels.[1]

Lave and Wenger define communities of practice as "a set of relations among persons, activity and world, over time in relation with other tangential and overlapping CoPs [communities of practice]."[2] By sharing information and experiences, members of the group are able to generate common knowledge, which would define both the group and its members. In fact, Lave and Wenger argue that this sharing is "an intrinsic condition for the existence of knowledge."[3] The specific cases that they analyzed were: nondrinking alcoholics, Goa tailors, quartermasters, butchers, and Yucatan midwives. The authors opened up a new perspective of analysis within the discipline of cognitive anthropology and the theory of social exchange.

Lave and Wenger define "situated learning" as the model of learning in a community of practice, which resulted from those practices as well as from the participation in the activities of a given group. Their proposal was well accepted, and the notion of

---

1. Lave and Wenger, *Situated Learning*.

2. Ibid., 98.

3. Ibid.

communities of practice became an analytical tool for sociology, anthropology, and innovation studies. Since then, diverse social and professional activities have been analyzed using such a conceptual framework: flute makers, photocopier technicians at Xerox, and international organizations.[4] In every single case, the resolution of any problem was obtained by claiming a previous knowledge gained from working and experience, which had been stored in the memory of some of the members of the community of practice. Otherwise, the problem was resolved by confronting it collectively and looking for a solution on a trial-and-error base (*learning by doing*, but collectively). This created a knowledge that became a common patrimony of the community of practice.

Initially, only those communities that have a physical presence were analyzed, but the model was soon applied to the study of spatially dispersed communities, including virtual communities on the Internet. A prime example of Internet communities is the Free Software movement, in which innovation and technological development is carried out by communities of practice that are distributed across cyberspace and interconnected by the Internet.

As seen, the application fields of this new concept were from the beginning quite varied. Paul M. Hildreth and Chris Kimble have analyzed in detail the diverse meanings of the notion "communities of practice" in recent years, evidencing its evolution to the point that a new concept, "knowledge networks," has emerged, becoming quite relevant to study the "network society."[5] Interactive learning processes and the development of activities on the Internet are two of the great changes provoked by the emergence of telematics networks. That is why communities that develop activities online are so significant. They create knowledge that is distributed among many knowledge networks.

In sum, Lave and Wenger's "communities of practice" conceptual innovation, which began studying learning processes, has increasingly widened its semantic meaning over the past few years. It has become an important analytical tool for the management and dissemination of knowledge. The same happened to the concept of "innovation," closely linked to the concept of communities of practice. Back in 1992, the Organisation for Economic Co-operation and Development's *Oslo Manual*, an international source of guidelines for empirical studies on innovation, only focused on the technological innovation of products. However, in its second version (1997), the manual began to address process innovation, while its 2003 version included another two types of innovation: organizational and marketing. As evidence shows that communities of practice act as innovation agents, their diverse connotations have to be studied parallel to the evolution of the concept of innovation, which in turn has increased its semantic meaning.

The goal of the book is to study the concept of communities of knowledge, which goes beyond the notion of communities of practice, as a way to analyze the structure of

---

4. Cook and Yanow, "Culture and Organizational Learning"; Orr, *Talking about Machines*; and Hildreth, Kimble, and Wright, "Communities of Practice in the Distributed International Environment."

5. Hildreth and Kimble, *Knowledge Networks*; Castells, *The Rise of the Network Society*.

the emergent knowledge societies. If we believe that a complex society has to be integrated by various and heterogeneous communities, *a knowledge society should be based on the plurality of communities of knowledge*. This was the main hypothesis behind the organization of the International Conference on Knowledge Communities, on which this book is based. A selection of updated versions of the papers presented at the conference is found in this volume. The conference took place at the Mathewson-IGT Knowledge Center, University of Nevada, Reno, on April 23–25, 2009, and was sponsored by the Center for Basque Studies.

Our intention was to examine the structure of knowledge-based societies, while exploring new modalities of innovation, in addition to those based on science (e.g., e-science) and engineering. To do so, we had to widen the concept of communities of practice, resulting in an examination of the concept of knowledge communities. Consequently, we called for original papers addressing scientific, engineering, and artistic communities as well as online communities with particular interest in the development of knowledge societies. There are knowledge communities such as the archivist ones or those in favor of free knowledge, whose work is essential for a knowledge society, because they link together other knowledge communities through the applications that they develop and share.

It was not possible to analyze all the relevant communities in a knowledge society in one book, so here we address four broad types of communities: "Science," "Free Knowledge," "Arts," and "Online." Seventeen scholars from multiple disciplines (e.g., art history, economics, fine arts, philosophy, physics, political science, social anthropology, and sociology) and fields (e.g., diaspora, Internet, migration, science, and Web studies) open a fresh academic dialogue on the complexity of knowledge communities. They explore whether such communities can generate real knowledge societies that could potentially contribute to economic, social, and political advantages for the whole population, facilitating technological development and innovation.

The book is divided into four parts as it focuses on the aforementioned four generic knowledge communities. It was our intention to present a wide range of interdisciplinary works on various knowledge communities in order to provide the reader diverse perspectives on the subject.

Part 1, "Science," compiles four chapters that focus on how science organizes communities of knowledge. Science and technology are among the main factors that explain how contemporary knowledge communities work as well as their significance. Historical perspective and case study are the two basic methodologies used in this first part of the book.

Javier Echeverría takes the Popperian notion of "intersubjective knowledge" in science to advance the concept of community as well as to identify different properties of communities of knowledge. Those properties require an examination of common questions such as what, when, and where (according to Aristotelian taxonomy). Basic knowledge communities are created first by languages that allow a flux of information among speakers, and at the same time can transform users into producers of knowledge. However, the naturalistic approach only partially explains communities of knowledge. Therefore, there is a need to include other factors such as civil structure, where values play a fundamental role. History shows us the emergence of different communities of knowledge and how they interact with urban spaces. Cities (*epistemopolis*) become the locus for knowledge communities, which rely on previous experiences as described by Tomas S. Kuhn. New spaces such as the digital open up new possibilities and accordingly new types of communities of knowledge. Meanwhile, values are defined by the need to transform knowledge into a public good because communities alone do not guarantee the free flow of information. Therefore, the main task of city governance is to embed values within those communities in order to ease the flow of information.

Probably one of the most fascinating knowledge communities at the present moment relates to the issue of global climate change, which is the subject of discussion in Mari Carmen Gallastegui and Ibon Galarraga's chapter. From an economic point of view, this issue has shown the need to modify some concepts such as "human capital," especially in relation to knowledge communities. Global climate change has also shown how knowledge communities have grown from different disciplines and sciences, increasing its value as knowledge. According to Gallastegui and Galarraga, global climate change is an example of the new or "weightless" economy. More sophisticated and aware consumers demand a correspondingly new and more respectful technology with regards to the environment. Yet at the same time, global climate change has introduced new elements into economic analysis such as the existence of a "global public bad" that affects everybody, as opposed to the "global public good" that represents the atmosphere itself. However, the authors argue that it is necessary to find new tools in order to be able to cope with a new set of problems such as uncertainty, internationalization of the issue, and the intra-generational and intergenerational legacy. Somehow, global climate change must be understood as an opportunity to tackle the most serious challenge we are confronting.

Alfonso Unceta and Marcelino Masa present a case study: how the educational network of *ikastolas* (Basque-language schools) can be read as a knowledge community. Education is a core element of knowledge and innovation communities but must be analyzed carefully. It is necessary to distinguish communities of practice from communities of knowledge. The latter requires the former, but the former does not guarantee the latter. To do so it is necessary to change schools from *gesellschaft* (organization) into *gemeinschaft* (community). This implies altering the roles of the different actors inside schools. Also, information and communication technologies (ICTs) fulfill a crucial role for that sense of community as they eliminate obstacles such as time and space and allow access to knowledge. The ikastola network includes 101 schools, 46,000 students, and 3,550 educators, a quite wide educational system in proportion to the Basque population of nearly 3 million. From the 1960s on, this network has undergone different stages due to political and economic changes. ICTs have become a crucial goal for the network with the idea of transforming them into a real community of knowledge.

Ander Gurrutxaga and Álvaro Luna's chapter addresses the interrelation between innovation and knowledge community. Communities, group, home, and other related concepts have a huge gamut of meaning; they are key concepts for sociological theory. Knowledge community implies a specific type of community based on a particular structural context, which is differentiated from other communities. Also, knowledge communities show specific dynamics for what represents "home," how members interact and organize themselves, what the pursued good is, and how information flux happens. The scenario that shelters that type of knowledge community on innovation is, as Echeverría points out, the city. Additionally, Gurrutxaga and Luna analyze three different types of innovation spaces and their own distinct features: American (e.g., Silicon Valley), European (e.g., Finland research spaces), and Asian *technopoles*. Those are successful examples of innovation partially explained by economic and/or technological factors; however, explaining innovation requires still more factors because it is the product of society as a whole.

Part 2, "Free Knowledge," is also arranged into four chapters and deals with the meaning of knowledge community from a philosophical, value-laden point of view. In other words, it addresses what elements—with particular emphasis on its anthropological, political, and ethical issues—are found inside a community of knowledge. Free Knowledge embraces a wide variety of communities of knowledge, distinguishing contemporary from older communities. Among these, Free Software and informal communities that produce knowledge are the most relevant.

Carl Mitcham gathers different definitions of the concept of "knowledge community" while attempting to distinguish different subtypes of communities: communities of practice, knowledge networks, and communities of knowledge. Moreover, Mitcham offers a brief review of the existent bibliography shedding light, from a historical point of view, on the understanding of contemporary knowledge communities. From universities and the "invisible college" (during the 1600s) a distinct knowledge community, maybe a new "invisible college," but with specific features, emerges: the *gesellschaft* substitutes the *gemeinschaft* because practices become increasingly disembedded during the twentieth century. However, ICTs seem to re-embed scattered individuals into what Howard Rheingold coins "virtual community."[6] Again those virtual communities have distinct features if compared to other types of communities. There are doubts about the power of ICTs to create actual communities. What is the strength of the virtual to favor the weight of civil society and the effectiveness to re-embed practices, individuals, and knowledge?

Copyright, patenting, copyleft, and free culture are main topics that attempt to understand knowledge communities produced by ICTs. According to Natxo Rodríguez the existence of a shrinking public domain poses an important challenge to the nature of future knowledge communities. Rodríguez examines, using the metaphor of computers, how to store, distribute, connect, and organize culture. As many of us have experienced,

---

6. Rheingold, *The Virtual Community*.

operating systems make errors, which metaphorically can be applied to explain how contemporary culture clashes with electronic knowledge communities. For instance, P2P culture (Napster, Pirate Bay, and others) has challenged the way that we distribute culture, provoking a harsh reaction from legal and economic realms. Free Software led by Richard Stallman can be read as a reaction against that increasingly oppressive situation created by industry and supported by legal changes. Somehow Free Software and culture should act as a resetting tool for an operating system that is blocked. There are new models to access and distribute knowledge that should be taken into account. Free licenses such as GPL, Creative Commons, and alike are the tools to do this.

The Free Software movement is maybe the most interesting contemporary knowledge community. Christopher Kelty proposes studying Free Software from an anthropological point of view. Because Free Software is a scattered community, it is important to see how its members began to think of themselves as part of a movement. Kelty identifies five elements that played a crucial role to reach the level of a movement. Firstly, there is a core of debates, aims, questions, and strategies that circulated among people. Secondly, sharing the same code was a key factor in promoting the existence of this kind of knowledge community. Thirdly, it was necessary to imagine how the infrastructure for Free Software would be. In other words, "going open" was what made such a community unique in comparison to competitors such as Microsoft. Fourthly, licensing and creating GPL was also an identifying element that differentiated them from competitors, whose products were based on strict copyright and patent legislation. Finally, collaboration and transforming the Internet into Web 2.0 allowed Free Software to disseminate and unite efforts to get a complete and reliable operating system.

Informal knowledge communities have an increasing presence in contemporary societies. Scientific knowledge is being produced and evaluated now not only by scientists and experts but also by laypeople. Knowledge is embedded into a society and has very different practical consequences. Politics and ethics are strong elements that cannot be neglected. Antonio Lafuente and Andoni Alsonso identify five different ethical and political values that are supported from different communities. The "right to know" means the right to have a plural, open, reliable, situated, and assessed knowledge. Environmentalist groups, movements on cryptography, electro-sensitivity, opposition to genetically modified organisms, and nuclear discussions are some examples of how knowledge is produced in an informal way by communities of knowledge as a combination between experts, scientists, and laypeople.

Part 3, "Arts," examines how artistic communities articulate knowledge. The chapters in this section provide an analysis of practical cases with broad reflections on how knowledge communities appear as well as about their values, relevance, and role in contemporary society. Peter Selz, who has devoted his entire life to art history as a professor, author, and curator of pioneering exhibitions, explores the work of the late Jorge Oteiza and Eduardo Chillida—two of the most prominent sculptors of our time. Selz's relation with Oteiza, for example, goes back to the early 1960s. Back then, he was the chief curator of painting and sculpture at the Museum of Modern Art in New York, when he introduced Oteiza's work into the United States as part of the museum's exhibition New Spanish Painting and Sculpture. As Selz walks us through much of the twentieth century's artistic communities in the European continent, he examines the evolution of sculpture and the modernist schools and their avant-garde networked movements, from abstract expressionism to geometric abstraction. Selz places both Basque artists Oteiza and Chillida at the center of an international artistic community immensely preoccupied with the development of sculpture as a three-dimensional artwork, its aesthetic values, and its fundaments regarding volume, "mass," space, and above all, the "void" as "an energy-producing element."

Anna María Guasch and Joseba Zulaika explore Basque artists' initiation trip to Paris, France, as an introduction to the universalizing project of modernity at the turn of the nineteenth century. This immersion into modernism helped Basque artists to build a new type of knowledge community that expanded beyond the geographical confines of the Basque Country. Basque artists met their European counterparts and their modernist trends on painting, sculpture, and architecture. In similar fashion to Selz, Guasch and Zulaika also invite the reader to travel through time as a way to analyze, through the Basque experience, the different layers making up the foundation of artistic communities and movements across Europe. In between local and global aesthetic values, Oteiza and Chillida became the paradigmatic figures who attempted to reconcile the aesthetic practices of contemporary art with the aesthetic practices of traditional art. The following generations riddled with ideological clashes, particularly during Francisco Franco's dictatorship, would also make an attempt to find a balance between tradition and modernity, between elitism and popular culture, between aesthetic values (in constant search for a Basque aesthetic identity) and political values through their own interpretation of social realism, postmodern eclecticism, and the new internationalism.

Part 4, "Online," explores the implication of new technologies for the formation of new types of communities-based knowledge such as crowdsourcing and online communities. Caroline Haythornthwaite analyzes the organization of knowledge communities (e.g., online academia and academic publishing) and knowledge crowds (e.g., Wikipedia) in order to examine the features that distinguish them in the following terms: commitment that an individual has to the collective activity, the networks of knowledge and expertise (e.g., knowledge structure), and the network practices. How are crowd- and community-based knowledge collectives established and maintained? Why do academic knowledge communities, for instance, shift their knowledge distribution practices, from print to online publications?

Haythornthwaite argues that the emergence of distributed communities that coalesce around topics of interest has been unparalleled since the creation of the Internet in quantitative as well as in qualitative terms. This is also true for academic and university library communities as well as for online publications and repositories. As the author states, "The whole notion of online academic publishing is tied to the larger issue of what motivates in their profession, and how orientation to the ideals of open science merges with ideas of open access and the legal platform of creative commons licensing to provide the underpinning change. The difference between a crowd and a community is not in what the collective does, but in how its participants need to pay attention to each other in order for the enterprise to succeed."

Finally, Pedro J. Oiarzabal examines, through the study of the Basque diaspora case, the institutional presence of migrant diasporic communities on the World Wide Web (Web) and the usage over time of various digital platforms such as social network sites. The author explores the establishment of online communities as webs of exchange of information and transfer of knowledge in both the physical and digital worlds. The chapter analyzes a longitudinal study that began in 2005 on the presence of the Basque institutional diaspora on the Web. As of March 2009, the Basque diaspora had formed 211 associations throughout twenty-four countries, of which 135 (or nearly 64 percent) had a presence in cyberspace in twenty countries (or over 83 percent of the total). Between 2005 and 2009 the author studied the evolution of the usage of different digital (networking) platforms by the Basque diaspora and their potential impact on online community-forming (e.g., communities of "friends" based primordially on a common ethnicity) and social networks of informal knowledge. In sum, Oiarzabal argues that the Basque diaspora, through multiple digital profiles, "is promoting a hybrid space [of participation and interaction] by combining different online and offline platforms in order to advance their institutions as well as their sociocultural, recreational, folkloric, linguistic, and political agendas."

Acknowledgments

Knowledge Communities would have not been possible without the support of the authors who took part in this collection, the Center for Basque Studies' staff, faculty, editorial board, and book production team at the University of Reno, Nevada (UNR), and the Mathewson-IGT Knowledge Center at the University of Nevada, Reno as well as the Autonomous Community of the Basque Country, whose financial help facilitated the organization of the International Conference on Knowledge Communities in 2009. We would like to specially acknowledge Jose Luis Agote, Kate Camino, Lisa Corcostegui, Daniel Montero, Howard Rheingold, Cameron Watson, and Steve Zink (Vice-President for Information Technology, and Dean of University Libraries, UNR).

Bibliography

Castells, Manuel. *The Rise of the Network Society*. Malden, MA: Blackwell, 1996.

Cook, S. D. N., and D. Yanow. "Culture and Organizational Learning." *Journal of Management Inquiry*, Vol. 2 (1993): 373–90.

Hildreth, Paul M., Chris Kimble, and Peter Wright. "Communities of Practice in the Distributed International Environment." *Journal of Knowledge Management*, Vol. 29, No. 3 (2000): 273–97.

Hildreth, Paul M. and Chris Kimble. *Knowledge Networks: Innovation through Communities of Practice*. London/Hershey: Idea Group Inc, 2004.

Kuhn, Thomas S. *The Essential Tension: Selected Studies in Scientific Tradition and Change*. Chicago: The University of Chicago Press, 1977.

Lave, Jean and Etienne Wenger. *Situated Learning: Legitimate Peripheral Participation*. Cambridge: Cambridge University Press, 1991.

Orr, J. E. *Talking about Machines*. Ithaca, NY: ILR Press, 1996.

Rheingold, Howard. *The Virtual Community: Homesteading on the Electronic Frontier*. Reading, MA: Addison-Wesley, 1993. Revised edition, Cambridge, MA: MIT Press, 2000.

Part 1
SCIENCE

1

Epistemopolis: From Knowledge Communities to Knowledge Cities

JAVIER ECHEVERRÍA

There are several criteria for determining varieties of knowledge. The most common philosophical distinction starts from the difference between subject and object. From this premise, one finds the opposition between subjective and objective knowledge in a wide range of subdivisions: the cognitive subject can be human or animal, and individual or collective; subjective knowledge can be tacit or explicit;[1] the known object can be natural, social, artificial, and so on. We thus come across an arborescent classification of knowledge that initially depends on the types of subject we are examining, but later subdivides in keeping with the ways of knowing and in accordance with the objects. A doctor, an artist, a scientist, an engineer, a politician, a jurist, and a theologian deal with different objects, and therefore produce different types of knowledge. Some traditional occupations in Europe created important knowledge communities (KCs), such as medieval monasteries or eighteenth-century freemasonry, to mention two antithetical examples. Industrial society gave rise to multiple professions, some of which became KCs, such as the scientific and engineering communities.

There is debate among epistemologists over the objectivity of knowledge. I believe there are greater and lesser degrees of subjectivity and objectivity, although I do not want to address here the controversial subject of epistemological relativism. Instead, I will just

---

1. Polanyi, *Personal Knowledge*.

rely on what Karl Popper observed about science: namely, that scientific communities generate *intersubjective knowledge*.[2] This idea can be extended without any problem to the remaining KCs, and indeed this is what I will do in this presentation where I am only concerned with intersubjective knowledge.

Another important philosophical question concerns the location of knowledge, both in space and time. There is a saying in Spanish, "*El saber no ocupa lugar*" (literally meaning "Knowledge does not take up space," and implying one can never know too much). This is true if we are thinking about physical spaces, but there are other kinds of places, such as social spaces, with their own topologies. Here I will concentrate on intersubjective knowledge *insofar that it is located in different subjects*, in other words, as regards *distributed knowledge*. One canonical example is that of languages, which are not located in any physical space but instead exist among those who speak them, that is, in a social space that is usually termed a *linguistic space*. These spaces are relational and, generally speaking, have a reticular structure with each speaker forming a node in the network. From an ontological point of view, languages are *intersubjectively* located *relational entities*.

Moreover, they are space-time entities because they develop in specific geographical areas and evolve through time. These properties of languages can be extended to other types of intersubjective knowledge. Put another way, intersubjective knowledge is something that is open in space and time, that changes and evolves, even though some of its structures are very stable. Knowledge is something that is well-distributed and cannot be fully possessed by any one subject, whether individual or collective. To paraphrase Heidegger, I would contend that knowledge is not *out there* (*dasein*) but that it is *among* (*zwischensein*). This form of being distributed is typical in relational and functional entities. *To be among* is the general philosophical category that I propose in order to analyze ontologically the different forms of knowledge shared by KCs. Knowledge is not something substantial but rather relational or, if one prefers, shared and distributed. *Gnoscere* is not the same as *cognoscere*. The Latin prefix "co-" adds an important dimension to knowledge: its shared or intersubjective nature. Something similar occurs with the idea of *community*. Here, however, I will just discuss intersubjective shared knowledge that evolves through time, independent of whether it may have a greater or lesser degree of objectivity or subjectivity.

Following these initial ontological reflections, I will offer two epistemological proposals. The first distinguishes three types of knowledge according to three types of environment or exterior world inhabited by human beings. I favor a naturalized epistemology[3] because knowledge, first of all, favors the survival of individuals and species in the biosphere, together with their best adaptation to the natural environment (*physis*). However, naturalized epistemology is not enough. Throughout history human beings have created more and more complex social and urban environments to which individuals as well as

---

2. See Popper, *Objective Knowledge*.

3. See Quine, *From Stimulus to Science*; and Giere, *Explaining Science*.

groups and collectives have had to adapt. Second, knowledge and epistemology are civil entities, since it is not just a question of surviving in nature but also in urban sites (*polis*).

Consequently, naturalized epistemology has to be implemented with a civil or, if one prefers, civilized epistemology. Furthermore, a third type of knowledge has been added to these two in recent decades. The emergence of information and communications technologies (ICTs) and, specifically, the Internet have led to the emergence of a third dimension in the world: the electronic space or the digital world to which human beings also have to adapt, both individually and collectively. Thus, third, epistemology has to be technological or, if one wants, informational, without ceasing to be naturalized or civilized. If we term *physis* (nature) the first environment, *polis* (city, nation, state) the second, and the digital world the third, today we must distinguish three major types of knowledge according to the environment or exterior world to which they refer: nature, the city, or electronic space.[4] As a general hypothesis, I argue that as human beings' environment changes structure, so different types of knowledge emerge, with consequent processes of experimentation, learning, and adaptation.

I will add another epistemological proposal to this distinction of three environments. Subjects make contact with different objects and with the environment, but some of them do so through a very specific cognitive attitude—*questioning* and *inquiry*—that has not been studied widely by logicians and epistemologists.[5] Knowledge is usually taken to mean the content raised by some question, rather than the question itself. However, the cognitive attitude that consists of raising questions and asking oneself about the world is one of the largest sources of creating knowledge. We can try to understand what the world is, what it is like, what its origins are, how big it is, who inhabits it, and so on. We can ask similar questions about ourselves and everyone else. Several kinds of knowledge can be distinguished on the basis of this erotetic criterion: *know what, know how, know how much, know where, know when, know who,* and, last but not least, *know why.* Aristotle and other Greek philosophers privileged this last type of knowledge and attributed it to their own community, that of philosophers. They termed it *episteme* and contrasted it with the *doxa* (opinion, *know what*) common to mortals, on the one hand, and the *techne* (*know how*) of artists and technicians on the other.

Nevertheless, Aristotle also underscored the importance of *know when* (*kairos*) for people's practical lives. It is not enough to have information and knowledge, but moreover one must know the best moment to apply them. Personally, I would also point out the historical importance of *know where* in both the animal and in the human world: for example, in the arts of hunting, fishing, mining, exploration, navigation, and even agriculture. Knowing where a certain resource is, knowing where there is danger, or determining the route to be followed are all forms of knowledge in the strongest sense of the word, since the survival of groups and individuals often depends on them, for example in the case of

---

4. For a more detailed explanation of these proposals, see Echeverría, *Los señores del aire*.

5. There are exceptions, such as erotetic logic.

migrations and exoduses. However, *know when* and *know where* do not normally generate knowledge communities, and are usually the attributes of exceptional individuals such as guides. Choosing the route and the right moment has been decisive for the survival of many people and many tribes throughout history, although such knowledge has not created specific communities, at least in principle.[6] By contrast, there are several occupations and professions that cultivate the concept of *know how much*, such as accountants, surveyors, economists, and statisticians. Just as Aristotle classified ten categories or predicaments for apophantic knowledge (substance, quality, quantity, relation, action, passion, place, time, situation, and custom), so questions might also be classified according to different ways of asking them: questioning or erotetic categories.

There is a third means of analyzing types of knowledge: from the axiological perspective. Before addressing this, I will comment briefly on certain knowledge communities that, in my opinion, should be considered canonical—specifically, linguistic communities and scientific communities.

Languages in the Economies and Societies of Knowledge

One essential kind of knowledge community emerges out of languages. Each language has a lexical and expressive treasure shared by its speakers that contributes a conception of the world (*weltanschauung*) and hence a kind of knowledge. Speaking a language implies possessing the capacity to enter this repository of knowledge. This is not in any specific place but, rather, flows among those who use the language, renewing and updating itself with the passage of generations. Speakers are users of this knowledge, but they also produce and distribute it, alongside storing it in their memory and transmitting it to their descendants. As regards knowledge, we might describe the basic properties of linguistic communities as follows:

- Linguistic communities share distributed knowledge, with this being a common possession that was produced and bequeathed by predecessors, and that must be maintained and developed by current speakers—all of this in every place and at each historic moment.

- Each speaker is a language user, that is, he or she uses the knowledge furnished by the language to relate to the world and the other speakers. Insofar as they are users, they appropriate part of this knowledge and, at the same time, embody it and update it—without the other members losing anything, but rather to the benefit of the community as a whole. Knowledge associated with a language is not diminished by use but instead grows the more people use it and the more often they do so. The economy of linguistic knowledge is not comparable to other economic goods that are usually scarce and tend to diminish the more they are used and consumed.

---

6. It would be beneficial to research more thoroughly whether there are examples of communities based on *know when* and *know where*.

- Beyond being users of this knowledge, speakers can also be its producers, suppliers, distributors, and transmitters. The pluralist model of innovation is applicable to the economy of linguistic knowledge.[7]

- Knowledge associated with a language is collective, but also individual, property. Since a number of languages exist, knowledge transfer among different communities is feasible in the same way that people can transfer knowledge among themselves.

- In each linguistic community there are expert users of the language in question, some of whom become authorities on the language through the creative and innovative ability they demonstrate when using it.

- Insofar as linguistic communities produce different kinds of knowledge (religious, scientific, artistic, social, historic, juridical, technical, environmental, and so forth) and are capable of integrating different sub-communities that cultivate these assorted types of knowledge, the KCs go beyond the purely communitarian phase and evolve into knowledge cities.

These six general properties are useful for common languages but are also applied to formal, computer, and, to cite another kind of example, musical languages. Whoever knows English, algebra, C++, or musical notation gains access to a *space of knowledge* shared by a whole, more or less extensive, community. This community might be open, closed, centralized, decentralized, national, international, and so on, but the knowledge accumulated and shared by those who make it up is always common property insofar as it is transferred among them. On the other hand, whoever practices a language can be a producer, supplier, distributor, user, or transmitter of knowledge, leading therefore to a *social value network* associated with this practice.[8] Such knowledge has the property of not wearing down or diminishing through use. Quite the contrary, in fact, because if there are no users the concept disappears and, inversely, the more users there are, the more shared knowledge grows. The result, then, is that linguistic communities contribute a *communitarian model* to the economies and societies of knowledge. In some cases, this communitarian model evolves into a citizen model, especially when the different communities make their respective knowledge public and are prepared to recognize the knowledge of other communities.

Consequently, I will use the term *cities based on knowledge* for those complex forms of association that develop on a foundation of a plurality of shared knowledge among different communities, and that maintain public spaces for the free exchange of knowledge. Therefore, I make a distinction between knowledge communities, societies, and cities. Like a society, a city based on knowledge must be capable of integrating diverse

---

7. On this model, see von Hippel, *Democratizing Innovation.*

8. In *Democratizing Innovation*, von Hippel uses the term "value chain." I prefer, however, the notion of a *value network* in which each user of the network nodes can contribute value to the whole, whether they are producers, suppliers, users, distributors, or transmitters of knowledge.

knowledge communities, each one of which cultivates specific kinds of knowledge. However, a knowledge city must also be able to maintain a specific space (*agora*) in which all these different types of knowledge can be expressed freely and accessed by any citizen. There are KCs that prefer to retain their knowledge in a private sphere instead of making it public in such an *agora*. When they take this step—for example, when the eighteenth-century enlightened thinkers published the *Encyclopédie*—KCs experience a sudden change by generating citizen spaces of knowledge, that is, an *epistemopolis* or a *knowledge republic*.[9] Wikipedia is another good example of an *epistemopolis* or a knowledge republic, originating in the telematic networks of the third environment.

To paraphrase Vannevar Bush in his *Science: The Endless Frontier* (1945), I would contend that all spaces of knowledge have their own endless frontier, not just scientific knowledge. Artistic knowledge is a canonical example of the unlimited space of knowledge where producers (artists), suppliers (museums, galleries), distributors (dealers, experts, critics), and users of different arts meet, with the latter being spectators and followers but also people who also carry out some kind of artistic practice. The "artistic area" of knowledge cities might be compared to a neighborhood where a series of practices based on artistic knowledge are carried out and create a specific kind of wealth: the arts. The urban metaphor can also be applied to different spaces of knowledge, in such a way that the traditional image of the tree of sciences and arts can be overcome. In the case of contemporary technosciences, knowledge cities are organized around networks, so not even the neighborhood metaphor is sufficient. Whatever the case, the important thing is that the boundaries of these spaces of knowledge are open or, if one prefers, endless.

Allow me to return to the subject of common languages, because they are especially relevant in the economies and societies of knowledge. Languages are a strategic recourse in this new kind of economy due to the fact that, regardless of what the language is in which certain knowledge is produced, to have any economic or social impact it must be circulated in markets and societies, which implies resorting to common languages. A typical example is that of computer languages. Because they are normally introduced in various idioms, they are *intercommunitarian languages*, without any detriment to the existence of a knowledge community that creates and cultivates them—for example, LINUX. To the extent that, when we speak of a knowledge society, we are referring to democratic rather than aristocratic societies, it is necessary for knowledge to be available to wide sections of the public that may use it freely.

Languages are the means par excellence to transmit and share knowledge. Throughout human history multiple communities have been created that, in sharing a common language, have been able to produce and transmit knowledge to both their contemporaries and to later generations, giving rise to stable cultures. Furthermore, the same

---

9. See Echeverría, "Las repúblicas del conocimiento." The idea of a "republic of science" was proposed by Polanyi, "The Republic of Science," and revisited by Rip, "The Republic of Science in the 1990s."

language makes room for several knowledge communities, even those opposed to one another. For there to be a society in the strictest sense of the word there must be several communities, not just one. The same should be said for cities where, moreover, there is also the indispensable requisite that they should be public spaces (*agoras*) for debate. Communities are usually very different among themselves, and they tend to ignore, or even criticize or oppose, one another. Knowledge societies and cities are more complex entities than communities. Therefore knowledge economies, societies, and cities must be capable of integrating different knowledge communities and especially different linguistic communities. We thus come to one of the key questions: knowledge transfer among different KCs and especially among different languages. To put this question another way, what is knowledge traffic like in an epistemopolis? What kind of governance dominates in knowledge republics? How much knowledge flows through the spaces of knowledge? From where to where, and by what means? These types of problem come under the rubric of *knowledge transfer*, which I will address later.

Insofar as this collective knowledge gradually settles down and develops in different languages, an epistemic complex takes shape out of which each speaker extracts what serves them and what does not. Evidently this "common epistemic treasure" is a complex entity consisting of internal conflicts and contradictions. Each language shapes a collective way of understanding the world and making contact with it. To employ another metaphor, we might say that languages generate *knowledge deposits* accessible to any of their speakers, albeit only partially. Through the mere fact of learning a language and making it one's own, one appropriates a part of this common treasure and uses it, without preventing the other speakers from doing the same. In contrast to other goods, the use of knowledge does not imply its deterioration or diminution, but in all likelihood its growth. Knowledge is not consumed but rather transformed. If the speaker is reflexive and critical, he or she can create new forms of knowledge that might occasionally go on to broaden the common heritage. In sum, language brings together a *knowledge community through time,* and from this languages contribute decisively to the creation of stable cultures. When they speak them, people use a common heritage and in some cases contribute improvements. Knowledge expressed linguistically is a typical example of *common property* although this is no obstacle to any speaker, on making the language their own, converting it into their *own knowledge*.

Since diverse human cultures have developed a plurality of languages, we might represent human knowledge as a diversity of deposits cultivated by the speakers of every language. Insofar as some cultures make contact with others, this results in knowledge flow, linguistic hybridization, and blending among knowledge communities. Insofar as, for example, the great works in one language are translated into others, *collective knowledge transfer* takes place. I will return to these considerations in the conclusion when I address cultural plurality in an epistemopolis.

Scientific Communities and Values

A second canonical example of knowledge communities is that of scientific communities. Robert K. Merton coined this term and drew up a sociological methodology to measure them, demonstrating that they were clearly disciplinary entities. He also argued that science has its own value system, the *ethos* of science, defined by four institutional imperatives: universalism, communism, disinterestedness, and organized skepticism.[10] Thomas S. Kuhn, meanwhile, correlates closely the notion of a scientific community with that of a paradigm: "A paradigm is what the members of a scientific community, and they alone, share; conversely, it is their possession of a common paradigm that constitutes a scientific community of a group of otherwise disparate men."[11] Furthermore, he argues that a scientific paradigm always has an axiological component and that scientists share values, even among different disciplines. Accuracy, consistency, scope, simplicity, and fruitfulness are five values that, according to Kuhn, scientists have always maintained throughout history. This is not an exhaustive list, however, and one might add other values such as utility, which Kuhn also underscores.[12]

These two authors, together with other philosophers and sociologists of science (such as Larry Laudan, Hilary Putnam, Andrew Pickering, and León Olivé) encouraged a line of research that modified the philosophy of science drastically at the close of the twentieth century and about which, for my own part, I have written extensively, especially in *Ciencia y valores* (Science and Values) and *La revolución tecnocientífica* (The Technoscientific Revolution). Instead of imagining a value-free science, as positivist philosophers argued in favor of throughout the twentieth century, one must recognize that science has its own values, *epistemic values*, as Hilary Putnam termed them. Scientific facts are charged with value, specifically epistemic values, because they have been recognized as scientific facts to satisfy these epistemic values. Scientific communities share some knowledge *because* they share a value system and because the knowledge they share satisfies these values. In Kuhn's words, such knowledge is scientific, and therefore valuable, because it is accurate, rigorous, consistent, of a broad scope, and fruitful, and also because it has been contrasted and verified empirically by other scientists, members of the same knowledge community of which one forms a part. Scientists think like this, but they are not alone in doing so.

Other knowledge communities (religious, artistic, technological, juridical, social, and so forth) also share kinds of knowledge, and do so because they consider them valuable, both for them individually and for their communities as a whole. I therefore come to one of the crucial points of my argument: *communities share knowledge because they share values.* Knowledge that satisfies the criteria of evaluation, whether *know how, know why, know what, know who,* or any other kind becomes valid and acceptable content for most

---

10. See Merton, *On Social Structure of Science*, mainly chapter 20, "The Ethos of Science," 267–76.

11. Kuhn, *The Essential Tension*, 294.

12. Ibid., 322.

of the community. The different value systems that distinct knowledge communities share determine the criterion that allows one to decide what is acceptable as knowledge (whether scientific, religious, technological, juridical, social, or artistic) in a given moment and what is not. Shared values are the key to defining what knowledge is shared by a community and what is not. The axiological perspective in the philosophy of science that I am summarizing briefly affirms these kinds of ideas and distinguishes different types of knowledge according to the diverse value systems shared by each community.

A scientific community can be studied from many perspectives: the axiological point of view is one of these. I do not deny the relevance of other lines of research, and I am simply suggesting that the axiological approach is rewarding when distinguishing different types of knowledge and therefore different knowledge communities. Scientific communities are a canonical example due to the social and economic relevance of scientific knowledge, especially at present, but also because the existence of these communities is based on shared value systems that allow one to discern what scientific knowledge is and what it is not. Always according to this approach, the system of peer evaluation is a scientific practice that reaffirms the validity of shared values in each specific situation, regardless of what is being evaluated (theories, instruments, research projects, people, and so forth). Scientific communities function like this, while other knowledge communities have relatively similar procedures, although their value systems might be quite different from scientists' epistemic values.

In sum, kinds of knowledge depend on the types of values that communities share, regardless of what objectives or questions interest the members of the community. Instead of classifying communities according to the objects they study, the axiological approach recognizes knowledge communities according to the types of knowledge they cultivate, and these in keeping with the kinds of values they share. Scientific communities can be (and have been) studied from this perspective. Here I contend that the axiological perspective is interesting for knowledge communities in general, not just for scientific communities. In fact, inasmuch as the value of the public is taken on board by a specific community, its space of knowledge usually evolves into an epistemopolis. If, moreover, governance principles for these knowledge *agoras* are taken on board, communities can end up forming knowledge republics where knowledge is not just common property but a *res publica* that everyone is responsible for administering.

Knowledge Transfer among Knowledge Communities

Translation is one of the most important means of transferring knowledge among different communities. Commerce is another method, in the same way as social coexistence. In fact, the greater capacity a city has to integrate different communities within its urban space and promote the exchange of knowledge among them, the more cosmopolitan it is. In similar fashion, an epistemopolis must promote, facilitate, and marshal knowledge flow among very different communities, each one of which has its own common property in the knowledge that it cultivates. There are no knowledge cities if different common properties have not come together in one public space, generating a *res publica* that must be administered by the communities as a whole, not just by one alone.

In the case of scientific communities, the languages of each one are usually very specialized. Furthermore, each one is guided by its own agreements and rules. The processes of knowledge transfer among different scientific disciplines are not easy to achieve, precisely because of this root diversity and autonomy. Let us briefly examine some relevant mechanisms for the intercommunitarian transfer of scientific knowledge.

Contemporary science—that has for the most part become technoscience—is characterized by the close collaboration between scientists and engineers, and in general among experts of varied disciplines. Consider the example of e-science, in which the cooperation between computer technicians and telematic engineers results in a condition sine qua non of scientific research. Instead of working with people of the same training and background, as has been customary in academic science, technoscience necessitates a *disciplinary convergence*. This transdisciplinarity takes shape in the tendency to form teams in which researchers from different scientific communities take part. The recent Converging Technologies programs in the United States and the European Union take it for granted that innovation requires a nano-bio-info-cogno convergence, and even more disciplines.[13] For these programs to continue it is essential to set up mechanisms of knowledge exchange and transfer within the teams that develop them. The result is that scientists from a certain discipline are expert users of knowledge generated by their colleagues from other backgrounds. This implies an important means of transferring knowledge.

Modern science has been characterized by a strong tendency toward specialization. Keeping up to date with the advances made in a certain specialty takes up a lot of time and requires a solid grounding in the material, because one must test and repeat observations and experiments just in case one has overlooked something or made a mistake. As Kuhn observes, normal science progresses in small steps through subtle improvements and advances. Such progress can only be fully comprehended by a few scientists, precisely those who follow the research attentively and who are capable of analyzing and criticizing fundamentally certain aspects of the results obtained. Normally these scientists cite one another, and they are frequently the anonymous evaluators of the contributions made by their colleagues. As Kuhn also points out, these communities of scientific knowledge are small, owing to the high degree of specialization that contemporary science has developed.

This process of producing knowledge is quite similar in the different disciplines. Journals indexed in databases such as ISI Thomson function on the basis of these *small scientific communities*. However, scientists are not just producers, but also users of knowledge.

---

13. I am alluding here to the Converging Technologies for Improving Human Performance program of the National Science Foundation in the United States, and the Converging Technologies for the European Knowledge Society program in the EU. Both promote the convergence of nanosciences, biotechnologies, information technology and communication, and cognitive sciences.

Given the degree of specialization in scientific research, an expert in a certain material cannot normally follow in detailed fashion the evolution of another discipline. Therefore when scientists have to use the advances made in another field different from their own, they become users of knowledge produced by their colleagues, in which, sometimes, they find a source of inspiration for their own work.

This procedure of knowledge transfer is very common in scientific activity, and is practically the norm. Scientists are knowledge producers in their area of specialization but at the same time they are users of knowledge that others have produced in different fields. Insofar as each scientific community maintains rigorous criteria for the quality control of the knowledge produced by that community, for the other communities the results are reliable and can be applied in different areas, even if they are not understood fully or have not been tested personally. Because there are shared values among the different scientific communities, trust in the validity of knowledge produced by other communities becomes the basic rule of governance that allows for knowledge transfer among different communities. Elsewhere there are scientists who are experts in transfer-ring knowledge from one field to another. These gatekeepers are extremely interested in researching knowledge transfer networks. Throughout the history of science, many advances have been made via this procedure, whose basic structure might be synthesized thus: *a scientist is a user of knowledge produced by others* (in different disciplines from his or her own) *and thanks to this is capable of producing advances in his or her own field of specialization.* Scientists are producers and users of knowledge, and both facets are indispensable for research. The use of scientific instruments—that are also usually improved by experts on the matter—is but one facet of this knowledge transfer process and has been a constitu-ent part of modern science. The mathematization of physics or economics or psychology might be some examples of this. A second example is that of the Newtonian paradigm that was circulated in various sciences, including the theory of electricity which, thanks to this, began to turn into a science in its own right.

Lacking more detailed historical studies, I will stick to the hypothesis that many small and major advances in scientific research have come as the result of knowledge transfer processes from one discipline to others. To support this claim, I will mention two possible case studies that need to be researched in depth.

The first of these refers to specialized scientific journals. These normally contain a high disciplinary element, that is, they are maintained by specialized knowledge com-munities. With some exceptions, a scientist is only capable of understanding fully (in the sense of making the knowledge of others his or her own) what is published in a few journals—those most relevant in his or her field of specialization. These sources are indis-pensable for the scientist's tasks, almost as much as his or her laboratory instruments. The diffusion of knowledge in a specialized discipline is carried out by these means, apart from conferences, symposia, and workshops, which are also scenes for interdisciplinary knowledge transfer.

Contemporary technoscience is marked profoundly by the existence of some journals that stand out clearly as knowledge distributors, for example *Nature* and *Science*. The singularity of such publications consists in the fact that they are not disciplinary but interdisciplinary. They are read by scientists from many disciplines and specialties, and they perform a basic function for transfer of knowledge: distributing the most important advances in knowledge generated by each discipline for producers in the other disciplines. The *Philosophical Transactions* of the Royal Society undertook a similar function historically: to inform the educated scientific public of the results stemming from the principal research in different sciences (physics, mathematics, biology, chemistry, geology, astronomy, meteorology, and so on). Nowadays, science is much more specialized, but these major knowledge media fulfill a similar function.

I am once more applying Eric von Hippel's ideas, in this case by suggesting that *Nature*, *Science*, and similar journals are *sources of knowledge transfer* for different scientific communities. To put it another way, they are means of interdisciplinary knowledge transfer, in the same way as the translators I previously referred to, but making up a public space as opposed to the translator's private work. The result, then, is that scientific knowledge is also a relational entity since it exists in the interrelation between various knowledge communities. There are journals that are means of knowledge transfer *for science as a whole* in that they publish the most relevant advances in different fields of scientific research swiftly and on the basis of quality control. All these forms of control form part of the governance of science or, if one prefers, the knowledge traffic system in the scientific epistemopolis. With the coming of the Internet and the possibility of diffusing preprints via the net (ArXiv, for example), intra- and inter-communitarian knowledge flow have grown considerably, to the extent that knowledge communities—formerly self-sufficient and separated among themselves—can connect with one another and transfer knowledge through networks to everyone's benefit.[14] To apply the citizen metaphor I have been using, previously isolated and separated villages and towns decide to join together by means of a city hall and lay out routes of communication and exchange through which they begin to generate knowledge cities.

One should extend von Hippel's ideas even further, arguing that knowledge suppliers are also sources of innovation in contemporary science. One of the most significant of these is Thomson ISI [now known as Thomson Reuters Web of Knowledge], to the extent that this business has created a huge database that includes an evaluation of scientific knowledge determining the impact factor of an author, an article, or a journal. The function of Thomson ISI is very different from that of *Nature* or *Science,* and yet it plays a decisive role when determining whether knowledge is transferred or not. Even without understanding the articles' content, something that is beyond the reach of nonspecialists, the Thomson ISI indexes determine the extent to which a given kind of knowledge has

14. For example, one might cite the large databases of scientific publications one can access via the Internet, such as SCIRUS.

been transferred to other researchers, and as a result of this its quality level. The methodology might be debatable, but it is true to say that it has prevailed in practice. Thomson ISI contributes a way of measuring knowledge transfer processes in contemporary science, and it therefore measures knowledge flow within the scientific epistemopolis, both inside and outside a community. Thanks to this, it has become an auxiliary instrument for scientific policies.

One should develop these ideas much more, but what I have explained thus far is sufficient to demonstrate that disciplinary convergence is also an important source of knowledge transfer, and hence the construction of a transport system from some knowledge spaces to others. In this way, the different knowledge cities begin to take shape, although what characterizes them is the maintenance of public spaces where knowledge can be presented, debated, and evaluated. Transfer in private spheres, as tends to occur in the case of technoscientific companies, is valid for KCs, but not for knowledge cities.

Knowledge Transfer to Other Technoscientific Agents

Up to now I have considered knowledge transfer processes among different scientific communities. However, technoscience is characterized by linking closely within it various kinds of agents: engineers, technicians, businesspeople, managers, politicians, and even military personnel. Their collaboration in joint projects and programs is constitutive of technoscientific practice.[15] Here I will offer some brief considerations about the exchange and transfer of property brought about by this new type of scientific practice, before presenting my conclusions. From the perspective of the philosophy of scientific practice, the important thing is to analyze transfer processes and how they are carried out, regardless of the content of what is transferred.

Greatly synthesizing this idea, I would contend that each of the agents involved in technoscience contributes his or her own values and hence their own properties: scientists contribute knowledge; engineers, technology; financers, money; businesspeople, management and economic gain; politicians, power; and military personnel, patriotism. In so doing, they generate value, yet not just for themselves but also for the other technoscientific agents. This mutual creation of value is one of the keys to the success of current technoscience. Technoscience is based on a value network that is markedly interprofessional and not just interdisciplinary.

I will offer this final point in a general and abridged way. Each one of the technoscientific agents has their own value system, and they are very different from one another. However, at least some of these values are reconcilable. Let us suppose, in order to simplify matters, that the scientist, the engineer, the financer, the businessperson, the politician, and the military representative have teamed up in the same technoscientific company and have defined projects and programs, making this decision because they are all thinking

---

15. In this regard, see Echeverría, *La revolución tecnocientífica*.

about gaining benefits from the collaboration. The scientist can achieve an advancement for knowledge in the sphere of his or her discipline, and hence prestige; the engineer will solve problems and invent more efficient artifacts or techniques; the investor hopes to make gains in the stock market, or publicity, or a growth in competitiveness in the market, in creating innovations based on research and development; the director of the techno-scientific company will be proud to optimize resources of all kinds (human, economic, equipment, administrative, and so forth) placed at his or her disposal, in accordance with his or her specific value system; the politician will demonstrate his or her decision-making power and will attempt to gain more power, besides resolving relevant problems that affect the society that has elected him or her to govern; and the military representative has to give priority to the defense and security of his or her country, the reason he or she must be up-to-date with the technoscientific innovations produced in these spheres, and also in accordance with his or her axiological commitments and convictions.

Therefore the six people I am outlining function according to their own value systems, trying to increase the level of satisfaction of those values they consider most relevant. However, they all end up sharing a series of different types of knowledge, despite the fact that their value systems are heterogeneous. This is possible because technoscientific practice facilitates *axiological convergence*, and hence knowledge convergence.

We usually distinguish twelve types of value in technoscientific activity: basic, epistemic, technological, economic, political, military, social, juridical, cultural, ecological, esthetic, and moral.[16] Using these, we can distinguish a number of different types of knowledge. Knowledge differs from simple information by having passed through more evaluative filters and by having been accepted and used by a given community. It is one thing to inform of the advances in one or another profession and quite another thing to appropriate and use knowledge generated by other communities. The appropriation and successful use of knowledge are distinctive signals that indicate transfer processes have been produced between some communities and others. Knowledge advances authentically when some professions make knowledge produced by others their own. They take it as valid and begin to apply it. This is possible when they partly take on board the values defended by other knowledge communities, recognizing that they also allow them to generate knowledge, albeit of a different sort from that produced by the original knowledge community itself.

Second, scientific progress does not just depend on knowledge production, but also on its supply and distribution to other communities, and especially on the use that other scientists make of this knowledge. The proposals of von Hippel are applicable here to the analysis of knowledge communities. Both distributors and users have their own evaluative criteria. Besides the internal peer system review of a community, it is necessary to satisfy other evaluative processes before a proposal becomes an advancement of knowledge.

---

16. See Echeverría, *La revolución tecnocientífica*, especially the third section.

Finally, not just scientific but also technological, juridical, administrative, cultural, artistic, and other kinds of knowledge are transferred. In particular, the knowledge that, besides having an intrinsic value for scientific communities, is of social and not just business or political or military use stands out. In contrast to Peter F. Drucker, who only refers to knowledge businesses,[17] one must maintain the notion of *knowledge communities*, some of which are scientific and others that are not. Insofar as such communities (for example, the artistic one) transfer their knowledge to society, they can generate a cultural or artistic market, yet the social or cultural value they produce is prior to their impact in markets. A cultural manager is also a knowledge manager although his or her basic reference might not be the market or industry but, for example, the success of a cultural proposal with the general public. The plurality of values allows one to characterize different types of knowledge, not just one.

Starting from these three suggestions, all of them based on previous hypotheses and proposals, a new means of inquiry opens up in the complex realm of the relations between science, technology, and society. Scientific communities must not just transfer knowledge to businesses but also to societies, or at least to some social sectors. Education is the typical route, but not the only one. Art and cultural critics also transfer knowledge, since they contribute to placing value on artistic and cultural works through their praise or criticism. The same could be said about suppliers of artistic knowledge, such as museums or art galleries, in that they promote certain painters and works of art, while they silence others. Against the romantic notion of the brilliant individual who created knowledge and masterpieces in his or her laboratory or workshop, I argue that we can only analyze knowledge transfer processes sufficiently if we distinguish who are the producers, suppliers, distributors, and users of knowledge. We might say the same for journalism and scientific communication, which also fulfill an important function in knowledge transfer to society.

Conclusion

Knowledge communities are very important for studies of science, technology, and society, especially when they involve one another and end up forming knowledge societies and in particular knowledge cities. The latter are distinguished from the former by the existence of public spaces for exchange and debate. From an axiological perspective, the condition of *common property* evolves and becomes *public property*, which is something quite different, because it implies *open spaces of knowledge*. Free and universal access to knowledge is not guaranteed in the case of knowledge communities, precisely because within them public value is less important than common value. Creating an epistemopolis implies attending to the maintenance of public spaces, and laying down rules of use and behavior within them. Above all, it implies considering knowledge as a *res publica*, the reason for

---

17. See Drucker, *Knowledge Work and Knowledge Society*.

which it must be disseminated to the public in general and not just a group of privileged knowledge aristocrats. This is my principal argument in this chapter.

At the same time I believe that this epistemological-political project I have termed epistemopolis is encouraged if we distinguish various nodes in the network of knowledge flow, and especially to the producers and suppliers, distributors, transmitters, and users of knowledge. The pluralist model von Hippel created to research sources of innovation is also valid to examine knowledge transfer processes.

My third proposal here has been only briefly noted, but it sets out a direction for the studies of science, technology, and society when they occupy knowledge spaces and flow. The plan to create various knowledge cities, not just in the scientific sphere but in other professional sectors, requires enabling systems of governance and quality control for knowledge that flows in the public *agora*. Finally, *knowledge policies* must be defined since knowledge cities are based on the convergence of various (for example, disciplinary) communities and on the presentation, exchange, and evaluation of their respective knowledge in the public sphere—something I have termed *knowledge agora*. Defining the values that must govern these policies is the most pressing task to undertake.

Bibliography

Bush, Vannevar. *Science: The Endless Frontier*. Washington, DC: United States Government Printing Office, 1945.

Drucker, Peter F. *Knowledge Work and Knowledge Society*. Cambridge, MA: John F. Kennedy School of Government, Harvard University, 1994.

Echeverría, Javier. *Ciencia y valores*. Barcelona: Destino, 2001.

——. "Las repúblicas del conocimiento." In *Sociedad del conocimiento: Propuestas para una agenda conceptual*, edited by Rodolfo Suárez, 27–62. Mexico City: UNAM, 2009.

——. *La revolución tecnocientífica*. Madrid: Fondo de Cultura Económica, 2003.

——. *Los señores del aire: Telépolis y el tercer entorno*. Barcelona: Destino, 2001.

Giere, Ronald N. *Explaining Science: A Cognitive Approach*. Chicago: University of Chicago Press, 1988.

Kuhn, Thomas S. *The Essential Tension: Selected Studies in Scientific Tradition and Change*. Chicago: The University of Chicago Press, 1977.

Merton, Robert K. *On Social Structure of Science*. Chicago: University of Chicago Press, 1996.

Olivé, León. *La ciencia y la tecnología en la sociedad del conocimiento*. México: FCE, 2007.

Pickering, Andrew. *The Mangle of Practice: Time, Agency and Science*. Chicago: University of Chicago Press, 1995.

——, ed. *Science as Practice and Culture*. Chicago: University of Chicago, 1992.

Polanyi, Michael. *Personal Knowledge*. London: Routledge, 1958.

——. "The Republic of Science. Its Political and Economic Theory." *Minerva* 1 (1962): 1–20.

Popper, Karl R. *Objective Knowledge: An Evolutionary Approach*. Oxford: Clarendon Press, 1972.

Putnam, Hilary. *Reason, Truth, and History*. Cambridge: Cambridge University Press, 1981.

Quine, W.V. *From Stimulus to Science*. Cambridge, MA: Harvard University Press, 1995.

Rip, Arie. "The Republic of Science in the 1990s." *Higher Education* 28, no. 1 (1994): 3–23.

von Hippel, Eric. *Democratizing Innovation*. New York: Oxford University Press, 1988.

——. *The Sources of Innovation*. Cambridge, MA: MIT Press, 2005.

2

Climate Change and Knowledge Communities

Mari Carmen Gallastegui and Ibon Galarraga

The 1990s saw major changes in the economic growth models used generally for theoretical and empirical analyses. Authors such as Paul Romer and Robert Lucas have shown how external economies of scale and knowledge spillover effects could increase the returns on accumulated private human capital.[1] This effect, in turn, enabled long-term endogenous growth of economies to be encouraged.

The idea stressed here is that knowledge is increasingly productive. This idea is based on the following argument: the creation of new knowledge by some corporations has positive external effects on others, increasing their potential for knowledge production, because it is impossible for all knowledge to be patented or kept secret. As a corollary it can be concluded that investing in knowledge gives rise to a natural external effect which, contrary to what economic theorists have long maintained under the name "law of decreasing marginal productivity," means that we now find that on an aggregate level knowledge has increasing marginal productivity. When this increasing marginal productivity for the intangible capital good known as scientific knowledge is substituted for the assumption of decreasing marginal productivity, the implications are far-reaching.

The most important implication can be put as follows: there is no reason why the economy should not be able to expand in terms of gross domestic product (GDP) if physical capital is combined with knowledge and science. This illustrates how little and how late we economists have included the importance of non-manmade capital (i.e., natural capital or environmental assets) into our analyses. It also illustrates how short-

---

1. Romer, "Increasing Returns and Long-Run Growth"; Lucas, "On the Mechanics of Economic Development."

sighted we have been in failing to realize that growth cannot be sustainable if non-man-made capital is overexploited or managed inefficiently. But leaving aside this unavoidable but, we believe, accurate comment, the need for knowledge and science to ensure GDP growth must be stressed.

When we speak of differences in technology between countries, the knowledge and science to which we refer is not usually general knowledge but the knowledge of specific people or of a specific subgroup of people who have dedicated themselves to the acquisition, production, and generation of knowledge. In this context Gary S. Becker of the University of Chicago developed a whole theory based on "human capital" that is still relevant today in explaining many differences in growth, productivity, and earnings between economies or geographical areas. Thanks to him, we know that it is the subgroups of people who dedicate themselves to the production and generation of knowledge that really matter. A prerequisite for such groups is the acquisition of knowledge through learning or research processes. These subgroups can be called "knowledge communities," and their endowment is known as "human capital," an asset that can be understood in aggregate form (e.g., at the national level) or disaggregate form (at the industrial level). The next section outlines some ideas as to why human capital is important for economic growth.

The Importance of Human Capital

As mentioned above, many recent economic models feature human capital as a driving force for growth. The introduction of this variable into theoretical models means that other aspects of our analysis must be developed. First of all, we must stop and consider how the different levels of human capital affect levels of production, and second, we must establish a model to show how the time allocated by each person affects the accumulation of this capital in the form of knowledge. But in the context of this chapter other aspects also need to be highlighted. On the one hand, in the accumulation of physical capital there is no counterpart to the group social activity that takes place when human capital accumulates. On the other hand, the analyses carried out as a result of Becker's pioneering work draw a distinction between "internal effects" and "external effects."

The internal effects of human capital can be thought of as the way in which investment in human capital translates into returns that are felt by individuals and their immediate families (salary effects, productivity, earnings throughout the life-cycle, etc.), while external effects are not appreciable at the micro-economic level but are visible at the aggregate level. In this regard, Lucas estimates the percentage of variation in US GDP due to the external effects of human capital as 0.4 percent, a figure which is certainly large enough to merit being taken into account.[2]

---

2. Lucas, "On the Mechanics of Economic Development," 37–38.

Another point of interest of this chapter is the following: in the context of economics, when we consider a technology through which the average skill level of a group of people affects the productivity of each individual within that group, the economic unit of analysis need not always be the national economy. Indeed, much smaller units such as regions, cities, communities, etc. may be used, which means that percentage of GDP is not a suitable variable. The idea is to capture the way in which the different groups that influence their respective productivity levels interact with one another.

Another factor that must be taken into account (because it conditions the way in which the analysis must continue) is that many external effects of knowledge can be internalized in small groups of people, that is, companies or families, though this is not necessarily the case. At the other end of the spectrum, certain discoveries may even be classed as having "common ownership," that is, once the knowledge in question has been created it is not considered as the property of a single owner or institution (company, family, etc.) but rather of a whole group of individuals or institutions.

The Learning Process

Most of what we learn is learned from others. Usually we pay our "teachers" directly, but there are also other, indirect forms of payment. Consider, for example, the option of accepting lower wages in exchange for benefiting from the knowledge held at the company where one works. However, most benefits are obtained free of charge and in ways that are mutually beneficial and interactive. Such "external effects" can be thought of as "learning by osmosis." This type of learning is common throughout the arts and sciences, that is, in what we might call "creative occupations," and the history of intellectual development is to some extent the history of these effects. One final idea remains to be added: for the most part, or at least to a large extent, economic activity is just as creative as art and science.[3] As Lucas puts it, "New York City's garment district, financial district, diamond district, advertising district and many more are as much intellectual centers as is Columbia or New York University."[4]

The specific ideas shared in these districts are different from those shared in academic circles, but the process is quite similar: a group of people doing practically the same thing, each emphasizing his/her own originality and uniqueness. A knowledge community can therefore be thought of merely as a focal point where creativity finds ideal conditions for growth and where the learning process is not necessarily formal, but may take place through the assimilation and spillover of creative attitudes and activities. For these knowledge units to bear fruit it is essential that they should contain a mix of cultures, religions, races, and genders. They must be communities where everyone learns from everyone else and where, ultimately, confidence rules because reference points can

3. Jacobs, *The Economy of Cities.*

4. Lucas, "On the Mechanics of Economic Development," 38.

be found regardless of who or what organization needs knowledge or wishes to contribute to knowledge.

This idea is relevant to the specific case examined here because we are attempting to show that climate change has given rise to a knowledge community in which the characteristics mentioned above can be identified, among others. Our knowledge of climate change, its causes, its implications, and its potential solutions is accompanied by an effort to pool knowledge from many different disciplines, areas of basic and applied science, institutions, and countries. The blending and sharing of the achievements of each party has been a constant feature in that effort ever since the United Nations set up the Intergovernmental Panel on Climate Change (IPCC). As explained below, the IPCC has conducted exhaustive studies into the problems and causes of climate change. But first let us analyze other ideas that may also be useful in explaining why a group of "sophisticated" consumers is a prerequisite for the success of certain technological developments and communities.

The Knowledge Economy (The "Weightless Economy")

In 2000, Danny T. Quah wondered about the reasons for certain developments that now seem easier to explain but that in their day required in-depth economic analysis.[5] Quah believes that the growth of the "weightless economy" explains why a special dynamic has arisen in the Internet economy, with online trading and an increasingly strong shift toward significant levels of trade based on mobile telephones. The clearest example of modern technology can be found in ICTs, which gave rise to what is known as the "productivity paradox," though the explanation of that paradox lies outside the scope of this chapter. However, one aspect of Quah's pioneering work that is of interest here is his definition of the "weightless economy," which does not coincide in all points with the definition of the knowledge economy. To understand the difference, consider the following stylized economic growth process.

Skills, education, and everything else involved in human capital and in the working population entail an allocation of time and energy between alternative uses. Thus, individuals who are "highly trained" or have "skills" may work in sectors that produce final goods and services for end users, or they may work as researchers, scientists, engineers, etc. The ideas that they generate provide a fundamental basis for growth and, in the terminology used by Quah, constitute intellectual assets subject to economic and social protection through intellectual property rights.

If ideas were transmitted through a free market, their price would tend to be equal to the marginal cost of reproducing them. This, in general, would give a price close to zero, which would therefore not provide any incentive to make new discoveries. But in the new economy the process of protecting ideas through intellectual property rights works

---

5. Information presented by Mr. Quah in a lecture at the Bilbao Stock Exchange.

differently. By contrast, consumers directly confront those sectors that produce knowledge, which means basically the ICT sector (the Internet, telecommunications, intellectual assets in the broad sense including patents, music, entertainment videos, advice on health matters and the like, databases, electronic libraries, etc.).

In all these cases, end users interact with products directly. Knowledge is incorporated not into the production process but into the end products: this is a major difference, and for the process to work knowledge must also be transferred to users. In other words, users must be sophisticated enough to appreciate, and therefore to demand, and be willing to pay for, knowledge-generated products. This contrasts sharply with, for example, an economy in which scientific and technological progress is driven by technological improvements in the manufacturing industry.

In a weightless economy, in which knowledge is incorporated directly into end products, the way in which demand is set up is crucial. Consumers must be capable of accepting complex, sophisticated new ideas, new products, goods, and services. The size of the market is also crucial. In terms of profit, whoever achieves the biggest market wins: local markets are too restrictive, so global markets must be sought.

The reader may be wondering how these developments are connected to the knowledge community established around the problem of climate change. The link can be found in the type of sophisticated alternatives being developed as potential solutions to mitigate the harmful consequences of climate change: houses that run on solar power, much more selective recycling, less-polluting products such as electric cars, carbon capture and sequestration, etc. Without sophisticated consumers well aware of biophysical problems many solutions are unlikely to be put into practice. Once again knowledge, in this case on the part of consumers, is crucial in responding to the global challenge of climate change.

The rest of this chapter focuses on the problem of climate change and seeks to provide a simple economic characterization for it, to show how the transfer of knowledge and the achieving of international agreements work.

Economic Characterization of the Problem of Climate Change

Government intervention to attempt to prevent the effects of greenhouse gases, or GHG, (especially CO_2) emissions on the Earth's climate is based on a sound foundation. From an economic viewpoint, however, certain points need to be taken into account. Earth's climate can be modeled as a public good. It meets the two requirements specified by Nobel laureate Paul A. Samuelson: nonrivalry and nonexclusion in consumption.[6] It affects us all and no one can be excluded from using it. Thus, in line with Samuelson's

---

6. Samuelson was the winner of the Nobel Prize in Economics in 1970.

thinking, we might expect it to be undersupplied, which would result in the existence of global warming or climate change.[7]

Moreover, the Earth's climate is a global public good. CO_2 emissions are known as "perfectly mixed" emissions: what matters most is the total amount of emissions generated all over the world, and not their point of origin. They are also persistent (i.e., the atmosphere is incapable of turning all CO_2 emissions into harmless forms), so it follows that when we analyze the problem we must take into account not only the flow (emissions) but also the stock (gases accumulated in the atmosphere that are not absorbed or assimilated) of pollution. An economic analysis of climate change therefore requires a dynamic, inter-temporal approach that must explicitly factor in the existence of uncertainty. It is also important to bear in mind that today's pollution is not produced today, but rather is the result of the build-up of gases over many decades. It is therefore essential not to put off until tomorrow measures to mitigate and solve the problem—urgent action is needed.

Another way of looking at the problem is to consider that the atmosphere is used by human beings as a free waste dump. Because the services provided by the atmosphere, and by the environment in general, are free, they are overused: not charging for the consumption or use of goods encourages their use to an extent greater than that which is economically efficient. Moreover, the fact that these are "perfectly mixed" emissions means that their sources are less important than their total amount. Countries that emit CO_2 harm not just themselves but also the people of other countries. To put it more technically, there are external effects that are reciprocal in nature.

Characterizing the Earth's climate and, by contrast, climate change as a public good (bad) or a situation in which there are harmful, reciprocal external effects between countries leads inevitably to the following corollary: *The workings of the market are unable to bring about an efficient allocation in the presence of public goods (bads) and when there are external effects in the economy. Global warming, the misuse of the atmosphere as a dumping ground for GHGs, is therefore a foreseeable consequence and not the result of bad luck or inevitable, "natural" changes in climate.*

Since it is foreseeable that countries, economic agents, and, ultimately, human beings will abuse the atmosphere and the environment and thus cause undesirable anthropogenic effects in the Earth's climate, it can be concluded that the only way of preventing such abuse is through regulation by the public authorities.

Regulation can be applied in many different ways. If we concentrate on emission control and/or mitigation, the measures adopted must meet two essential requirements:

1. They must be global in the sense that they must affect all the countries in the world; and

---

7. The fact that the Earth's climate is a global public good does not imply that the effects of climate change must also be considered as a public good. Those effects may be unevenly distributed across geographical areas, which vary according to the extent of the temperature increases involved.

2. They must also be global in the sense that they must cover all sectors of production and consumption (emissions are produced by all sectors, including domestic and residential).

On the other hand, there is a basic equation which, in its simplest form, reads as follows: CO_2/output = Efficiency (energy/output) * Carbonization (CO_2/energy).

From this it can be deduced that regulating climate change calls for a decarbonization of the economy and for energy efficiency.

Both these requirements may be expensive to achieve, so the challenge is to carry them out in such a way as to minimize transition costs, harmful economic adjustments, impacts on poorer countries, and the impacts of the "losers" on the wealthier countries, and to assure the welfare of future generations. Achieving regulation in such a way as to minimize anthropogenic impacts on the Earth's climate (a public good that must be safeguarded) is a complex business, as the basic characteristics indicated above make clear. The global nature of the problem means that the solution needs to be negotiated worldwide, in a process of negotiation that can tackle the distribution of the benefits and costs arising from cooperation.

However, cooperation is extremely hard to achieve. Consider the following points:

- It is individually rational not to take part in control or mitigation policies implemented by other countries (which goes some way toward explaining the current positions of the United States, China, India, and Australia).
- Negotiation costs are very high, because there are many countries involved and the costs of controlling the damage caused by climate change and monitoring mitigation efforts are distributed unevenly.
- There is a high degree of uncertainty. For example, mitigation costs are incurred immediately while the benefits of preventing or mitigating climate change are felt only in the future.
- The likelihood of deception and nonfulfillment is high.
- There is no international body that can guarantee the fulfillment of the agreements reached.

Moreover, numerous actions are required to achieve decarbonization and efficiency. Energy sources not based on fossil fuels must be used, technological improvements must be introduced to foster energy efficiency, changes in consumer habits must be encouraged, and carbon capture and sequestration (CCS) technologies must be researched and implemented. Mitigating emissions, changing consumer habits, shifting to less harmful energy sources, conducting research in CCS technologies, and so on, all have internal economic impacts of their own, since the economy is a mechanism that must be analyzed from the viewpoint of general equilibrium. Everything influences everything else. The production of renewable energy sources such as biofuels, for instance, gives rise to changes in the prices of basic products such as corn, and increases the price of edible oils and other foodstuffs.

The new transport policies that must be implemented are another case in point: they are bound to have an impact on the automotive industry, on the mobility of economic agents, on the prices charged for road journeys, etc. New consumer habits have implications for the service sector, and it is estimated that the market for low-carbon emission products could be worth up to €500 billion by the year 2050. Nor should we forget the implications of the appearance of new opportunities or niche markets for business, new investment opportunities, new technological advances, and new products that may affect insurance companies, financial analysts, investment firms, and others. In short, mitigation and regulation measures must be considered in a highly general context that includes all their potential side effects.

The Instruments Available

Once it is accepted that there is a need for regulation and for global agreements, and given the lack of any international regulatory body, cooperation is the only way in which efficient results can be assured. However, as mentioned above, cooperation is hard to achieve because it is individually rational to act noncooperatively. The political efforts required to achieve cooperation are huge but fundamental. "Compensations" and "transfers" are crucial elements in this process.

Furthermore, the instruments to be used in mitigating emissions must be chosen with great care. From an economic viewpoint, once it is accepted that efficiency is unattainable, the use of environmental policy measures to achieve objectives at minimal cost is proposed. The scenario is such that objectives must be selected by society through its political representatives (based on scientific reports). These objectives constitute minimum levels (e.g., keeping the average temperature of the planet from increasing by more than two degrees) that must be reached in such a way that the costs inevitably entailed by emission mitigation processes are minimized.

It has been amply proven that market instruments (prices, taxes, creation of markets) are cost-effective, but it is clear that they must be designed and implemented with the maximum rigor and based on reliable, comprehensive studies. In short, maintaining the Earth's climate calls for well-designed, well-planned, well-implemented government intervention. The actions taken must be global, the instruments used must be cost-effective, and uncertainty must be explicitly taken into account.

To take our examination of the matter of instruments a little further, let us now pause briefly to consider the Emissions Trading Scheme (ETS) selected as part of the package of measures introduced by the Kyoto Protocol, which will be considered in more detail in the next section. The ETS covers only part of the CO_2 emissions produced in the EU. Specifically, it affects emissions from around four thousand facilities in the energy, cement, glass, ceramic, steel, and paper industries. In all, the emissions covered amount to around 45 percent of the total. Within Europe, electricity generation from fossil fuels is the biggest individual cause of CO_2 emissions from industry. It involves large, static emission sources.[8]

Economic analysis suggests that the relative effectiveness of this policy instrument will depend on the context in which it is used.[9] Specifically, the relative extent of uncertainty as to the benefits and costs of reducing emissions may tip the balance in favor of mechanisms such as the ETS or in favor of taxes/subsidies. The arguments in support of each option can be summed up as follows:

- If a tax on CO_2 is set too low, too much CO_2 will be emitted. But because the environmental damage done by GHGs builds up over time, short-term excesses have little influence on the overall path of global warming; the tax can be raised before much damage is done to the environment. By contrast, setting the wrong levels in emission trading may cause the price of permits to rocket or plummet, with immediate, costly economic consequences. These markets usually have volatility levels in excess of 40 percent, so this may translate into significant fluctuations in inflation or domestic spending, and may slow down investment in clean technologies. On the other hand, in an emission trading market, inflation is adjusted for automatically, which is not the case when taxation is used.

- Taxation provides a clearly lower threshold for CO_2 prices and thus a minimum return for any innovation. By contrast, in an emission trading market an invention that cuts CO_2 emission costs could force the price of trading rights down and thus reduce the return on investments.

- A tax on CO_2 raises tax revenue. Governments can use this additional revenue to cut other, less efficient taxes and thus reduce the financial cost of reducing emissions (the double dividend hypothesis). Alternatively, they can use the revenue to compensate those people (e.g., the poorest members of society) who are affected disproportionately by increased fuel costs. Cap-and-trade systems can do likewise, provided that the initial assignation of emission rights takes place by auction (the form recommended by economists). In practice, however, political considerations have resulted in trading rights being given away at the initial stage of the process.

Another possible form of mitigation is to use standards, such as establishing caps on CO_2 emission levels. This can force firms to make changes, for instance, in electricity generation technology. Thus, a cap of 600g CO_2/kWh will remove a coal-fired power station from the grid and encourage its owner to replace it with a natural gas–fired station.

---

8. The transport and residential sectors and others remain outside the ETS. This is due largely to how difficult they are to regulate in view of their disperse nature, the fact that they are mobile emitters, and other considerations. These characteristics could be taken as an argument for a tax on CO_2 instead of or in addition to a cap-and-trade system.

9. The sectors covered by the ETS operate on a cap-and-trade basis, under which the relevant authority sets the total admissible volume of emissions (the cap) and issues the corresponding number of CO_2 credits. From there on the working of the market itself (trade) guides those credits into the hands of those willing to pay most for them (i.e., the corporations with the biggest emission reduction costs). For the same reason, firms with lower reduction costs sell their rights (on which they place less value) and cut their emission levels. This means that emissions are reduced at the lowest possible cost.

A still more restrictive cap of 400g CO_2/kWh will remove a conventional gas-fired power station from the grid and force the owner to install CO_2 capture technology.

These three instruments can be used jointly or separately, so there is a wide range of mitigation options. Some degree of substitution between them is also possible. For example, replacing coal-fired power stations with cleaner, gas-fired facilities begins to make sense at CO_2 prices in excess of 33/ t CO_2, regardless of whether or not there is a limit on quantities. Similarly, a restrictive limit may be compatible with a low level of taxation on CO_2. Note, however, that although the same level of mitigation may be achieved by each of these three instruments, the cost of electricity will not be the same in all three cases.

There are other complications that affect environmental policies on climate change which are not considered here due to lack of space, but which also have a substantial effect on the complex matter of policy design.[10] Moreover, aside from specific environmental policies there are measures typical of fiscal (taxes and subsidies) and financial (bonds, insurance) policies that can also be used in the struggle against climate change.

Climate Change Policy in International Forums

Given the complexity of climate change and the policies for dealing with it, we felt that we should devote a section of this chapter to outlining the course that matters have taken on the international stage in regard to the problem. Concern for changes in climate patterns were first aired at the World Climate Conference in Geneva (Switzerland) in 1979. Since then, the following are the main landmark dates:

- The Greenhouse Gas Conference in Austria in 1985;
- The founding of the Intergovernmental Panel on Climate Change in 1988; and
- The establishment of the United Nations Framework Convention on Climate Change (UNFCCC) at the Rio Summit in 1992 (though it came into force in 1994).

Kyoto and International Negotiations

The Kyoto Protocol, to which we have referred above, was drawn up in 1997 and takes its name from the Japanese city in which it was signed. It is a major international agreement that sets industrialized countries a target of reducing their greenhouse gas (GHG) emissions by 5.2 percent from 1990 levels in the period 2008–2012.[11] Thirty-eight countries initially signed the protocol. Under the distribution of efforts to meet this objective, the EU as a whole was set a target of reducing emissions by 8 percent. The way in which

---

10. Cost benefit functions tend to be highly nonlinear, so it is inadvisable to trust calculations based on average or expected levels. Environmental policies entail major irreversibility, which interact with uncertainty, sometimes in a complex fashion. Environmental policies cover long timeframes, which exacerbates the uncertainty concerning their costs and benefits and greatly increases uncertainly as to what the right discount rate might be.

11. The main GHGs are carbon dioxide (CO_2), methane (CH4), nitrous oxide (N2O), hydro-fluorocarbons (HFCs), per-fluorocarbons (PFCs), and sulphur hexafluoride (SF6).

this target was then broken down among Member States resulted in Spain being allowed to increase its emissions by 15 percent. The Protocol established a legal framework for a commitment to reduce GHG levels that is binding on those countries that approved and then ratified it. Mechanisms were also established for achieving the targets set.

The Kyoto Protocol draws a distinction between "Annex I" countries (industrialized countries that are legally obliged to implement the reductions agreed upon once they have ratified the protocol) and the rest, which are to make voluntary commitments. The process of negotiation focused mainly on working out conditions under which non-Annex I countries could make a significant contribution to achieving target levels. The conditions established cover many aspects, from the distribution of the financial burden among developed countries (which are historically responsible for most emissions) to effective technology transfer systems, the role of deforestation, and the establishment of funding for adaptation to changes which are already taking place as a result of climate change as well as changes that will be unavoidable in the coming years. Among the instruments established under Kyoto are the "flexible mechanisms," three market-based mechanisms (one of which is discussed the previous section) that go beyond national-level policies in each individual country.

Emissions Trading

The best example of this mechanism is the European Emissions Trading System (ETS), a general system that accompanies the protocol and establishes the levels of CO_2 emissions permitted in each country in line with its targets, expressed in AAUs (Assigned Amount Units). One AAU equals one tonne of CO_2 equivalent (a generic unit which enables comparisons to be drawn between the six gases). These units can be traded between countries or between companies that fall short of or exceed their emission limits at the end of each year. Emissions can also be traded in certified emission reductions (CERs, used in the Clean Development Mechanism), emission reduction units (ERUs, used in Joint Implementation), and European monetary units (EMUs, used in reforestation projects).

The Clean Development Mechanism (CDM)

Under this mechanism companies or governments from Annex I countries undertake emission reduction projects in non–Annex I countries, that is, in developing countries, to enable the latter to achieve additional GHG reductions. These projects are usually concerned with energy efficiency, fostering the use of renewable energies, or encouraging sustainable transport. The additional reductions achieved can then be traded on the market.

Joint Implementation

This is similar to the CDM, but refers to projects in the industrialized countries listed in Annex B of Kyoto Protocol.

As explained in the previous section, the possibility of trading in emission rights means that in a context of efficient allocation CO_2 can be reduced in those sectors and areas where it is most cost efficient to do so.

Implementing policies of this type is extremely complex, so the regulatory framework has had to be discussed and developed subsequently at various Conferences of Parties (CoPs). These conferences are held annually to monitor progress in commitments and undertake new challenges. Apart from the CoPs (which are the "supreme body" of the UNFCCC), the worldwide negotiation process includes conferences of parties serving as the meeting of the Parties to the Kyoto Protocol (CMPs, which are the "supreme body" of the Protocol) and meetings of the subsidiary bodies, which monitor the technical workings of the system.[12] For the Kyoto Protocol to be implemented it had to be ratified by at least fifty-five countries representing at least 55 percent of all emissions. This figure was achieved when Russia decided to sign up, and the Protocol eventually came into force on February 16, 2005. Its subsequent ratification by Australia in 2007 provided a further substantial boost. At CoP 12, held in Nairobi in 2006, a commitment was made to approve a new protocol for the post-Kyoto period at CoP 15, held in Copenhagen in 2009.

CoP 13 in Bali in 2007 set out a path for the culmination in 2009 of negotiations on the post-Kyoto period, approved the launch of the Adaptation Fund, promoted measures for the effective transfer of technology to developing countries, and specified policies for reducing emissions due to deforestation. The CoP 14, held in Poznan, reiterated the commitment to approve a new protocol at the 2009 Conference in Copenhagen (CoP 15). The developed countries are hoping that the developing countries, especially those with the fastest-growing economies (China, Brazil, and India), will commit to achieving significant reductions, while the latter in turn are hoping for major commitments from the developed countries in emission reductions and in providing them with financial, political, and technological support in reaching their targets.

The agenda undertaken by U.S. president Barack Obama and the triumph of the view that climate change is not a zero-sum game, but instead one requiring that forward-looking, cooperative geopolitical strategies be worked out, mean that some hope exists regarding the results expected from the Copenhagen Conference (paraphrasing T. Santarius).[13] The issues examined above illustrate how hard it is to reach clear international agreements on matters as complex as climate change.

The Role of the Intergovernmental Panel on Climate Change

In terms of policy action, it should be recognized that the IPCC has played a vital role in promoting the gathering of all the necessary scientific knowledge and the use of the

---

12. The Subsidiary Body for Scientific and Technological Advice (SBSTA) and the Subsidiary Body for Implementation (SBI).

13. Santarius et al., "Pit Stop Poznan," 22.

evidence gathered for policy making, by organizing detailed assessments of all the scientific, technical, and socioeconomic aspects of climate change by leading scientists around the world.

The IPCC has effectively contributed to the use of "science for policy making" and to the mainstreaming of the science of climate change, which has allowed policy makers to adopt ambitious policies to combat climate change. The Norwegian Nobel Committee recognized these efforts "to build up and disseminate greater knowledge about man-made climate change, and to lay the foundations for the measures that are needed to counteract such change" in awarding the IPCC the Nobel Peace Prize for 2007 (shared with former U.S. vice president Al Gore).

The IPCC's main assessment reports were published in 1990, 1995, 2001, and 2007. Each report is divided into three main chapters, referred to as Working Groups 1 (The Physical Science Basis), 2 (Impacts, Adaptation, and Vulnerability), and 3 (Mitigation of Climate Change). As an illustration of just how ambitious this task is, note that the fourth Assessment Report involved over six years of contributions from more than 2,500 expert scientific reviewers, more than eight hundred contributing authors, and more than 450 lead authors from 130 countries.

Thanks to these reports there is now a clear consensus regarding the following aspects:

- Over the last century the Earth's climate has changed.
- Most global warming is the result of human activity.
- Temperatures will continue rising over the twenty-first century.
- There will be many impacts but they cannot be predicted on a regional scale.
- The greater the emissions the more global warming will occur.
- The greater and faster the warming the greater and more severe the effects will be.
- The more global warming there is the more irreversible the process will become.

Science has also established that the main challenge is to stabilize the stock of greenhouse gases at between 500 and 550 parts per million (ppm), which will result in a temperature increase of 2°C. Taking into account that the current level is 430 ppm and that before the Industrial Revolution the level was 280 ppm, the immensity of the challenge is clear. Policies should thus be designed with a view to succeeding in this effort using all available policy instruments and offsetting costs and benefits. All countries at all levels of governance have a duty to contribute to the struggle against climate change.

Other pieces of research such as the *Stern Review* have contributed to our understanding that the cost of failing to act may be five times higher than the investment necessary for effective, global action. The *Stern Review* estimates "the annual costs of stabilisation at 500–550ppm CO_2e to be around 1% of GDP by 2050" while "climate change will reduce welfare by an amount equivalent to a reduction in consumption per head of between

5 and 20%."[14] These conclusions have filtered through to the population, companies, institutions, and NGOs and have helped establish a common understanding that the fight against climate change is one of the biggest challenges that humanity faces in this century.

But what knowledge communities have contributed to this? What mechanisms have been crucial in acting as a catalyst for paradigm shifts? We believe that all this transfer of knowledge has been possible thanks to the confidence generated by the way in which the IPPC reports have been produced. We all know that the reports are based on meta-analyses undertaken by researchers who have taken into account only those conclusions that have sound foundations and are backed by good research.

Although it has taken longer than predicted, governments have also been able to convey the relevant empirical findings to the relevant institutions and to all interested parties in the community. Almost everyone knows that we must change our pattern of behavior if we are to overcome climate change, that the energy model adopted is crucial, that fossil fuels must be replaced by other sources of energy—mainly renewable energy—and that if we are to do our duty to future generations we cannot continue living according to our present habits. We are aware that transport is a major contributor to the problem of CO_2 emissions, thus we need to travel by public transport rather than private cars, and governments need to continue with policies for managing the demand for transport. Rail transport is an alternative that will be developed to a large extent before long. All this knowledge has been and is still being transferred to individuals in developed countries, increasing their awareness of the problems that climate change will cause.

There is also a knowledge community that understands that climate change is a global problem and as such needs global solutions, though that does not imply that local actions are unnecessary. The globality of the problem means that there is a need for coordination and cooperation between the countries of the world, albeit in a way that admits the possibility of different responses, because not all countries are in the same position in terms of income and wealth, and they are, therefore, not all capable of undertaking the same efforts to mitigate emissions.

Climate Change as a Challenge and an Opportunity

Human capital brings a new dimension to the traditional concept of economic growth and development as dealt with by economists. This is not a new conclusion, but it is significant if we are to understand the role that the protection of our environment and our natural resources may (and should) play in the new concept of welfare.

A subgroup of individuals gathered in a knowledge community provides fertile ground for the acceleration of learning processes that can thus help create not just internal effects (for individuals and for their surroundings) but also external effects for

---

14. Stern, *The Stern Review*, xii, executive summary.

the community as a whole. Those external effects may even extend beyond national borders.

In this sense, this chapter seeks to illustrate why climate change is a good example of this process, or in other words why the theories of Becker and Lucas are certainly valid in explaining the process of knowledge creation and globalization that is taking place in the field of climate change. The establishment of the IPCC by the UN in 1988, with the duty of reviewing all existing scientific knowledge on climate change and drawing up rigorous reports on the state of knowledge and its repercussions for the quality of human life, has been a determinant factor in this process. There can now be no doubt that climate change exists, or that its main cause is probably the burning of fossil fuels as part of human activity.

The existence of what we have called "sophisticated consumers" helps explain the underlying reasons for encouraging the complex technological and political alternatives that exist to combat this global problem. From the viewpoint of an economist, climate change can be modeled as a global, perfectly mixed "public bad" (as opposed to the concept of a "public good," which in this case means the atmosphere). As a result, no one can be excluded from its effects (or from the consumption of the resource of "air" or "atmosphere" in the public good), and it will always be over-supplied if the market is allowed to act unhindered, that is, if there is no public-sector intervention.

This characterization reveals how tremendously difficult it is to design and implement a public-sector policy that results in an appropriate allocation. The difficulties include the large number of actions required to tackle climate change, the need to find a global solution, the complexity of sharing the costs and benefits of the policies implemented and their interaction with other policies. The uncertainty that still surrounds estimates of the effects and consequences of climate change and the extremely long-term nature of the problem also clearly hinder actions by planners.

We have sought to highlight the market-based mechanisms that currently top the list of policy instruments in use for tackling the problem: emissions trading, subsidies, and taxation. The examples given show that they can be cost-efficient and can all achieve the same results in terms of mitigating emissions, but that the consequences as regards the distribution of burdens may be very different. The design of the instruments to be used is therefore crucially important in achieving policies that are effective and take into account such concepts as intergenerational, international, and intra-generational equity.

Finally, we have sought to illustrate the debate by providing further information on the international context and design of climate policy in the framework of the United Nations, highlighting the role of the IPCC as a driver and prescriber in globalizing and disseminating knowledge to solve the problem. The IPCC has helped to analyze, bring together, sum up, and above all spread existing scientific knowledge and instill a realization of the seriousness of the situation by getting its message through to the community of policy makers and the general public. The contribution of the *Stern Review* must also be noted.

Climate change is probably the biggest challenge facing humanity, in view of the global nature of the problem and, especially, the seriousness of its potential impacts. If the most pessimistic scenarios forecast by scientists come true, then the very habitability of our planet and therefore our own survival are at risk. The magnitude of the challenge contrasts with the great opportunity that it may provide to bring about a paradigm shift and begin to redefine society and our way of life toward models that are more in balance with and fairer to present and future generations.

Bibliography

Becker, Gary S. *Human Capital: A Theoretical and Empirical Analysis, with Special Reference to Education.* New York: National Bureau of Economic Research; distributed by Columbia University Press, 1968.

Jacobs, Jane. *The Economy of Cities.* New York: Random House, 1969.

Lucas, Robert E. "On the Mechanics of Economic Development." *Journal of Monetary Economics* 22 (1988), 3–42.

Quah, Danny. *Technology Discrimination and Economic Growth: Some Lessons for the New Economy.* Center for Economic Performance Discussion Papers 0522. London: Centre for Economic Performance, LSE, 2002.

———. *The Weightless Economy in Economic Development.* Center for Economic Performance Discussion Papers 2094. London: Center for Economic Performance, 1999.

Romer, Paul M. "Endogenous Technological Change." *Journal of Political Economy* 98, no. 5 (1991): 70–102.

———. "Increasing Returns and Long-Run Growth." *Journal of Political Economy* 94, no. 5 (October 1986): 62–83.

Samuelson, Paul A. "The Pure Theory of Public Expenditure." *Review of Economics and Statistics* 36, no. 4 (1954): 387–89.

Santarius, Tilman, Christof Arens, Urda Eichhorst, Dagmar Kiyar, Florian Mersmann, Hermann E. Ott, Frederic Rudolph, Wolfgang Sterk, and Rie Watanabe. "Pit Stop Poznan: An Analysis of Negotiations on the Bali Action Plan at the Stopover to Copenhagen." Wuppertal Institute Working Paper Series. Berlin: Wuppertal Institute, 2009. Available at www.wupperinst.org/uploads/tx_wibeitrag/Pit-Stop-Poznan.pdf.

Stern, Nicholas. *The Stern Review: The Economics of Climate Change.* London: HM Treasury, UK Government, 2006.

3

The *Ikastola* from Community to Knowledge Community: Learning and Organizational Changes

ALFONSO UNCETA and MARCELINO MASA

Community, considered in its widest possible meaning, has been the object of study of diverse branches of knowledge that have analyzed numerous problems connected to it, such as methodologies, perspectives, criteria, and various other concerns. However, possibly one of the most surprising characteristics of the community is its capacity to subsist and transfer some of its peculiarities throughout time and thus historical events mold new ways of being and making a community.

Bearing in mind the above, there is sufficient evidence to regard as an analytical mistake any effort that tries to dilute the concept of community in the simple confrontation between tradition and modernity, *gemeinschaft* and *gesellchaft,* in the sense used by Ferdinand Tönnies in his classic text of 1887.[1] This conceptual confrontation, or rather the use by sociology to account for these two types of ideals, can only be understood as an attempt to explain far-reaching social processes, and especially the process of modernization.

Therefore, the existence of the forms of community sociality is absolutely self-evident. Graham Crow and Graham Allan state that:

> Community figures in many aspects of our everyday lives. Much of what we do is engaged in through the interlocking social networks of neighbourhood, kinship and friendship, networks which together make up "community life" as it is conventionally understood. . . . Community ties may be structured around links between people with common residence,

---

1. Tönnies, *Gemeinschaft und gesellschaft.*

common interests, common attachments or some other shared experience generating a sense of belonging.[2]

The multiple, constant evidence that highlights the community's persistence and capacity of adaptation cannot, however, prevent the unresolved controversy between "a body of theory which constantly predicts the collapse of community and a body of empirical studies which finds community alive and well."[3]

Beyond the recognition of such a controversy, there is little doubt that far from being in decline, there are signs of community's persistence and its capacity to transform and express in very diverse ways, together with the search for "methods of social relationship characterised by a high degree of personal privacy, emotional depth, moral commitment, social cohesion . . . with man envisaged as a whole rather than as one or another of his roles," as so magnificently asserted by Robert Nisbet.[4]

In a certain way, persistence of community in modernity and the many terms that have been used to convey its different radicals—post-modernity, post-industrial society, radicalized modernity, late modernity, knowledge society, and so on—denote the power and the value that community has on people within the framework of their daily lives. In this sense, Crow and Allan uphold the view that community persistence (stubborness) in modern society is due to both its proximity and mediatory nature between the individual and the institutional. Consequently, "a significant reason why the notion of community does have a salience for people is that it represents a term of social organization which mediates between the personal and the institutional, between household and familial issues which many feel they have a degree of control over and the large-scale social and economic structures which are dominated by events and processes outside ordinary people's influence."[5]

We must not forget that Max Weber pointed out in 1922 that the ideal types of social action (and among them traditional action) are interrelated in everyday life and that they also have an effect on the modern condition. This outlook leads him to say in *Economy and Society* that "the concept of communal relationship has been intentionally defined in very general terms and hence includes a very heterogeneous group of phenomenon."[6] This broad, diverse and dynamic vision of community referred to by Weber—that the community does not have one single meaning but many—is the basis for this approach to the study of the *ikastola* and its process of adaptation as a knowledge community.

---

2. Crow and Allan, *Community Life*, 1.

3. Abrams, "Introduction," 12. Willmot's work is also included within these empirical studies. See, especially, Young and Willmot, *Family Kinship in East London*; and Willmot, *Community Initiatives.*

4. Nisbet, *La formación del pensamiento sociológico*, 71–72. In this line of interest, see Calhoun, "Community."

5. Crow and Allan, *Community Life*, 193.

6. Weber, *Economy and Society*, 42.

The Difference between Knowledge Communities and Communities of Practice

A standard definition of knowledge communities such as that of Peter Senge and Katrin Kaufer—"people in diverse positions who collectively help the members of an enterprise shape their future"[7]—reflects one of the key and differential aspects of knowledge communities: the existence of an organization. However, the communities of practice resemble groups of social relations marked by informality, that is, not necessarily reflected or objectified in an organization, yet present in all places where the individual develops his or her social daily life throughout his or her career or biographical data.

It is true that knowledge-based communities are essential to the creation of communities of practice. Likewise, communities of practice could constitute an intermediate step in the setting up of formal organizations. As Etienne Wenger says:

> "We all belong to communities of practice. At home, at work, at school, in our hobbies. . . . And the communities of practice to which we belong change over the course of our lives. In fact, communities of practice are everywhere. . . . Communities of practice are an integral part of our daily lives. They are so informal and so pervasive that they rarely come into explicit focus, but for the same reasons they are also quite familiar. Although the term may be new, the experience is not. Most communities of practice do not have a name and do not issue membership cards."[8]

Knowledge communities are forms of organization and collective action. Organizational forms are crucial precisely because knowledge, in order to be shared, requires structures that are capable of energizing and distributing knowledge. The organization then takes on the features of a living system, open and stable, whose evolution is the result of changes caused by interactive processes. That is why knowledge resides in human networks that comprise organizations as they respond to the need to produce and transfer knowledge, and also provide vital support—something that is obvious in the field of education and which is the subject of our chapter.

Schools as Knowledge Communities

The context of knowledge community, combined with the problems caused by the quantitative expansion of education and concurrent need to renew, increase, and update knowledge, have stimulated interest in debates on the present and future of methodologies, teaching practices, content, and above all the very management of education. If increasingly the management of knowledge works as a core organizer of contemporary

---

7. Senge and Kaufer, "Communities of Leadersor No Leadership at All," 1. The classic reference text is Senge, *The Fifth Discipline,* which carries a certain application in schools, both in the first work of this quote, for example, in Senge et al., *Schools That Learn.*

8. Wenger, *Communities of Practice,* 6–7. Equally interesting is the text by Lesser and Prusak, "Communities of Practice."

educational culture, it seems to indicate that schools must develop new ways to access, produce, transmit, and distribute knowledge. This immediately suggests the possibility of applying the concept of knowledge communities to the schooling environment, namely, to a group of schools. After all, an educational system is itself a forum of debate in which many points of view are expressed. Not only are problems of a technical nature addressed, but also the fact that it is strongly influenced by social and cultural issues combined with the intense incorporation of information and communication technologies (ICTs).[9]

It is our understanding that, for a school to transition from community to knowledge community, compliance with a number of conditions is required. First, the possibility for a school, through its practices, to become a "*gemeinschaft* place." Second, the possible evolution of this "*gemeinschaft* place" toward a model that adopts the distinguishing characteristics of a knowledge community. Finally, the intensive use of ICTs, which can facilitate access to processes and practices typical of a knowledge community.

Schools as Gemeinschaft *Places*

Today more than ever, schools, as visible and unique educational institutions, have become more valued over the more systematic and traditional conceptions of education. We are referring to their increased capacity to cooperate in independent areas associated with specific forms of knowledge management, areas where community practices tend to be developed. As Thomas Sergiovani pointed out in referring to the transition from the school *gesellschaft* to school *gemeinschaft*, "it is time that the school was moved from the *gesellschaft* side of the ledger to the *gemeninschaft* side. It is time that the metaphor for school was changed from formal organisation to community."[10]

The truth is that in many schools there is an opportunity for the development of community practices, which are actually community within a wider social setting. The need for cooperation is at its maximum level in an environment where knowledge expands at high speed, and the ability to transform information into specific knowledge becomes crucial. And community-based organizational forms can be adapted fairly appropriately to the new reference model described by Andy Hargreaves: "the kinds of organisations most likely to prosper in the post-industrial, post-modern world, it is argued, are ones characterised by flexibility, adaptability, creativity, opportunism, collaboration, continuous improvement, a positive orientation towards problem-solving and commitment to maximising their capacity to learn about their environment and themselves."[11]

In fact, a paradigm change is occurring in the conception and interpretation of the role of education, which guides us toward a broader conception of education, expressed

---

9. European Union Commision, *Teaching and Learning.*

10. Sergiovani, *Building Community in Schools,* 14.

11. A. Hargreaves, *Changing Teachers, Changing Times*, 93.

by Emile Durkheim in his understanding of the role of education as socialization.[12] The intensity in the use of knowledge, a deep transformation resulting from the introduction of ICTs, and the consequent education and training demands of citizens in the context of a knowledge society marked by globalization and directed toward lifelong learning, increasingly demonstrate the need for collaboration and cooperation. The future is written with the word *network*, and networks are also built collectively.

As expressed by Joette Stefl-Mabry and Barbara Lynch in *Knowledge Communities: Bringing the Village into the Classroom,*[13] schools have created a need for conceptual and methodological tools to aid in the effective development of citizens. The compliance of this task depends largely on the center's connections and capacity to take part in more extensive projects. That is why the understanding of schools as *gemeinschaft* places can certainly be a good mechanism to increase the effectiveness of educational action and of the schools themselves. All this implies a process of organizational learning, which requires the development of certain elements.[14]

Knowledge Creation as a Social Process

The increase in knowledge is driving new processes that are especially affecting the way we understand organizations. Knowledge management—how to create and disperse knowledge—is a process that affects all areas of society. In fact, the knowledge society needs modern institutions and organizations in which communities of individuals carry out exchange activities and generate knowledge. Thomas H. Davenport and Laurence Prusak have accurately stated the scope of this new paradigm: "Knowledge is a fluid mix of framed experience, values, contextual information and expert insight that provides a framework for evaluating and incorporating new experiences and information. It originates and is applied to the minds of knowers. In organisations, it often becomes embedded not only in documents or repositories but also in organisational routines, processes, practices and norms."[15]

From this definition, and being deliberately synthetic, as mentioned by Sami Paavola, Lasse Liponen, and Kai Hakkarainen: "There are two main ways of thinking about the genesis of new knowledge, namely, the 'acquisition' and the 'participation metaphors.' Behind these two metaphors is the debate between cognitive and situated perspectives on learning and human activity"[16]; we would be more comfortable within the latter perspective.

So it seems there are two common, or cross-sectional, aspects in the models of knowledge generation, including the usual distinction between explicit knowledge and

---

12. Durkheim, *Education and Sociology.*

13. Stefl-Mabry and Lynch, *Knowledge Communities.*

14. Brown and Duguid, "Organizational Learning and Communities-of-Practice," 40–57.

15. Davenport and Prusak, *Working Knowledge,* 5.

16. Paavola, Liponen, and Hakkarainen, "Models of Innovative Knowledge Communities and Three Metaphors of Learning," 557.

tacit knowledge on the one hand, and the confirmation in varying degrees of its social character on the other. Therefore, if knowledge is always socially situated, and situations coproduce knowledge, then "new ideas and innovations emerge between rather than within people. . . . Knowledge creation is not primarily a matter of creative individuals but instead requires fundamental reorganisation of the practices of a whole community. Epistemological processes require supporting social processes and vice versa."[17] On the other hand, there are four levels of entities that operate in knowledge creation: the individual, group, organizational, and inter-organizational levels. According to Ikujiro Nonaka and Hirokata Takeuchi, knowledge is created and transformed in an ascending process or spiral from the individual level to the group and organizational levels, and finally among organizations.[18]

Thus, in this concrete case, knowledge creation as an institutionalized social process must commence within organizations. Within the organizational framework of education, conditions should be set for generating the process of spiral knowledge creation.[19] We will refer to four of them.

Collaborative Culture: Integrating All Parties Involved at School

In the context of schools as knowledge communities, the social process of institutionalization of knowledge requires the existence of a "collaborative culture." Thus, active participation—open or, if preferred, democratic regarding all parties or social agents that make up the school system—constitutes another of the main characteristics of this kind of school. The text of Stefl-Mabry and Lynch, which is key in understanding this set of proposals, explicitly states that "each person can contribute towards the building and maintenance of a Knowledge Community because everyone in the community arrives with baggage."[20]

But if all the agents involved in the school organization have something to contribute to the benefit of the organization itself, it will have a different nature in accordance with their respective baggage, as mentioned above. In the case of students, one of the most relevant questions is the change in the concept of their role, not as customers but as active members of the organization. "For if schools are to constitute the learning organizations," according to Marlene Scardamalia and Carl Bereiter, "in which students gain experience, the role of students must change from that of clients to that of members. This means changing the function of the school from that of service provider to that of a productive enterprise to which the students are contributors."[21]

---

17. Ibid., 564.

18. Nonaka and Takeuchi, *The Knowledge-Creating Company*.

19. Brown, Collins, and Duguid, "Situated Cognition and the Culture of Learning," 32–42; Anderson, Reder, and Simon, "Situated Learning and Education, 5–11; and D. Hargreaves, "The Knowledge-Creating School," 122–24.

20. Stefl-Mabry and Lynch, *Knowledge Communities*, 23.

21. Scardamalia and Bereiter, "Schools as Knowledge Building Organizations," 275.

And regarding teachers, specifically in their role as managers of a school organization, one of the issues that is most emphasized is not only the need for their leadership but also a model of governance capable of developing a culture of collaboration where active integration of students in the daily dynamics of the school is the main challenge. Thus, as Sergiovani stated, "students are not clients, customers or cases, but objects of stewardship. Stewardship requires that adults have a personal stake in the academic success and the social welfare of each student. Stewardship requires that adults bring a collective orientation rather than self-orientation to bear in their relationships to students and with each other, placing common good over their own particular interest."[22]

Cultural Change: Schools Ready for Change

One of the characteristics of schools as knowledge communities is their ability to create collaborative environments, where knowledge is dynamic and shared, and there is a process of flowing and feedback of both tacit and explicit dimensions. It can only take place in organizations permanently ready to take on change, dynamic and multidirectional organizations where innovation is part of their culture. Hence, "the basic aim of creating Knowledge Communities is to bring together not only educators and students into classrooms, but to create an environment where knowledge flows in a multidirectional manner inside, outside and around the classroom. This can be accomplished by collaborating with parents, professionals, community members, and many diverse and underutilised resources located in and around the local and global community."[23]

Share the Organization's Values: Sense of Belonging

Sharing the values of an organization is not that simple. It requires a significant degree of integration and also of dependency on certain mechanisms that order the conduct of individuals as members and participants of a group. The willingness to share is not in itself sufficient. There should be core values, clearly defined and recognisable, giving rise to a noticeable and general degree of commitment. Sergiovani raises this as a condition sine qua non for the generation of a knowledge community in the educational field: "Where does one begin the process of becoming a purposeful community? One popular strategy is for schools to identify and commit to 'core values.'"[24]

Even in the presentation of the text the author reinforces this collective approach (we) versus individuality (I), which is like going back to defending community perspectives in the specific context of managing educational organizations. According to Sergiovani, "We are in authentic community when community becomes embodied in the school's policy structure itself, when community values are at the centre of our thinking . . . Community can help teachers and students be transformed from a collection of

22. Sergiovani, *Building Community in Schools,* 102.

23. Stefl-Mabry and Lynch, *Knowledge Communities,* xi.

24. Sergiovani, *Building Community in Schools,* 72.

'I' to a collective 'we', thus providing them with a unique and enduring sense of identity, belonging and place."[25]

The Role of Information and Communication Technologies

The previous defense of a restricted view (due to being organizational) of knowledge communities and their differentiation from communities of practice is closely linked to the role that information and communication technologies (ICTs) have in reshaping schools as knowledge communities.

Without at the moment going into the importance and relevance that ICTs, and especially the Internet, have had in the transformation of our societies[26] and its forms of social relationship or sociality,[27] both on a global scale and in the context of our daily lives,[28] it is however true that the new city shaped by these technological innovations— suitably named "telepolis" by Javier Echeverría,[29] has also affected, as one might expect, schools themselves.

There can be different interpretations and views on the depth, impact, and degree of acceptance and diffusion of ICTs in education, but nobody can dispute that ICTs are a huge factor in the construction of a new model of school organization when promoting, among other aspects, the plurality of information sources and thus an unlimited access to knowledge by the various agents involved in the schooling process. Stefl-Mabry and Lynch argue that "new technologies foster opportunities to grow Knowledge Communities that defy the constraints of time and distance as they provide access to knowledge that was difficult to obtain."[30]

Furthermore, while one of the main contributions of the Internet is the ability to establish large scale or long-distance relationships,[31] its impact and that of ICTs on a local level or in local networks is most certainly a relevant matter. This causes Keith N. Hampton to conclude that the Internet is a local facilitating factor and not just global.[32] Specifically concerning education, the role of the Internet and ICTs as local facilitators is of great importance in the implementation of dynamics of collaboration and knowledge exchange not only within schools but also in the relationship they established among themselves.

---

25. Ibid., xiii.

26. Castells, *La galaxia internet*; Briggs and Burke, *Social History of the Media*.

27. Meyrowitz, *No Sense of Place*.

28. Wellman and Haythornthwaite, eds., *The Internet and Everyday Life*; and Castaño, *Las mujeres y las tecnologías de la información*.

29. Echeverría, *Telépolis*. From the same author, see *Cosmopolitas domésticos* and *Los señores del aire*.

30. Stefl-Mabry and Lynch, *Knowledge Communities*, xxi.

31. Calhoun, "Indirect Relationships and Imagined Communities."

32. Hampton, "Networked Sociability Online, Off-line," 284.

The *Ikastola*: A Unique Educational Community

Ikastolas are a kind of school developed in the 1960s in *Euskal Herria*, the Basque Country, that are an educational and cultural reality with their own identity. Currently, the ikastola movement consists of 101 schools, 46,000 students, and 3,550 education professionals encompassing managers and teachers. The network of ikastolas identifies its geographical range within Euskal Herria. For this purpose, it acts in accordance with the right of each language community to organize its teaching so as to be able to transmit its cultural heritage beyond the administrative boundaries.

Genesis and Evolution

According to Mario Onaindia:

> Ikastolas constitute the most innovative socio-linguistic movement in the history of the Basque language to the extent that they represent a break with the major endogenous obstacles which Basque has ever encountered in its development, namely, the lack of social esteem, as it was a language associated with the more humble and undeveloped classes, in particular, the primary sector. For the first time in the history of the Basque Country, social sectors emerge which are interested in using Basque as a vehicle of enlightenment, culture and progress. . . . These new feelings toward the Basque language made thousands of Basque people want their children to learn the language in the only possible setting during the Franco period. The regime forbade not only Basque nationalism but also any linguistic, cultural, or even folk-related manifestation; in other words, anything to do with Basque was not allowed. . . . Therefore, it was impossible to imagine that these new concerns toward the Basque language would take the form of claims against the Franco regime so that Basque could be taught in national schools, and hence they organized themselves aside from and in parallel to national schools under the only institution that could provide shelter during the Franco regime, namely, the Church.[33]

The evolution of ikastolas can be ordered in different stages,[34] depending on various benchmarks, but nonetheless what all authors point out as the main characteristic during the sixties and much of the seventies is their phenomenal expansion in number of both students and schools. In approximately fifteen years between 1960 and 1975, 144 ikastolas[35] were founded in Araba, Gipuzkoa, Bizkaia, and Nafarroa, which gives an idea of the intensity of the movement. It appears that the relationship between the representation of the movement and the action taken is very close. Action and activity are the references from which to understand the commitment of the members of the movement. Félix Basurto even designates one of the features of the movement in the 1960–70 time period

---

33. Onaindia, "La Escuela Pública Vasca," 11.

34. Some examples are Arpal, Asua, and Dávila, *Educación y sociedad en el País Vasco*. From page 45 on it refers to three stages: secrecy, tolerance, and recognition; Basurto, "La normalización de las ikastolas." On page 143 he distinguishes between the time of secrecy, expansion and legalization, and legal normalization and public equality.

35. Arrien, *Las ikastolas de Bizkaia, 1957–1972*, 255.

as "improvised and precarious,"[36] which seems to reinforce the idea that commitment, activism, and action are fundamental ways to understand the social and educational activity that the ikastola movement represents.

The seventies were essentially a time for debate on the legal embodiment of the movement and the schools themselves, and also on financial, educational, and organizational issues. In other words, in a time of remarkable institutional stagnation, ikastolas were a place of organizational and educational experimentation and represented a definition of new models of operation. This is one of the questions that most reinforces the social interest in the movement, which is perceived as the bearer of a new system of rules, educational procedures, and cultural contents in such a way that it produces a displacement of the objective of the action but not of the value of the action.

The apparent willingness for historical autonomy that characterizes the ikastola movement has proven its tenacity in prevailing over any attempt at social, political, or institutional subordination, to the extent that the ikastola movement and the agencies that currently represent it are still a force capable of asserting new forms of sharing public resources in education, and of proposing formulas of institutional integration that seek to overcome the public-private divide. The formulation of a third option is the result of constant resistance of a sector of the ikastola movement to being located within the public-private dichotomy. And, in fact, the existence of these three types of educational levels constitutes a special feature of the Basque Country.

The long process that has led ikastolas to their present status has always been portrayed by its actors in collective and community terms as a social response in the field of education to those needs—also social and educational—that could not be satisfied within the public or private educational institutions. Trying to express this in an understandable way within its complexity, it could be argued that the ikastola is an inter-subjective social-identity educational space as opposed to the public-state-political model.

Organizational Culture

Ikastolas are grouped into federations under the format of educational cooperatives, and as they are school entities they share between themselves a number of common features. The governing bodies of each ikastola are the assembly, the governing council, and the presidency. The most noteworthy fact is that they rely on the tradition of social participation regarding management and organization. Thus, there is a "differentiation of roles" between parents and teachers. The parents, who are the true owners on a cooperative basis, have always been more focused on managing economic and material aspects (buildings, grants, and legal status, among others) while teachers have more autonomy in academic and educational matters. Based on these organizational principles, each ikastola is:

---

36. Basurto, "La normalización de las ikastolas," 145.

- A school establishment with its own legal personality
- An educational community
- Managed on a cooperative basis
- A unit that functions as part of a whole along with the other ikastolas
- In charge of devising its own educational plan.

Figure 3.1. Ikastola's organizational structure

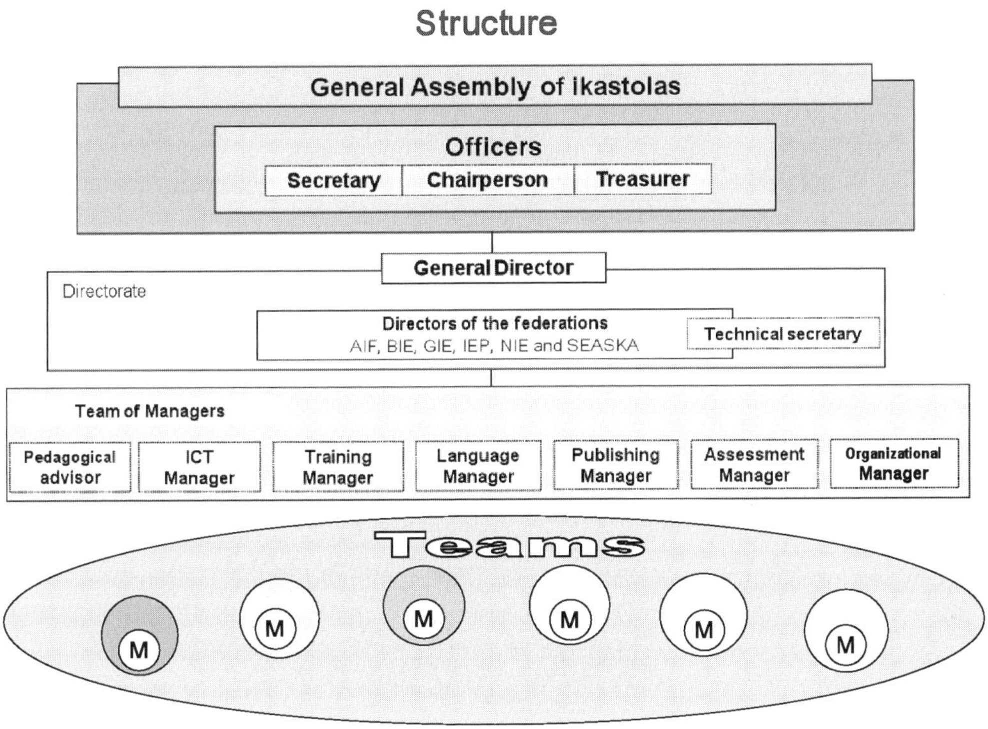

Structure

The network of ikastolas is headed by an owners' organization that carries out its joint educational plan, helps schools develop their own teaching plan, represents them collectively, and promotes Basque education within society. In fact, it is a cooperatively-managed organization that actively cooperates with other social, educational, and cultural agents in developing the Basque Country in its widest meaning. It has its own range of common services that are organized as follows:

- Services are organized through close inter-ikastola liaison. The needs arising in each specific context are identified, solutions are planned, developed, and implemented, and the results are reported.
- Services are approved and assessed by the ikastolas through governing bodies.
- The shared services are exclusively for ikastolas and/or they will be performed so as to promote Basque language education beyond the ikastolas' own boundaries.

- The tasks of researching, developing, innovating, and managing shared services are executed by professionals who combine expertise with a commitment to the character, mission, and vision of the ikastolas.
- Those professionals follow the guidelines set by the ikastolas' governing bodies.

Educational Model

The educational model of the ikastolas has a high degree of specificity; it is an integral model that manages all the constituent elements of the educational ecosystem. The educational model of ikastolas is characterized by the following features:[37]

- *Euskaldunidad.* Basque language and culture is the basis on which ikastolas carry out their integral, multilingual, and intercultural teaching.
- *Civil Nature.* Ownership and management are based on each individual educational community, which neither depends on the public administrative authorities nor conforms to the traditional private model.
- *Active Participation.* Members of the Educational Community of each ikastola take an active part in its government and operation.
- *Autonomous Management.* The will of each educational community is the only decision-making engine for the development and implementation of the educational plan in each ikastola.
- *Inter-Ikastola Cooperation.* Ikastolas cooperate with each other by sharing their autonomy in a collective organization, namely, the Federation.
- *Solidarity Fund.* There is a community chest to address problems that each ikastola might have.
- *Forms of Social Economy.* The principles of social economy are the foundations on which the management of schools is based.
- *Specific Work Context.* Ikastolas are equipped with their own specific working framework and context.
- *Training Plan.* Ikastolas have a training plan adjusted to their educational model.
- *Production of Teaching Materials.* Ikastolas create and produce materials and tools appropriate for their educational model.
- *RDI (Research, Development, and Technological Innovation).* The ikastola is a defined project of continuous improvement and thus subject to research and development.
- *Opting for ICTs.* The integral use of ICTs began around twenty years ago and constitutes a reference point for other centers, independent of educational level and geographic location. So, in this matter ikastolas are one of the most important examples.

---

37. "Sketch for the normalisation of ikastolas in the educational system," Internal document.

Ikastola as a Knowledge Community

It is ironic that such a classic concept as "community" now holds a place of such importance. Indeed, the fairly widespread emergence of knowledge communities seems to be the best indicator that the community remains an appropriate mode of being in society—communities of a very diverse character.[38] Hence, while new communities with an individual or private characteristic are activated, others with a more self-defining profile adapt their practices from experience and the solid anchorage provided by the life experience of a long community history. This is the case of the ikastolas, which through the use of presence communication or by means of technological tools and networks have been able to use ICTs to progressively transform into a knowledge community.

This transformation began in the early 1980s when ikastolas made the strategic decision to become a center for educational services. This idea led to the development of systematic processes for the creation of knowledge. The attempt to turn the intangible (ideas) into tangible (materials serving the community) has generated a specific pattern of knowledge creation, followed up to the present time, that can be expressed as follows:

- Choice of a project.
- The project is developed into an experimental model to be tested in three or four ikastolas.
- Work teams are set up.
- Specific materials are established.
- Materials that have been tested are distributed to the rest of the ikastolas.
- The project must always have a beneficial outcome or economic output.

The Specific Role of ICTs in Ikastolas

Ikastolas strengthened their community ties for years while increasing their capabilities, all through systematic processes. Thus, there was an experience of creating, sharing, and knowledge management in which a large number of individuals and groups were involved—an experience that would expand when the intensive use of ICTs made it possible.

We are also referring to a community in which, since the beginning, commitment, activism, and action have established essential forms of understanding social-educational activities. It should be understood as a lifestyle that we might recognize as an assessment of closeness or proximity of everyday life in which the culture of collaboration, the feeling of belonging, and change as an objective are part of the corporate identity. This is in turn a community accustomed to sharing experiences through interrelationships of collective learning as a knowledge community.

---

38. Suttles, *The Social Construction of Communities*; Cohen, *The Symbolic Construction of Community*; and Anderson, *Imagined Communities*.

It is therefore not surprising that the intensive use of ICTs in ikastolas was a prime target, because it clearly accelerated social relations, cross-learning, and knowledge construction. Moreover, as mentioned earlier, the characteristics of the *ikastola model* require a close connection in both its content and methodology between what each ikastola needs and the educational service that ikastolas can offer through the Federations or Confederation of Ikastolas. It should be remembered that what ikastolas understand by an educational service is the total knowledge and support necessary to develop the educational project of each ikastola, including services related to the teaching/learning process and those connected to its support (internal/external communication, legal and economic stability, and administration). [39]

The intensive use of ICTs in ikastolas has enabled the updating of their specific pattern of knowledge creation by developing a model-type typical of knowledge communities, a model that is the backbone of the ikastolas' management in the field of RDI (Research, Development, and Technological Innovation) and that also is carried out based on processes and sub-processes stated in figure 3.2.

Figure 3.2. Processes and subprocesses of RDI
(research, development, and technological innovation in ikastolas)

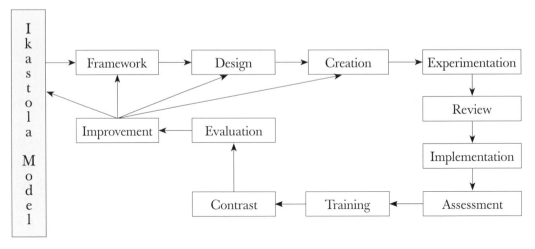

Based on this general model, ikastolas are currently developing a total of nine projects whose development can only strengthen the consideration of this educational community as a knowledge community. As shown in figure 3.3, the aim of such projects is to design, build, test, edit, implement, assess, provide training for, contrast, evaluate, and improve curriculum materials (for use by students, professionals, and families) in a cooperative manner using professionals at each ikastola and specialists from the Confederation of Ikastolas.

---

39. Report titled *Las ikastolas, presente y futuro*, approved on January 24, 2009, by the 6th Congress of Ikastolas.

Figure 3.3. Main projects, forums, and participants

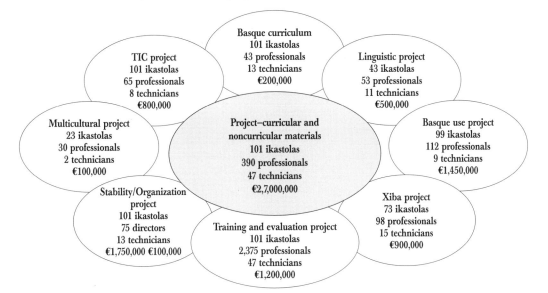

These projects are supplemented by frequent personal contact in forums, an exchange network based on ICTs consisting of forums individualized by projects (in which forum members interact) and open forums. All are managed by a panel called e-ikastola. The subscribers include over 80 percent of the professional group.

On another level, each individual ikastola has an internal computer application (called IKASDAT) that manages on-site databases for that ikastola and energizes the internal life of each school; 75 percent of ikastolas have their own RDI application.

Conclusion

We conclude by pointing out that it is difficult to discern when an organization can be considered a knowledge community. As we know, the social process for the effective creation of a specific type of organizational culture still remains a very complex issue. Erving Goffman had stated with masterly sarcasm in his speech as president of the American Sociological Association in 1982 (which he unfortunately could not present due to his passing away some months before) that social scientists "would be happy if we change everything we have produced up to now for a couple of good conceptual distinctions and a cold beer."[40]

While all organizations have some degree of complexity, any person who has had experience in the operation of schools in different roles or responsibilities is very much aware of the inherent difficulties in daily management, probably because of the complex-

---

40. Goffman, "The Interaction Order," 17.

ity of the material in question on both a students' and parents' level, without forgetting the various interests of teachers. As Stefl-Mabry and Lynch pointed out, "The building of a culture that is 'knowledge enabled' and sincerely dedicated to learning is not a quick-fix solution. It will take hard work, time, sincerity, patience, and the willingness to constantly reflect, rethink, and recharge. It will take a full community effort wherein learning relationships and social connectiveness are a priority. Hard work no doubt, but doable."[41] Furthermore, as Sergiovani highlights, "community cannot be borrowed or bought."[42]

In sum, the transformation of schools into knowledge communities can form one of the most appropriate strategies to handle the swarm of interests, expectations, and aspirations that are concentrated in this social place one academic year after another. Perhaps the prospect of community or *gemeinschaft* in schools enables them to maximize the effectiveness of their educational action, undoubtedly recognized as a key action in the context of a knowledge society. But it does not seem easy, much less on a day-to-day basis, to create an organization steeped in collaborative culture, a culture prepared to change, open to innovation, and capable of creating shared core values and generating a sense of belonging—capable, in short, of sharing knowledge.

As noted earlier, considering its genesis and historical evolution up to the present, its organizational culture, its educational model, the existence of a specific pattern of knowledge creation at the heart of each school based on its autonomy, although always conveyed by the federal and confederate network, as well as using ICTs intensively, everything seems to point to the existence of sufficient objective conditions to consider ikastolas as a knowledge community.

At this point, and finally, it is very important to indicate the specific role that ICTs have within an ikastola. They are without a doubt a reference model in education regarding the use of ICTs. Ikastolas have a conception of them as tools or means and never as an end in themselves. Aware that the pace of technological change is much more intense than the pace of change in education; those responsible in ikastolas know that it is the educational dimension and not technology that defines the social function of their schools. Therefore, ICTs are key drivers in the creation and consolidation of each ikastola as a knowledge community, but always as dependent variables subject to the established criteria of management's vision and mission.

Bibliography

Abrams, Philip. "Introduction: Social Facts and Sociological Analysis." In *Work, Urbanism and Inequality,* edited by Philip Abrams. London: Weidenfeld and Nicolson, 1978.

Anderson, Benedict. *Imagined Communities: Reflections on the Origin and Spread of Nationalism.* London: Verso, 1991.

---

41. Stefl-Mabry and Lynch, *Knowledge Communities*, 254.

42. Sergiovani, *Building Community in Schools,* 5.

Anderson, John R., Lynne M. Reder, and Herbert A. Simon. "Situated Learning and Education." *Educational Researcher* 25, no. 4 (1996): 5–11.

Arpal, Jesús, Begoña Asua, and Paulí Dávila. *Educación y sociedad en el País Vasco.* Donostia-San Sebastián: Txertoa, 1982.

Arrien, Gregorio. *Las ikastolas de Bizkaia, 1957–1972: Sus orígenes y organización.* Donostia: Eusko Ikaskuntza, 1992.

Basurto, Félix. "La normalización de las ikastolas: Breve historia y estado de la cuestión de la escuela pública vasca." In *Historia de la educación: Revista interuniversitaria*, no. 8 (January–December 1989): 139–65.

Briggs, Asa and Peter Burke. *Social History of the Media: From Gutenberg to the Internet.* Cambridge, UK: Polity, 2002.

Brown, John Seely, Allan Collins, and Paul Duguid. "Situated Cognition and the Culture of Learning." *Education Researcher* 18, no. 1 (1989): 32–42.

Brown, John Seely and Paul Duguid. "Organizational Learning and Communities-of-Practice: Toward a Unified View of Working, Learning, and Innovation." *Organization Science* 2, no. 1 (1991): 40–57.

Calhoun, Craig J. "Community: Toward a Variable Conceptualization for Comparative Research." *Social History* 5, no. 1 (1980): 105–29. Reprinted in *History and Class: Essential Readings in Theory and Intrepetation*, edited by R. S. Neale. Oxford: Blackwell, 1983.

——. "Indirect Relationships and Imagined Communities: Large-Scale Social Interaction and the Transformation of Everyday Life." In *Social Theory for a Changing Society*, edited by P. Bourdieu and J. S. Coleman. New York: Westview Press, 1991.

Castaño, Cecilia. *Las mujeres y las tecnologías de la información. Internet y la trama de nuestra vida.* Madrid: Alianza Editorial, 2005.

Castells, Manuel. *La galaxia internet. Reflexiones sobre Internet, empresa y sociedad.* Barcelona: Plaza y Janés, 2001.

Cohen, Anthony. *The Symbolic Construction of Community.* London: Tavistock, 1985.

Crow, Graham and Graham Allan. *Community Life. An Introduction to Local Social Relations.* London: Haverster Wheatsheaf, 1994.

Davenport, Thomas H. and Laurence Prusak. *Working Knowledge: How Organizations Manage What They Know.* Boston: Harvard Business School Press, 1998.

Durkheim, Emile. *Education and Sociology.* New York: The Free Press, 1956.

Echeverría, Javier. *Cosmopolitas domésticos.* Barcelona: Anagrama, 1994.

——. *Los señores del aire: Telépolis y el tercer entorno.* Destino: Barcelona, 1999.

——. *Telépolis.* Barcelona: Destino, 1994.

European Union Commission. *Teaching and Learning: Towards the Learning Society.* White Paper on Education and Training. Brussels: European Union Commission, 1995. http://europa.eu/documents/comm/white_papers/pdf/com95_590_en.pdf.

Goffman, Erving. "The Interaction Order." *American Sociological Review* 48, no. 1 (1983): 1–17.

Hampton, Keith N. "Networked Sociability Online, Off-line." In *The Network Society: A Cross-cultural Perspective,* edited by Manuel Castells. Northampton, MA: Edward Elgar Publishers, 2004.

Hargreaves, Andy. *Changing Teachers, Changing Times: Teacher's Work and Culture in the Postmodern Age.* New York: Teachers College Press, 1994.

Hargreaves, David H. "The Knowledge-Creating School." *British Journal of Educational Studies* 47, no. 2 (1999): 122–24.

Lesser, Eric and Larry Prusak. "Communities of Practice, Social Capital and Organizational Knowledge." In *Knowledge and Communities,* edited by Eric Lesser. Boston: Butterworth/Heinemann, 2000.

Meyrowitz, Joshua. *No Sense of Place: The Impact of Electronic Media on Social Behavior.* New York: Oxford University Press, 1985.

Nisbet, Robert A. *La formación del pensamiento sociológico,* vol. 1. Buenos Aires: Amorrortu, 1986.

Nonaka, Ikujiro and Takeuchi, Hirotaka. *The Knowledge-Creating Company: How Japanese Companies Create the Dynamics of Innovation.* New York: Oxford University Press, 1995.

Onaindia, Mario. "La Escuela Pública Vasca y la construcción nacional." *Cuadernos de Alzate,* no. 20 (1994): 9–63.

Paavola, Sami, Lasse Liponen, and Kai Hakkarainen. "Models of Innovative Knowledge Communities and Three Metaphors of Learning." *Review of Educational Research* winter, vol. 74, no. 4 (2004): 557–76.

Scardamalia, Marlene and Carl Bereiter. "Schools as Knowledge Building Organizations." In *The Development Health and The Wealth of Nations. Social, Biological and Educational Dynamics,* edited by D. Keating and C. Hertzman. New York: Guilford, 1999.

Senge, Peter M. *The Fifth Discipline. The Art and Practice of the Learning Organizations.* New York: Doubleday/Currency, 1990.

Senge, Peter M., et al. *Schools That Learn: A Fifth Discipline Filed Book for Educators, Parents and Everyone Who Cares about Education.* New York: Doubleday, 2000.

Senge, Peter M. and Katrin H. Kaufer. "Communities of Leaders or No Leadership at All." In *Cutting Edge: Leadership,* edited by Barbara Kellerman and Larraine R. Matusak. College Park, MD: James McGregor Burns Academy of Leadership Press, 2000.

Sergiovani, Thomas J. *Building Community in Schools.* San Francisco: Jossey-Bass, 1994.

Stefl-Mabry, Joette and Barbara L. Lynch. *Knowledge Communities: Bringing the Village into the Classroom.* Toronto: The Scarecrow Press, 2006.

Suttles, Gerald D. *The Social Construction of Communities.* Chicago: University of Chicago Press, 1972.

Tönnies, Ferdinand. *Gemeinschaft und gesellschaft.* Leipzig: Fues's Verlag, 1887. Translated by Charles P. Loomis as *Community and Society.* East Lansing: Michigan State University Press, 1957.

Weber, Max. *Economy and Society: An Outline of Interpretive Sociology.* Vol. 1, edited by Guenther Roth and Claus Wittich. Berkeley and Los Angeles: University of California Press, 1978.

Wellman, Barry and Caroline Haythornthwaite, eds. *The Internet in Everyday Life.* Oxford: Oxford Blackwell, 2002.

Wenger, Etienne. *Communities of Practice: Learning, Meaning and Identity.* Cambridge: Cambridge University Press, 1998.

Willmot, Peter. *Community Initiatives: Patterns and Prospects.* London: Policy Studies Institute, 1989.

Young, Michael and Peter Willmot. *Family and Kinship in East London.* London: Routledge and Kegan Paul, 1957.

4

Knowledge Communities, Structural Contexts, and Innovation Spaces

ANDER GURRUTXAGA and ÁLVARO LUNA

The discourse concerning community is a resource of the sociological perspective. In societies of knowledge a certain type of community emerges: these are groups that are formed by individuals that recognize themselves by the jobs they hold, by the places they occupy—laboratories turned into homes—and the *sanctuaries* they transit—the institutions where research and development (R&D) work happens. The groups recognize each other because:

- They have a "good"; they create and reproduce technical and abstract knowledge.
- They demonstrate a great capacity to manipulate ideas and create new knowledge.
- They create the idea of "us" that moves and expands around global networks. The network is the means and the instrument of communication that differentiates them from other groups.
- The Internet is the instrument of action; through it, they transfer their knowledge and discoveries.
- The acknowledgment strategy does not end in the adscription to the network; members search for one another, and see and recognize each other using face to face interaction.
- The chosen moments and places to celebrate the ritual of interaction are scientific encounters, conferences, congresses, and seminars. At these events, the members meet, recognize and see each other, and interact, with community being the

instrument that traces the singularity of each one. The encounters are part of the acknowledgement strategy of the idea of "us."

- Individuality is not dissolved; on the contrary, the persistence of community requires interaction between individuals.
- The community holds onto the tension of creativity and discovery, and needs to generate a certain feedback between them. The communities of knowledge are, from this perspective, "communities of individuals."

Our hypothesis is that community emerges in the societies and places that are able to build social spaces of innovation based on knowledge, learning, and experimentation. These spaces are developed in structural contexts equipped with institutional systems of innovation; they also have university systems of high performance and quality research. They are able to constitute political societies where quality of life and social welfare are guaranteed to their citizens. They possess a culture of innovation where networks of trust, intangible values, and teamwork prevail. They also provide financial sources based on risk capital and public initiatives managed by the state.

We are forming historical communities that are the product of the institutionalization of knowledge societies. They make knowledge into their own good, networks into their own means, and the individuality of discovery becomes their strategy of acknowledgement. Success is guaranteed if the goal is endorsed by the spaces of innovation where abstract knowledge is produced, by a university system that provides intelligent sources for the necessities and requirements of the system of innovation, by an innovative culture that institutionalizes creativity, and by a financing system that supports R&D in the *home*—laboratories—and the *sanctuary*—institutional system—of these types of communities.

The path that we propose begins with a discussion about the place of community in sociological discourse; it also touches on the definition of structural contexts that make community possible, and finishes with the analysis of the role of social spaces in the emergence of this type of groups.

The Persistence of Community

Community is an unclosed remnant, a fragment of the "theoretical home" and of the conceptual references of sociology. Its links are everywhere, they go through time, history, and sociology to remain as one of the *ahistorical* concepts, which historicity transforms into one of the commonalities of social science. Who does not identify himself as a member of a certain type of community? To mention some empirical references: this identity is formed by the strategists of big enterprise that discover in social responsibility the support to germinate informal associations in complex organizations; it is formed by those who give heed to social capital to find the *home* in complex organizations; it is formed by the analysts and prophets of political change who dedicate millions of pages to cosmopolitan community or to the communal relationship that is generated in political participation; we can find it in migratory movements inspired by diasporas to produce ties; it is also the resource of those who see in God's metamorphosis the links of earthly union through a community of believers.

The home for community is also found in the behaviors of private sociability, in the industries of paradoxical happiness that articulate the praxis of consumption, in the practices that recognize themselves by means of secret codes based on the network language, or, alternately, as a response to the coldness of the computer keyboard in the creation of virtual communities. In this case, the response is a temporary space, where the links are urgently created and are set to cover specialized needs in a leisure universe. In other cases, the discourse impregnates the networks of communication technologies; the Internet is the home, and interactive communication the format, while the *others* keep themselves within the communicative space. Knowledge societies integrate other types of communities: those that articulate in the innovation spaces hosting R&D initiatives, and those that see in knowledge the most desired and sought-for good.

Zigmund Bauman says, "Words have meanings: some words however, also have a 'feel.' The word 'community' is one of them. It feels good: whatever the word 'community' may mean, it is good 'to have a community,' 'to be in a community.' In short, 'community' stands for the kind of world which is not, regrettably, available to us—but which we dearly wish to inhabit and which we hope to repossess."[1]

From this perspective, the idea we are trying to defend is that building community relations is like building a home. Quoting Alfred Schutz, "Home is starting-point as well as terminus. It is the null-point of the system of coordinates which we ascribe to the world in order to find our bearings in it. Geographically 'home' means a certain spot on the surface of the earth. Where I happen to be is my 'abode'; where I intend to stay is my 'residence'; where I come from and where I want to return is my 'home.' Yet home is not merely the homestead—my house, my room, my garden, my town—but everything it stands for."[2] The concept is not limited to the empirical meanings that it projects, but it has the capacity to hold meanings for the praxis it sets into action. Schutz expresses this idea when he warns us about the dangers that the unidimensional perspective has concerning that complex phenomena: "Home means different things to different people. It means, of course, father-house and mother-tongue, the family, the sweetheart, the friends; it means a beloved landscape, 'songs my mother taught me,' food prepared in a particular way, familiar things for daily use, folkways and personal habits—briefly, a peculiar way of life composed of small and important elements, likewise cherished."[3]

The concepts of home and community are like "the content and the continent." From this deduction we can extract the following hypothesis: community needs "home" and the format it adopts is communal. Hence, the "symbolic notion of 'home' is emotion-

---

1. Bauman, *Community*, 1–3.

2. Schutz, "The Homecomer," in *Collected Papers II*, 107–8.

3. Ibid., 108.

ally evocative and difficult to describe."[4] Authors like Richard Sennet relate this notion, so dense and enfolding, with the *sanctuary* perspective. For this author, the explanation resides in the social encounter background of acknowledgement strategies: "The coming of the Industrial Revolution aroused a great longing for sanctuary, 'home' became the secular version of spiritual refuge; the geography of safety shifted from a sanctuary in the urban center to the domestic interior."[5]

The conclusion is that the notion of "home" is built into the new sanctuary. Modernity sets out the bases for an extended opinion where the interior and the exterior of modern social life reflect different ways of being in the world and positioning toward different forms of life. As a result, community spaces are warm and secluded places where individuals can find what they cannot seek in the production world, in their job, or in the public spaces that they frequent. It is not unusual, in light of the empirical evidence residing in communal processes, to agree with Robert Nisbet when he writes, "The most fundamental and far-reaching of sociology's unit-ideas is community."[6] The fact is that tracking communal elements in collective behaviors is an arduous and protracted labor because it is a concept used with profusion.[7]

In the dominant discourse, community has it is own characteristics. On the one hand, we emphasize the presence of "group," where individuals see themselves as global personalities, apart from their own roles and statuses. On the other hand, the members of the group hold dense ties and bonds because community implies mutual knowledge. This state can only be reached if the interaction lasts through time. Also, the members of the group need to be recognized not in their individuality but as members of the collectivity. The collectivity—the group that builds itself—gives name to the individual. A deviation from what the group does is penalized, as members' behaviors are controlled by group solidarity.

Communal forms create a sense of belonging. The group sticks together, it develops a consciousness of "us," its outlines are defined and identified by the "others." The communal group needs the "other" in order to secure the acknowledgement that the consciousness of "us" produces and reproduces. This makes it able to hold internal cohesion. The members hope that what the group assures is relevant is also recognized as relevant. If they say they act as A, in contrast with B, they hope to be treated according to the definition they give themselves. This aspect is important because through it they constitute the

---

4. Ibid.

5. Sennet, *The Conscience of the Eye*, 21.

6. Nisbet, *The Sociological Tradition*, 47.

7. Sociologists, anthropologists, historians, political scientists, moral and social philosophers, and even economists use the term "community." Among the most suggestive is—leaving aside the classics—Charles C. Cooley. The text of Theodorson, *Studies of Human Ecology* is a magnificent exponent of the contributions of this school. We also need to cite some of the classics like Lynd and his analysis of the Middletown community. Community studies are also relevant in the analysis of ethnic relations. To mention some of the most important: Misra and Preston, eds., *Community, Self and Identity*; Farley, *Majority-Minority Relations*; Glazer and Moynihan, *Ethnicity*; Cohen, *The Symbolic Construction of Community*.

symbolic frontier. The community members manage these limits, although the "others"—those who do not belong to the group—have to differ and interiorize them as distinctive signs of the group "us." This guarantees the persistence of the communication structure from which we negotiate social reference frames and the differences that might be established. For the type of group maintaining a frontier—the symbolic us/them frontier—this implies that one and the other are transformed into the conditions for communal survival. The forms of sociality project rituals that highlight many differences when the group creates its exclusive language, its peculiar esthetics, its distinctive behaviors, and so forth. In conclusion, community condenses and synthesizes feelings and reason, tradition and modernity. Indeed, there is no primary or secondary institution, macro-, meso-, or micro-, where we cannot find form, content, and social communal spaces.

The discourse on community cannot escape a degree of complexity that is achieved by social processes of innovation, and by the uncertain contexts that knowledge societies define better than any other. Our thesis is that the community's praxis responds to the functioning of "emerging systems," that is to say, communal systems evolve from "simple to complex rules."[8] As Steven Johnson states, "Such a system would define the most elemental form of *complex* behavior: a system with multiple agents dynamically interacting in multiple ways, following local rules and oblivious to any higher-level instructions. But it would not fully be considered *emergent* until those local interactions resulted in some kind of discernable macro-behavior."[9]

In these patterns of living, the communal discourses focus on the problems and paradoxes that emerge thanks to the success of individualization. In fact, many communal expressions feed and recycle themselves through the use of individualization, as if the individual and the community were not opposing elements but perspectives in fusion. Maybe, as author Norbert Elias believes, we should quote the "community of individuals."[10] The human being has to choose among the opportunities offered by life, gender, identity, religion, blood relationship, social bonds, marriage; all of them become decision objects.

In these landscapes and in presence of this view, what is left of the discourse on community? Has it disappeared? Has it transformed? How has this happened? Community, just as we described, invades all social scenarios. Just as in the world of early modernity, the present forms itself to the conditions of contemporary time. It is as if we had passed from community organized by tradition to community highlighted by the common expressions of life. This does not imply that tradition is unimportant or that the expression of individualized forms invades everything. It so happens that there is a place for everyone; it is as if we were guarding a vortex that gobbles everything, absorbing it but not digesting anything.

---

8. Johnson, *Emergence.*

9. Ibid., 19.

10. Elias, *Society of Individuals.*

Knowledge Communities and Innovation Spaces

From the general perspective of the community discourse traversed by the concept of "home," sheltered in the sanctuary of innovation systems, limited in its expressive capacity and conditioned by individualization, a certain type of community is created—the community of knowledge. These knowledge communities grow in innovation spaces that are built within intelligent cities.[11] The hypothesis is that innovation is the context that leads to the construction of knowledge communities. When these communities are built we become part of social spaces of innovation. This means that the groups that sustain these types of communities require innovation and learning spaces to develop. In them, knowledge, experimentation, and apprenticeship are linked. They contain the human capital that accumulates specialized knowledge based on applied sciences and technologies, which is used to develop new knowledge.

The specific factor of "group," the element that characterizes it, is the possession of the most valued "good": abstract knowledge. This element is highly valued in innovation spaces. Moreover, the possession of this "good" is key to knowledge societies. These types of expression require the creation of innovation spaces—social places where individuals "learn to learn" within specific structural contexts and within a culture based on creative values as the expressive resource and atmosphere of a knowledge society.

Communities of knowledge are set up as expressive communities, that is, the groups emerge through their work, they exhibit and represent in the network and through the network. We could say that the Internet is the means to exhibit the goods that they hold. Being part of the network and the Internet become the supporting elements of community. Knowledge does not need, except in extraordinary circumstances, face-to-face interaction, but requires us to be in the network, have access to the Internet, and be able to communicate through it. In this manner, what do these groups exhibit? They exhibit the most precious good: *knowledge*. This is the product of work and the distinctive sign that articulates its presence in the network. The specific knowledge is specialized knowledge; to possess it gives us status and singularity within the network.

If the means to exist is being in the network, the method to do it is knowledge transference. The meeting point is in the virtual network space. However, the localization of network also has fixed geographic anchors. Why do we say this? The community finds itself in order to recognize itself, and not only by knowledge transference or virtual network spaces. Scientific encounters conform to interactive spaces whether they are conferences, congresses, and so on. This is the moment in which knowledge transference acquires physical presence and in which face-to-face interaction transforms the manner of recognition. Membership is based on interactive criteria, in the moment in which community anchors itself to physical and material reality, in the instant that it relates to

---

11. It is important to mention the following publications: Castells and Himmanen, "Modelos institucionales"; Edquist and Hommen, eds., *Small Country Innovation Systems*; Hamalainen and Heskala, eds., *Social Innovations, Institutional Change and Economic Performance*; Saxenian, *The New Argonauts*; and Van Den Berg et al., *European Cities in a Knowledge Economy*.

certain geographic space. In this particular case, the strategies of acknowledgement are based on face-to-face interaction processes. In them personal knowledge is valued—in fact, the discovery of the "others" happens in the processes of face-to-face interaction and not through the network or through the acquisition of knowledge within it.

The recurrent space is located in the urban center. The city designates a specific space where it admits the infrastructures that community shelters. The laboratory, as we said, is the "home," "motherland." Nevertheless, the city is not the specialized place for the establishment of these types of communities. The laboratory is the natural shelter. The social saloons where communities are exhibited are extrapolations of laboratory. Communities of knowledge are not articulated by geography; they are managed by the significance that the home/work/laboratory acquires and by the connections formed through the network. Knowledge transference is the unmistakable sign that confirms that we belong and we are part of the network.

Knowledge cities shelter and protect themselves through the distinct aspects that characterize them. From the perspective of those who defend the "intelligent territory" theory, knowledge cities are defined as follows: cities that, within their geographic territory, are planned and managed according to a strategy involving both the society and the government.[12] These actors have a common goal: to build an economy based on knowledge development. The characteristics that best describe these cities are:

- They consider their citizens to be creative inhabitants.
- They are attractive to creators—scientists, artists, knowledge companies—that come from other places and cities.
- They are the nodes that compose the whole knowledge network, having high-level resources to facilitate the formation and education of new knowledge workers.
- They have different technological and cultural instruments to make knowledge accessible to the creators.
- They consider every resource and every space as an opportunity to create new networks where innovation is produced and knowledge is accessible.
- They connect institutions with urban infrastructure to create a network of innovation builders.

It is important that we understand that knowledge cities defined from this perspective not only facilitate the creation of innovation spaces, they also make possible the creation of opportunity structures in which knowledge becomes the leitmotif of urban actions. In these types of cities, knowledge communities can be easily created. This kind of habitat defines an urban structure that accepts housing developments where housing is not an exclusive project; that contains important universities—although this is not the most important factor; that is not built exclusively for researchers, even if they are

---

12. There is a wide range of bibliographic production concerning this matter. We can find very interesting texts such as: Vegara and de las Rivas, *Territorios inteligentes*; Sassen, *Globalization and Its Discontents*; Sassen, *Global Networks*; Soja, *Post-metrópolis*; Carrillo, "Capital Cities"; and Landry, *The Creative Cities*.

key to the work structure; that is not based solely on Internet resources, even though it must then acquire important infrastructures; that is able to define a long-term project that considers future changes. All these are factors indicative of knowledge-based cities, and they must be in equilibrium. It is in this balance that knowledge communities find a good social repertoire for understanding themselves as containers and homes for the mentioned groups.

Knowledge communities do not deny or reject individuality. On the contrary, the individual needs to recreate knowledge communities. Individuality is not dissolved in the act of belonging as a member. Individuality must be recognized, it cannot be denied by community membership. My hypothesis is that the characteristics of these types of groups cause us to consider them as individualized communities—that is, they do not shun the individual, rather they need his or her creativity and entrepreneurial capacity. Individuality is required by the urban environment to create different goods and values such as: diversity, tolerance, access to different goods and sources, and an avant-garde esthetic. Thus, the knowledge community assembles the individual in the symbolic universe but does not dissolve it; on the contrary, it is integrated within it, and the community preconceives individuality.

We are defining a group that defends individuality, that claims it, knowing that community is not possible without it. The individual introduces creativity and innovative capacity. Creating communities is impossible if we do not also recreate them. In this case, community does not dissolve the individual, and he or she does not live life apart from the community. Although it may seem paradoxical, we are not considering the terrains of community and individuality in the sense of modern tradition. In that reality, individual action builds community and anchors it to the goods they possess, that is, scientific knowledge.

The Structural Contexts of the Knowledge Community

In knowledge social structure, the labor class is a minority and its size decreases in parallel to the diminishing of the service sector. While the upper class diversifies, the middle class has differentiated itself on an internal level. In its place, new divisions and occupations based on social and technological changes have appeared. Approximately two-thirds of the jobs generated by the new economy require technical knowledge in ICT, and other special abilities. This class of work positions is increasingly more abundant and demanding in relative terms. From 1995 to 2004, the proportion of jobs requiring specific technical knowledge—"Apple Mac" jobs—has increased from 20 percent to 24 percent. Many people also work in "Big Mac" occupations such as public service jobs in cafes, stores, malls, gas stations, households, and so on.

Social hierarchy places a certain set of social groups at the top of society. These groups are formed by elites whose power has increased, especially in global European and North American cities. The influence of this model is national and transnational. A minimum of 50 percent of the jobs in the knowledge economy require a high grade of cognitive and personal abilities, which affects the duties of "connected workers," that is, those who use computers during most of their working day. These categories include those who work for the state administration or public-state companies.

Generally, class divisions in a knowledge society are determined by differences in lifetime opportunities. This is a significant transformation in contrast with industrial society. Differences in life conditions are common, but different ways of life often influence these more than purely economic limitations. Today we have democratization of everyday life, but this does not imply more security or more sense of security. The majority of people now expect more of their lives than did past generations, which implies they are induced to have aspirations and expectations that cannot always be fulfilled. The democratization of expectations is distributed among social classes; they are distinguished by the access to opportunities that will enable them to achieve their expectations.

The amount of security that we experience in the different social groups causes ideological breaks. Those who have success feel comfortable with diversity and adopt cosmopolitan ways of life. They can be excited by the idea of changing jobs, by not expecting a traditional labor career. The creative industries, the high-tech jobs, finance and bank jobs, and other professional occupations are labor environments where individuals of different groups can encounter each other more readily. A significant example is what Richard Florida calls the "creative class." According to his calculations, the "creative class" represents more than 20 percent of the workforce and is concentrated in the R&D sectors of metropolitan areas. In order to measure this group, Florida has developed a creativity index based on four factors:

- The percentage of members of the "creative class" in contrast with the local working population
- The percentage of workers occupied in the high-tech sector
- The measurement of innovation in terms of patents in proportion to GDP
- The measurement of diversity in terms of the proportion of homosexual people, as representative of the amount of "openness" of a zone or local territory

The application of this index finds that cities at the top of the list are world leaders in economic prosperity and employment generation. Their economies are characterized by the three Ts: talent, technology, and tolerance. The groups that constitute the creative class are, mainly, cosmopolitan and mobile. They gravitate toward cities that offer what they seek in their lifestyle. But it is also true that we can find local groups that develop attitudes of rejection toward everything new—people who look for a "whipping boy" they can blame for their problems. These people are usually attracted by political populism.

The social structure of an innovation society—in other words, that place where knowledge communities live and develop—defines a radical diversification process, a process where the argument about lifestyles and cultural conflicts plays a central part. The materialization of new social divisions does not derive from cultural class codes, but rather from lifestyles related to the specific employments that knowledge communities enjoy and to the framework of expectations, possibilities, and real opportunities they posses. While expectations democratize and trespass frontiers and social divisions, opportunities are limited by the type of employment they develop. Self-programmed knowledge workers have a life status and can access expectations that generic and replaceable workers cannot enjoy or afford. They move in the magma of the service sector, enjoy the democratic right to dream, and participate in the society of expectations, even when objective life conditions deny the chances that are announced in almost all formal and informal communication channels. Consequently, a society of innovation enables the dreams of some to come true but denies the dreams of many others.

At times, the discourse of innovation becomes the rhetoric of social sectors occupying elite positions in knowledge societies' social structure, as the elite social sectors have the best jobs and the best cultural resources to accomplish their objectives successfully. The opportunity framework does not run through the inside network toward sectors that occupy subordinate positions. The low-cost society lightens the society cut that democratizes expectations and installs the idea of "access" in the "tool-box" operation center of knowledge societies. However, they do not create sufficient opportunities for expectations to be developed, and when they do, they only install the "bait" access. This is an important factor to consider when we analyze the "tool-box" with which an innovation society operates—that is, the social, cultural, and economic logic of the generic workers and workers of the service sector, who are replaceable. These workers are "one-thousand-euro earners" who have little possibility of leaving their jobs for those that the society of expectations offers.

The Contexts of Innovation

The gaze to the territories where knowledge communities are celebrated warns that there is no universal recipe that explains the reasons for their emergence; on the contrary, it conceptualizes the mosaic of experiences and situations that in many cases cannot be extended to other contexts. The analysis is registered in the background, where the knowledge society builds as a socioeconomic referent. This happens when the framework of industrial societies' socioeconomic organization is disarranged. In this sense, innovation spaces are those that are able to channel innovation, education, knowledge transference, and information treatment toward economic, political, social, and cultural development. What appears in different studies and experiences is that the contexts are conditioned by a series of variables. Examples include the high levels of cooperation between actors at the local, regional, and national levels, that is, in public and private institutions, educational institutions, research centers, dense associations, and a rich and well-managed civil society; the capacity to create mechanisms of vision and social consensus by those groups that promote change; the adoption of "good practices" by seeking an equilibrium between social, economic, and cultural innovations; good systems of local governance that create effective social policies with citizen input and participation; the professional qualifications of the population in the area; high educational level of its citizens; low levels of social exclusion; high concentration of employment rates in the ICT sector (knowledge companies and industries); good transportation systems; high-quality cultural institutions; high-quality educational systems; the production of results and new discoveries in scientific research—patents, scientific publications, research centers; young age demographic rates; good logistic and international connections; decentralization and local autonomy of the different municipalities and quarters in decision-making processes; and good planning and urban design of the cities where knowledge companies and laboratories are settled.

To this effect, the mentioned variables act together in an interdependent manner. It is not necessary that all these variables appear in the situations that innovation spaces create, but it is important that some of them emerge. As a result of this situation, many of these societies are able to guide their socioeconomic structures toward an intensive use and increased value of knowledge, being capable of responding to and overcoming the specific difficulties of their territories. Having present the characteristics that the contexts of innovation posses, there are three main models that differ in the way they manage the relationship among:

- The regulations and functions that the state holds to itself
- The role of market
- Finance regulation and investment
- The institutional system they adopt
- The institutions and infrastructures built to favor knowledge transference
- The culture of innovation

The characterization of these patterns allows us to identify the main forms in which intelligent territories appear. These territories have a different and varied impact over the geographical environments they influence by acting as referent models in their regions.

The first model has to do with the appearance of an intelligent experience like Silicon Valley in the southern area of San Francisco Bay in the United States. Without doubt it is one of the better-known and representative cases concerning intelligent territories. This model is similar to others developed in the United States, for example, Route 128 in Massachusetts. Silicon Valley has become the avant-garde in the historical transition toward a knowledge society; this model has been imitated in other countries, yet failing to have the same relevance as the first. The model's characteristics are related to minimization of state regulations concerning economy. The point of this action is to offer the market a free space and a context where it can operate freely.

The system is oriented toward an equal but individual opportunity perspective; it rewards those that gain success and excludes those who fail to obtain it. One of the many characteristics that explains the development of the Silicon Valley experience is the five-university network that exists in the region providing the concentration, cooperation, and competition between the well-educated people in technological knowledge and social innovation. This network also supplies the needs of the critical mass companies working in the area. It is very important to consider the significant role that risk capital plays, being the real engine that makes creative innovation funding work in the North American framework. In short, it is the conjunction between deregulation, the individual success option, financing by means of risk capital operations, an existing university framework leading excellence in research and innovation, and the permeability of the institutional system that simplifies knowledge transfer. All these factors explain the success of the Silicon Valley system.

Another model is that of Nordic countries. In contrast with the previous model, this model is built upon the combination of three important elements: economic growth, welfare state development, and the creation of strategic scenarios for the development of R&D spaces. Although there are differences between countries, we can say there is a common pattern that influences all the countries in the European Union. Due to its singularity, the most popular case is Finland; we can use it as a representative case in which we find all the characteristics of the Nordic model. Among these, it is important to mention the conception of state and market that these countries have, with a clear social orientation that is not understood as a limiting factor but as a way to leave possibilities open.

Social welfare is placed in the center of the system and the acquired state functions are an example of it, for instance the educational and sanitary systems. Concerning Finland, the governmental actions are directed to design strategic action plans in which the basic objective is to guide the country toward knowledge societies and technological development, with governmental agencies having a protagonist role: the Council of Scientific and Technological Politics, the National Agency of Technology (TEKES), and the Fund for Research and Development (SITRA). These three have been capable of generating a chain of "good practices," with very impressing results in terms of economic development and social innovation. Yet, in this case the most important elements are: the role of the state; the capacity of the state to design an appropriate institutional system for the requirements of a knowledge society; an educational system that trains its students for future challenges; and the financing managed by the public administration and private companies, especially those that are oriented to the fabrication of their own knowledge products. We cannot understand this system without the crucial role that the Nokia company has played; it is the main sign of economic development and the engine of Finland's technological success. The result of this process is a symbiosis between state, institutional system, educational system, "good practice" financing, and corporate development—all this without leaving aside the implicit welfare state logic.

The third case extends through the eastern and Pacific countries of Asia, such as Taiwan, Singapore, South Korea, and Hong Kong—the well known Asiatic Tigers. These countries have followed the Japanese trail that now is extending to other parts of the Chinese coast. Therefore, the Asiatic model is rooted in countries of small dimensions, except for China. The growing poles are located in those regions with very special particularities. This is an important fact for understanding the role that the state plays in these countries, taking control of all aspects of economic, social, political, and cultural life. The corporate and political elites are closely interrelated with the system of family clans, to the point that it is difficult to make a distinction. In this context, the governmental institutional practices and the design of public policies are managed by these elites and are oriented—as with Singapore—toward intensive activities in technology, petro-chemistry, financing services, and exportation, demanding significant investment in the educational system. This makes these countries perfect examples of rapid economic development, as they are among the most paradigmatic examples of the way to escape underdevelopment and, consequently, break the binomial of west-modernization.

What are the most relevant aspects of these three examples? First of all, it is the capacity of the countries' innovation systems. The capacity for innovation, like the cited experiences demonstrate, does not happen in an isolated manner in companies or specific sectors, it is originated by innovation means that are territorially articulated and connected. This occurs through the computing and transportation networks, with other means and innovation models that are mobilized in other spaces in the interior of global networks. The contexts of innovation are linked to others and interconnected through global networks, in a way that the interdependent connections become the distinctive signs of those spaces. To know who your allies are, who your neighbors are, and with whom to be (or not be) associated are questions that must find answers in the countries that transit through the innovation spaces of a knowledge society.

Second, it is important to mention the quality of the universities and the effectiveness of the articulation mechanisms within the different companies. Universities are very important for the production and diffusion of knowledge and for the creation of high-quality human resources. These are necessary for applied knowledge in science and technology. When the university system is weak or deficient, there are two options: On the one hand, we can make a public effort to create and maintain high-quality research universities, adapted to the surrounding characteristics and the demands that society makes of itself. It is important to succeed with the given model and build excellence. On the other hand, it assigns the coordination and articulation of research and discovery between universities, companies, and public administration. If there is not any relationship it is crucial to promote it. This relationship does not have to do with the exclusion of one of the integrated parts; on the contrary, every part has to have its own autonomy. It is central to applying the learned knowledge in each sphere. This is the way to maintain a fluid relationship, knowing that it must be built through the years.

Third, the matter of human resources is significant in the innovation and knowledge economy. This translates into crucial facts that need to be considered, such as the importance of the education and living conditions of the workers. In this case, the referents vary. Why? Because while in Finland the welfare state is the decisive factor in providing high quality, stable jobs, in the United States, by contrast, the poor public education conditions and an underdeveloped welfare state force the country to look on immigration as a basic and necessary human resource/talent management. In comparison, in Southeast

Asia, the importance of the state and its capacity to manage development strategies is essential.

Fourth, it is common to mention the need to have an enterprising culture based on innovation values. This is true, if we do not make a myth of it or transform it into public rhetoric. In the above examples, such as that of Silicon Valley, the innovators moved there; they were not born there. They went in search of the opportunities that the innovation space offered, through the universities of the region and the facilities given to creativity and risk. First they created small companies that later became huge. In Finland, the big companies like Nokia gave birth to the entrepreneurs. What this experience demonstrates—especially in the case of Southeast Asia—is that innovation and entrepreneurial culture are products of necessity. We get motivated when there is no other alternative and we must take the risk. Moreover, innovation is not a unique attribute of the production cycle. There are innovations and innovators that are not born in the production cycle; they play with the cultural dimension. An innovative culture is built through the pleasure of creating and sharing with those who belong to the knowledge community; the hacker culture is a good example of this. Sometimes, the technological knowledge acquired by society is more important than the productive cycle. An innovative culture and a vivid, high quality, and flexible university system are sine qua non conditions for the emergence and reproduction of entrepreneurial spirit.

Fifth, there are the financial resources invested in the system's development. In all innovation systems there is a system of risk capital and public aid for the best initiatives. In the majority of the successful regional policy cases centered on innovation, the financing of this kind of initiative has become a key factor.

The conclusion is that every context has special matters that need to be valued. The industrial structure of the different countries is not the same, nor are the business opportunities, the social structure, and the cultural tradition. Each country responds to different parameters. The five mentioned factors can be found in all of the given examples: high educational level, freedom to innovate, creative culture, institutional flexibility, and company financing are the main elements to build stable communities of knowledge and autonomic innovation spaces. In other words, without clear innovation politics, a good educational system, a social structure capable of adapting to the environment, and a culture that activates and protects creativity, the construction of innovation spaces and knowledge communities is impossible. If society builds a productive project based on culture and education, it will move ahead in the globalization era by uniting quality of life, economic development, and a creative capacity.

The Social Spaces of Innovation

We depart from the viewpoint of something that is accepted by the majority of the authors that work in this field of study: there is an extended idea that in knowledge societies the competitive advantage lies in the productive use of the input we receive from the socioeconomic environment. In this context, innovation is considered a key tool to favor the adaptation and competitiveness of the companies, expanding in the geographic spaces where it is located. Interactive learning has strong social and territorial roots; this implies that competitiveness builds thanks to the interaction established in the local space and in concrete territories, although in both cases the objective is to obtain a global projection. We know that the local geographic spaces are different and generate diverse forms of knowledge tracing differences with the innovative capacity of social agents, companies, territories, and most important, with the competitive advantage of every particular environment.

As a result, the competitive advantages derive from local factors—like the knowledge that is generated in certain places or regions, social relationships, and trustful networks—that transform the territory in a single differentiated fact. Some of the localized spaces store innovation resources, building the environments that make the emergence of innovative knowledge and its transference easy. We also have to mention the fertilization of ideas in interaction with other agents and territories and, consequently, an effective response to the challenges of the moment and the assets that emerge at every instant. The spaces that result from this interdependence game are conceptualized as "regions that learn," due to their capacity to mold the socioeconomic structures by adapting to innovation requirements.

As previously pointed out, the R&D policies, the educational and formation programs, the public infrastructure, the marketing strategies, and the fiscal policies, among other instruments, are perceived as efficient factors if they are designed from the established relationship between local and regional institutions. In this way, and to mention an example, the industrial networks are benefited by the regional institutional structures if they allow the development of solid trustful and cooperative relationships to improve competitiveness. What we know is that innovation processes tend to concentrate in some territories, especially those of urban and metropolitan character. Why does this happen? Because they are given the conditions that allow the emergence of innovative places and practices—for example, the accumulation of technical support, qualified human resources, technological infrastructures, universities, help centers, risk capital, and so on—apart from special proximity advantages and the concentration of different agents and resources.

How are the innovation and learning effects that favor productivity and competitiveness between companies and social environments generated? Is it enough to gather in the same place the agents, resources, and infrastructures that participate in these effects? Our hypothesis is that the innovation processes exceed the extreme narrowness of the technological and economic interpretation, in a way that they capture the complexity of the processes that happen in spaces and scales not directly related to economic matters—ecosystem, sociocultural spaces (artistic, educational social services), and the institutional context—and that they jointly and constantly interact following multiple and complex processes.

Therefore, we must pay attention to the diversity of innovation sources and the spaces where innovation is possible—companies, the economy, the social, cultural, and artistic spaces. We must not lose sight of the fact that innovation implies creating a cultural system based on tolerance with the purpose of accepting the modification of basic existing aspects, such as tangible "goods"—processes, products, technology, marketing— or intangible values, ideas, emotions, and institutions. This is done in such a way that when the processes are successful they can acquire new uses and senses. In this situation, the uses and the open possibilities look like innovation engines, trying to escape from the exclusive interpretation that technology grants and from the responsibility that the economic cycles have toward them.

This perspective proposes that innovative societies blend in their spaces well-instructed human capital, a high-quality educational system that is extended to the majority of the citizens, a public policy system, institutional environments that promote the assumption of risks, and a reward for new ideas and enterprise incentives. An example of this are the mechanisms that build opportunity structures reinforcing the relationship between R&D systems and the university system. All these elements enhance welfare and quality of life. To innovate does not mean to follow the premeditated direction that public and private institutions build; it means that the dynamic where it lies acquires different features. Not every society innovates under the same criteria; the institutional bases can adopt different trajectories. The problem emerges when we observe that some societies lack the dynamics for innovation. This problem is common to those societies that are not able to find the strategies and paths that improve the quality of life of their citizens.

There is no doubt that the social dynamic that starts innovations rests in the processes with a high sociocultural component. The identification, the confidence, the recognition, the security, the collaboration, and even the competition play a key role in innovative moments. The exchange and the interaction under reciprocity and association rules provide the fundamental base from which the culture of innovation grows and, definitively, from which socioeconomic development is encouraged. Florida suggests that competitive and dynamic cities know how to create environments open to creativity and diversity. The synergies that result from the combinations of cultural and artistic creativity with entrepreneurial and technological capacity is the key to prosperity in the knowledge era. The synergies happen in localized environments where people with talent choose not only to work but also to live—the already mentioned case of Silicon Valley is representative of this. The competitive advantage of cities rests in their capacity to create, attract, and retain the workforce that creates knowledge development.

However, the talent is retained in special city-regions. In the globalized economy one part of the creation of value in many sectors is based on intangible assets; this is why the decisive factors are related to the attributes and characteristics of the places that make them especially attractive for the creative class. This working force is attracted toward the places that have a critical mass of people and creative activities. That is to say, these people are attracted to the communities and populations where other creative people live, and where diversity and multiple identities abound.

In contrast with human capital, understood as an individual good, creativity emerges as a collective and relational good; it is the visible part of the process and the result of the communitarian usages that require teamwork and social bonds. The decisive element in economic behavior and city competitiveness is the social character of cities, that is, the places that offer a higher quality of life and that best adapt to diversity. These are the places that are able to retain talent and the most effective in the generation of intensive technological activities. In this manner, when we emphasize creative ecosystems and the necessary conditions for their creation, the role of tolerance stands out as the social variable that determines creativity.

According to the empirical analysis of the US regions, the most developed knowledge communities are those where tolerance is the social characteristic that best distinguishes when it comes to creating an adequate ecosystem to attract and retain talent. The territorial spaces that transform in social spaces and create a tolerant culture are "creative ecosystems," which from the social point of view are opened to new people. These people are free to interact and relate without frontiers or preconceptions to produce new knowledge—immigrants, bohemians, and active minorities. Consequently, the type of social space open to innovation on any level—artistic, sexual, and so forth—fits well with the lifestyle of that knowledge community. According to Florida, this community upholds the traditional label of knowledge workers: scientists, engineers, and so on, plus the creative professionals—architects, designers, artists, musicians, and so on.[13] These groups are all attracted by open and tolerant ecosystems. In fact, due to their way of understanding the world and enjoying life, the technological innovators are attracted by the social innovators. The reason for this is that both groups believe the key to personal development is the exercise of individual autonomy. Thus, tolerance and talent are reinforced. In particular, there is an open and positive relationship between the social capital they absorb, socioeconomic development, and the culture of innovation. This last becomes the cultural broth of open society in which social relationships prevail based on soft but very consistent links and in generalized confidence.

In this way, we can say the knowledge dynamic economies are not the basis of social cohesion; instead, what happens is that certain forms of social cohesion are the basis for knowledge economies. Authors that come from the perspective of the new regionalism have reached similar conclusions; the maintenance of social cohesion and integration, more than a burden for the states, is a decisive mechanism to motivate socioeconomic development. The specific culture of the different spaces is an identity and integration social resource. It simplifies the production of public goods and the elements that place the city-region in the specific niche in the international markets. The dissolution of intangible factors in the region is a risk for the appearance of social fragmentation problems.

---

13. Florida, *Cities and the Creative Class.*

In these cases, the consequence is the construction of a vicious circle that slows the production of social capital and essential public goods for regional development.

Conclusion

Knowledge communities need the resources that ease structural contexts where knowledge society, innovation spaces, and opportunities are better defined and created. These appear as the resources for the constitution of a specific type of community. This means that it follows the progression that the sociological perspective opens up about community. The emergence of this type of groups depends on the amount of institutionalization that is reached by knowledge societies. This implies that the most significant data is that given by the structural contexts that create objective and subjective conditions so that these types of communities can be built. In all cases, the groups are associated with the construction of social spaces of innovation. From this perspective, societies, regions, and the spaces and places in which the institution of the knowledge society best grows, are those that are best prepared for the development of these communities. We could end this article by making another conclusion: these communities are the "daughters" of the knowledge society, given the capacity they have to manage social spaces of innovation. In them, these communities are born and better reproduced.

Identity is related to the type of work one carries out, to the knowledge and abilities one possesses, and to the functions one fulfills in his or her home, that is, the laboratory. The strategy of acknowledgement plays with the network abilities and transfers the knowledge that that person acquires to the research projects in which he or she participates. The network is the instrument of communication and acknowledgement. Face-to-face interaction is held in the congresses, conferences, and seminars where those who belong to that reality meet. In general, the knowledge community is individualized. It does not annul the subjects but revalorizes them and discovers in them a creative and innovative resource: they are true pillars of this type of community. From this perspective they are communities of individuals.

Bibliography

Bauman, Zygmunt. *Community: Seeking Safety in an Insecure World.* Maiden, MA: Blackwell, 2001.

Carrillo, Francisco J. "Capital Cities: A Taxonomy of Capital Accounts for Knowledge Cities." *Journal of Knowledge Management* 8, no. 5 (2004): 28–46.

——. *Knowledge Cities. Concepts, Approaches and Practices.* Bradford: Butterwood-Heinemann, 2006.

Castells, Manuel and Pekka Himmanen. "Modelos institucionales de sociedad red: Silicon Valley y Finlandia." In *La sociedad red: Una visión global,* edited by Manuel Castells. Madrid: Alianza, 2006.

Cohen, Anthony. *The Symbolic Construction of Community*. Chester: Ellis Horwood Limited, 1985.

Edquist, Charles and Leif Hommen, eds. *Small Country Innovation Systems: Globalization, Change and Policy in Asia and Europe*. London: Edward Elgar Publishing, 2008.

Elias, Norbert. *The Society of Individuals*. Oxford: Basil Blackwell, 1991.

Farley, John. *Majority-Minority Relations*. New Jersey: Prentice Hall, 1988.

Florida, Richard. *The Rise and Fall of the Creative Class*. New York: Basic Books, 2004.

Glazer, Nathan and Daniel P. Moynihan. *Ethnicity: Theory and Experience*. Cambridge, MA: Harvard University Press, 1975.

Hamalainen, Timo J. and Risto Heskala, eds. *Social Innovations, Institutional Change and Economic Performance: Making Sense of Structural Adjustment Processes in Industrial Sectors, Regions and Societies*. Finland: SITRA/Edward Elgar Publishing, 2007.

Johnson, Steven. *Emergence: The Connected Lives of Ants, Brains, Cities and Software*. New York: Scribner, 2001.

Landry, Charles. *The Creative Cities*. London: Earthscan, 2000.

Misra, Bhabagrahi and James Preston. eds. *Community, Self and Identity*. Chicago: Mouton, 1978.

Nisbet, Robert A. *The Sociological Tradition*. New York: Basic Books, 1966.

Sassen, Saskia. *Globalization and Its Discontents*. New York: The New Press, 1998.

——. *Global Networks: Linked Cities*. London: Routledge, 2002.

Saxenian, Anna Lee. *The New Argonauts: Regional Advantage Culture and Competition in Silicon Valley and Route 128*. Cambridge, MA: Harvard University Press, 1996.

Schutz, Alfred. *Collected Papers II*. Netherlands: Mealinus Nihoff, 1971.

Sennet, Richard. *The Conscience of the Eye: The Design and Social Life of Cities*. New York: Alfred A. Knopf, 1990.

Soja, Edward W. *Postmetrópolis*. Madrid: Mapas, 2008.

Theodorson, George A. *Studies of Human Ecology*. New York: Harper & Row, 1975.

Van Den Berg, Leo, M. J. Pol Peter, Winden Van, and Paulus Woets. *European Cities in a Knowledge Economy*. Netherlands: Aldershot Ashgate, 2005.

Vegara, Alfonso and José Luis de las Rivas. *Territorios inteligentes*. Madrid: Fundación Metrópoli, 2004.

Part 2

FREE KNOWLEDGE

5

Knowledge Communities: From Conceptual Issues to Ethical-Political Questions

CARL MITCHAM

Contemporary social orders are producing data, information, and knowledge in greater quantities and at greater rates than ever before in human history; additionally, social orders are trending toward increased dependence on such production. Indeed, there exists no previous period in which social commentators have referenced perceptive and cognitive activities in such terms or identified data, information, and knowledge production and use as issues calling for socio-critical reflection. Among the concepts that have emerged in this discourse are combinations of the three key concepts—data, information, and knowledge—with other terms such as "business," "community," "economy," "engineering," "management," "machine," "network," "society," "worker," and more. As a contribution to more general reflection, the present discussion will focus on one of these combinations: "knowledge community." The trajectory of analysis will move from an introduction of conceptual qualifiers through a review of related historico-philosophical perspectives toward ethical-political criticism. It deserves to be emphasized, however, that what follows is heavily dependent on the work of, especially, Javier Echeverría and Andoni Alonso, while making claims to function as no more than a provisional effort to advance understanding of the character and meaning of the increasingly knowledge-based, information-rich, and data-saturated world in which we live and move and have our mediated if not altered being.

Conceptual Qualifications

With regard to conceptual qualifications, it is useful to note the origin of the term "knowledge community." Here it is possible to draw, appropriately enough, on an account from

Wikipedia. According to a Wikipedia article on this topic, the "knowledge community" concept was constructed as a result of "the convergence of knowledge management as a field of study and social exchange theory." Having evolved originally from in vivo and virtual forums, and once termed "discourse communities," knowledge communities are now often referred to as communities (or virtual communities) of practice:

> As a web or virtual construct, knowledge communities can be said to have evolved from bulletin board systems, web forums and online discourse communities through the 80s and 90s. When framed with the scores of social networking sites coming online at the turn of the millennia, knowledge communities can be described as another form of social media. The biggest difference between social network sites and knowledge communities is [that] social network sites typically lack moderation or an outcome orientation.

In social exchange theory, knowledge communities are analyzed as information exchanges stimulated to meet diverse needs. In one common instance the need is the production of innovation, in which case knowledge communities are conceived as an organized means for introducing change into a system. This is perhaps the most common management interpretation of knowledge communities:

> From an organizational perspective, knowledge communities serve to maintain the strong ties and weak ties of [an] organization with many diverse publics; they help feed quality back into the organization (via more timely feedback and narrative analysis of discussions), drive organization credibility (via more rich exposure and building public trust by incorporating diverse opinion) and speed knowledge transfer, . . . knowledge utilization [and knowledge mobilization].[1]

The linguistic descriptors here are revealing of a kind of crude pragmatism. Knowledge communities are conceived not in epistemic but in lower-level instrumental or operational terms. From this perspective, the "knowledge ecosystem" becomes simply another instrument in the production process, with questions seldom asked about the reasons for the production—even when the cognitive ecosystem becomes parasitic or destructive of the natural ecosystem.

Stepping just slightly beyond Wikipedia, Tobias Müeller-Prothmann, in the *Encyclopedia of Communities of Practice in Information and Knowledge Management*, provides a complementary analysis of the management literature that distinguishes knowledge communities, communities of practice, and knowledge networks. Knowledge communities are defined as "self-organized, altruistic relationships of trust between people for research, development, and innovation-oriented knowledge exchange within a wide domain of knowledge." That is, knowledge communities—also termed "communities of knowing"—are equivalent to academic disciplines, insofar as such disciplines are not tied directly to practical application or goods production. By contrast, communities of practice are

---

1. Wikipedia, "Knowledge communities," at http://en.wikipedia.org/wiki/Knowledge_community (last modified April 10, 2010).

constituted by "relatively small groups of people who focus on a specific topic and are strongly bound together by trust, shared work practice, and a common goal." Communities of practice thus appear to be little distinguished from corporations or economic firms. Finally, knowledge networks are described as "relationships of a large number of loosely coupled participants with a diffuse common domain of knowledge and without clearly defined boundaries."[2]

Drawing again on Wikipedia (with some "poetic license") from the pragmatist perspective,

> Knowledge communities and communities of practice suffer from the same pitfalls as all communities. To some, the mission-driven orientation can detract from creativity. To others, the exchange aspects reek of the over commodification of culture. And the pooling of experts or like-minded persons in knowledge communities and communities of practice often creates communities that are less diverse than traditional ones. One response has been the emergence of knowledge networks with their more loose structures.[3]

This fluidity of conceptual differentiation among knowledge communities, practice communities, and knowledge networks is further complicated by data-information-knowledge distinctions. Although there are numerous antecedents, Russell Ackoff, in a presidential address to the International Society of General Systems Research, is often credited with formulating the conceptual distinction as a hierarchic one that can be restated as follows: human sensing via instrumentally mediated structures yields data (e.g., thermometer readings); the interpretation of sensations and data yields information (e.g., "It is hot."); recognition of information patterns yields knowledge (e.g., the law of how increases in heat on a confined volume of gas increase pressure). On top of knowledge, Ackoff adds understanding (answering "why" questions) and wisdom (evaluated understanding). Such relations can be given graphic (knowledge) representation in the form of a pyramid as shown in figure 5.1.

Figure 5.1. Knowledge pyramid.

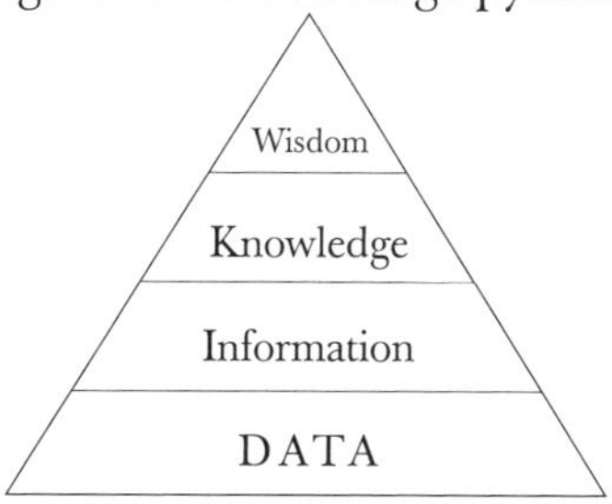

Source: Based on Ackoff, "From Data to Wisdom."

---

2. Müeller-Prothmann, "Knowledge Communities, Communities of Practice, and Knowledge Networks," 264–65.

3. Wikipedia, "Knowledge communities."

In light of these distinctions, questions readily arise about possibilities for and relations among data communities, information communities, knowledge communities, and wisdom communities. With regard to the instrumental or technological mediation of data and information production and their potentials for community construction, analyses by Don Ihde and Peter Galison are particularly relevant. Ackoff's argument for the hierarchical character of data-information-knowledge relationships also suggests the possibility of hierarchical integration of such cognitively differentiated communities.[4]

Historico-Philosophical Perspectives

Against the background of this complicating analysis of the knowledge communities' concept, it is appropriate to turn to the much more expansive historico-philosophical perspective advanced by Javier Echeverría in *Los señores del aire: Telépolis y el tercer entorno*. This book culminated a series of efforts to appreciate the social implications of networked communications. Extending Marshall McLuhan's notion of a television-based "global village," Echeverría argued for a more general "politics at a distance" based in a host of communications media:

> The central thesis of *Telépolis* as well as my subsequent book *Cosmopolitas domésticos*, may be summarized in the prefix "tele": the most important difference between the third framework [*el tercer entorno*] and the other two lies in the possibility of interrelating and interacting at a distance. Over against the natural or urban scenarios, in which human beings are physically present and close to one another, which permits them to speak, to see one another, and to communicate among themselves, the scenarios of the third framework are based on tele-voice, tele-sound, tele-vision, tele-money, and tele-communications, with it being possible to imagine in the more or less distant future a tele-touch, tele-smell, and tele-taste, in which case the proposed third environment would lose its heuristic character, and be transformed into a precise description of what happens in the new social space.[5]

As Echeverría notes, the conceptual advance of this over his two previous engagements with the theme of tele-politics is the theory of three *entornos*. In painting *entorno* refers to the background or frame; in philosophy it names that ensemble of things related to something without actually forming part of it. It is thus difficult to translate, with "milieu," "environment," and "system" being reasonable correlates. The modestly awkward "framework" is used here in part to call attention to its technical status.

After a brief prologue, *Los señores del aire* is divided into three roughly equal parts. Part 1, "The Three Frameworks of Humanity," provides a broad historico-philosophical overview in which to situate the contemporary emergence of telepolis. For Echeverría

---

4. Ihde, *Technology and the Lifeworld* and *Expanding Hermeneutics*; Galison, *Image and Logic*; Ackoff, "From Data to Wisdom."

5. Echeverría, *Los señores del aire*, 14. All translations by the author.

the first framework for human beings was that of nature. The second is an urban world created by humans themselves, which becomes a kind of mediation between humans and nature. With the emergence of the third framework of electronic communications there also arises what Echeverría calls a "neofeudalism" in which the "lords of the air"—that is, the multinational telecommunications corporations based in advanced capitalist countries—both develop and dominate the new telecommunications networks. It is against this neofeudalism that the democratization of telepolis will have to be asserted.

Part 2, "Human Activities in the Third Framework," examines how the networked and tele-connected world influences and transforms the character of war, finance, work and economics, science, architecture, leisure, education, medicine, literature, art and culture, journalism, and even the human body. With the phenomenon of virtual reality, Echeverría suggests, tele-transformations become internalized in the body, and there emerges not just the cyborg but the tele-body that experiences itself in cyberspace.

Part 3, "Toward a Constitution for Telepolis," is concerned with how to move from the neofeudalism of the present toward a democratic telepolis or teledemocracy. Echeverría's aim is thus not simply descriptive but normative. He not only describes the new human environment, the networked tele-world that is emerging on top of the natural and urbanized worlds, but seeks to assess and judge its political character, to point out how such a world may be truly humanized. Globalization alone, for instance, does not lead to a democratic telepolis.

As Echeverría observes in his prologue, on the one side are those who think that the Internet prefigures the new democratic world order, which will bring about great progress because it will empower direct democracy and shrink the importance of nationalism and States. Other authors call themselves cyberanarchists and see in the Internet the historical realization of anarchism, affirming that there should not be any type of regulation on the Web, apart from strictly technological regulation. Echeverría himself opposes both interpretations, and suggests that "the current power structure of the third framework . . . does not allow us to be at all optimistic about the level of democratization of the new social space." [6]

Part 3 further considers what actions might be undertaken to promote democracy. Echeverría concludes "that a profound restructuring of power and wealth is being produced, through which there is emerging a series of great lords of information and telecommunications (as well the sectors connected to them), those whom we may call the "lords of the air," given that their influence is not based on the dominion of territories or national markets, but in the control of satellites, networks, and flows of information and communication." [7] This process is both dangerous and able to be changed. Yet before advancing political or moral evaluations, it is appropriate to analyze the causes

6. Ibid.

7. Ibid., 374.

of such social changes of power. As a result, for instance, Echeverría describes in detail technical debates about how to structure and organize the Internet, and in this context concludes by proposing basic principles for a constitution of telepolis. With regard to these arguments, connections perhaps deserve to be made with the ideas and analyses of Lawrence Lessig.

In arguments that can be read as complementary to Echeverría's, Andoni Alonso has also argued some distinctive characteristics for the digital world. Writing with Iñaki Arzoz, his *La nueva ciudad de Dios* interprets what might be called extreme computer culture as a new religiosity or vision of this-worldly transcendence, with *La quinta columna digital* examining the political potential of the digital lifeworld. By contrast, Alonso's own *Basque Cyberculture* seeks to appreciate the practical political value of a digital network diaspora that could also be described as a knowledge community.

Historico-Philosophical Qualifications

Venturing commentary on Echeverría's historico-philosophical argument, it may be noted that his three-framework structure—nature, urbanism, and telecommunication networks—has marked affinities with such other divisions as those of European history in its many permutations of ancient, medieval, and modern. Compare, for instance, G. W. F. Hegel's pre-Greek, Greek, and Christian worlds; Auguste Comte's theological, metaphysical, and positive stages in intellectual history; and especially with Jacques Ellul's distinction between three milieux: natural, social, and technological. Echeverría is clearly working in the tradition not just of cultural studies deriving from McLuhan, but advancing a social criticism influenced by Karl Marx and Max Weber.[8]

As Echeverría's structure itself suggests, there are grounds for uneasiness with regard to any inclusive concept that would equate traditional and modern communities as equally knowledge based. Although groups as different as those of traditional ethnic communities and modern artistic, scientific, and engineering associations have produced and shared various world views, their cognitive elements have been shared by practices that have ranged from legends, songs, and recipes to science and engineering itself. From the perspective of the classic definition of knowledge as justified true belief—which was formulated initially in Plato's *Theaetetus* but still functions as a point of departure in much contemporary analytic philosophy—to equate legend and song with knowledge would be to conflate *mythos* and *logos*.

Using the classical definition of knowledge, it could be argued as inappropriate prior to the 1600s to refer to any community as a knowledge community. Not until the 1600s was an informal "invisible college" given institutional form by the founders of modern science at the Royal Academy in London, and as national academies of science in a series of other countries. Perhaps universities, as they arose across Europe in the

---

8. For Hegel, Comte, McLuhan, Marx, and Weber, see standard texts; Ellul, *Perspectives on Our Age*.

1200s, could also have been described as communities of knowledge, but they were even more communities of religion or faith and professional practice.

Prior to the creation of modern natural science, human cognition was so embodied and embedded in a material context that it would have been difficult to think of knowledge as independent of some particular human experience. There may have existed knowledge of communities but no communities of knowledge. That is, communities created knowledge; knowledge did not create communities.

Even more pointedly, for thousands of years, communities of hunters and gatherers defined themselves in terms of kinship relationships, by distinctive plant and animal engagements, and by their techniques—as tools were fashioned first from stone, then bronze, and finally iron. In each instance perception and cognition were embedded in pre-existing communities, rather than communities arising from perception and cognition. The agricultural revolution was one not so much of knowledge as practical skill, which only in a derivative sense could be called knowledge.

One argued exception to this interpretation can be found in *Vom ursprung und ziel der geschichte*, in which Karl Jaspers presents the Axial Age (800–200 BCE) as a period in which new understandings of the human condition arose independently in China, India, and the eastern Mediterranean—with Laotze, Confucius, the *Upanishads* and the Buddha, Socrates-Plato, and Isaiah—to generate a series of analogous cultural transformations. But the resulting "wisdom communities" as unities of insight and practice aimed at emancipating human experience from family or tribal delimitations are, again, something distinct from knowledge communities.

An analysis of closer provenance has been that developed in the sociology of science, especially in relation to studies of the diffusion and production of knowledge. Here the work of Derek J. de Solla Price and Diana Crane has been especially influential. As the developer of empirical methods for citation analysis, de Solla Price actually preferred to refer to "networks of scientific papers" over knowledge communities.[9] In her minor classic on *Invisible Colleges*, Crane built on de Solla Price's argument for a logistic curve in the growth and leveling off of knowledge production in any scientific specialization to ask a further question:

> Why should the growth of scientific knowledge take this form? Price does not offer an explanation. The thesis [of Crane's book] is that the logistic growth of scientific knowledge is the result of the exploitation of intellectual innovations by a particular type of social community.[10]

In other words, for Crane, forms of communication create types of knowledge production rather than knowledge production creating types of communities. Crane goes on

---

9. de Solla Price, "Networks of Scientific Papers."

10. Crane, *Invisible Colleges*, 2.

to suggest that "the term that best describes the social organization of the entire set of members of a research area is the concept of the 'social circle' [—the] exact boundaries [of which] are difficult to define."[11] Sociologically, what is crucial with regard to a cognitively productive social circle is that its members "are geographically separated to such an extent that face-to-face contact never occurs between all members and occurs only periodically among some."[12] Instead, what is more characteristic is indirect and mediated interaction. Indeed, this is precisely why such social orders are not properly described as communities but as networks.

In subsequent work Crane carries this theory of the priority of communicating media over the communicated content to media and cultural studies in general. In an analysis of *The Production of Culture* (1992), she writes,

> Instead of viewing the media as neutral instruments for transmitting information and ideas, there is now considerable debate about how the media transform and interpret reality in the process of disseminating news and entertainment to the public. The principal objective of previous research was to assess whether or not individuals had absorbed specific items of information from the media. In the new theories, the impact of the media is seen as the outcome of interaction between the media and its audience. Audiences belonging to different social groups, ranging from dominant to marginal, interpret the same messages in very different ways.[13]

Again, social relationships trump cognitive content. The concept of the invisible college invites at least two comments: First, the notion of a college connotes more a collection of individuals than a community in the strict sense. The term comes from the Latin *collegium*, meaning an association of *collegae* (*com-* "with" + *leg-*, stem of *legare*, "to choose," thus one who chooses to work with another), and in one common usage refers to a university faculty or group of individuals with certain powers and duties centered on the shared pursuit of a task. Thus it is clearly something less united than a community. Compare, for example, "community," from the Latin *communitatem* (*communitas*), meaning "community, fellowship," from *communis*, "common, public, general, shared by all." In classic German sociology the close-knit community as *gemeinschaft* is contrasted with the loose association of society or *gesellschaft*. Second, as a term of art for the precursors and prolongations of the Royal Society, "invisible college" is historically associated with the notion of a secret or hermetic society separated from any material cultural embedding.[14] This is also a feature of what might be called cyber-polities, as explored by Alonso and Arzoz.[15] The typically modern hermeticism involves what

---

11. Ibid., 13.

12. Ibid.

13. Crane, *The Production of Culture*, 14.

14. Lomas, *The Invisible College*.

15. Alonso and Arzoz, *La nueva ciudad de Dios*.

might be called the Masonic or active, this-worldly hermeticism of a secret society that aims to infuse into the world revolutionary, transformative ideas. This is in marked contrast to premodern hermeticism, which instead sought to protect the world from dangerous ideas and forbidden knowledge.

Both points can be described as imbedded in Caroline Wagner's somewhat idealistic description of globalized scientists in *The New Invisible College*:

> Self-organizing networks that span the globe are the most notable feature of science today. These networks constitute an invisible college of researchers who collaborate not because they are told to but because they want to, who work together not because they share a laboratory or even a discipline but because they can offer each other complementary insight, knowledge, or skills.[16]

Such scientific research networks lack the traditional features of shared material culture in the form of laboratories or even college campuses. But insofar as "the new invisible college . . . gives developing countries a second chance to create strategies for tapping into the accumulated store of scientific knowledge and applying what they learn to local problems," they may well share an ideology of development that echoes the early Royal Society hermetic mysticism of science.[17]

To draw on the terminology of another social scientist, Karl Polanyi (1944), the college as a circle or network of scientists is socially disembedded, not to say disembodied. Indeed, it can be argued that any association of human beings based on knowledge production or diffusion is likely to exhibit a measure of disembeddedness, precisely because disembeddedness is a central feature of knowledge itself—knowledge qua knowledge being more separated from materiality than imagination or construction and the manifolds of material culture.

As has been argued elsewhere, disembedding may be read as a distinctive aspect of the trajectory of modern social history.[18] It can be found manifested not only in economics (where Polanyi initially identified it), but also in the technological production of goods as well as in epistemological production and communication (the aspects of experience most relevant to the present context). One summary way to describe disembedding as it is manifest in exchange is that the marketplace is replaced by the market. Surely something analogous is manifest, as technics gives way to technology and embedded-embodied social relationships to disembedded-disembodied ones. By way of a simplified sketch of analogies of disembedding across economic exchange, technological production, and epistemological production and communication, consider the following matrix:

---

16. Wagner, *The New Invisible College*, 2.

17. Ibid.

18. See, e.g., Briggle and Mitcham, "Embedding and Networking."

Table 5.1. Matrix Comparison of Disembedded Practices

Economic exchange of goods	Technological production of goods	Epistemological production and communication
Takes place at a distance from the household, sometimes even outside the city on the margins of society	Takes place at a distance from the household or the artisan's workshop, in the industrial factory	Takes place at an instrumentally mediated distance from the senses, communication via tele-communication systems
Oriented less toward meeting basic needs and more toward making a profit (money)	Oriented less toward meeting basic needs and more toward making a profit (money)	Oriented less toward meeting basic needs and more toward making a profit (money)
Becomes increasingly impersonal, based on prices	Becomes increasingly impersonal, based on input/output analyses (pursuit of efficiency)	Becomes disembodied, instrumentally mediated, and media based
Ceases to be restrained or limited by non-economic mores (family or ethnic relations, religion, etc.)	Ceases to be restrained or limited by non-technological factors (such as social relationships)	Ceases to be restrained by time, space, or material culture

Insofar as the disembedding of economic exchange and technological production are commonly understood to undermine traditional (*gemeinschaft*) community in favor of modern (*gesellschaft*) society, how could the disembedding of epistemological productivity and communication not help but have similar implications? In distinct opposition to such questioning, however, is a persistent evolutionary affirmation represented, for example, in the thought of Pierre Teilhard de Chardin's developmental trajectory from geosphere through biosphere to creation of what he terms a "noosphere" via the human phenomenon.[19] For Teilhard, as for many others, the mind and its intellective activities are the basis for a unique and unprecedented form of community—one perhaps better indicated by the increasingly ubiquitous and globalizing term, "networks."

Ethical-Political Questions

One burden of the previous analysis is to argue for clarification of the concept of "knowledge community" and to suggest that the phenomenon might not be precisely what the term initially appeared to imply. One alternative term is "knowledge networks"—or, more accurately, "information networks"—highlighting a distinctive kind of social-intellectual relationship, independent of the question of whether information is the basis of the

---

19. See Teilhard de Chardin, *Le phénomène humain*.

relationship or the relationship the basis of information—thus acknowledging mutual influence and interaction. There nevertheless remain an indefinite number of ethical and political questions that can be raised with regard to such knowledge/information networks.

First, one might well argue that the new information media, in their intensity and broad spectrum availability, actually re-embed knowledge in new forms of community, networked community. Social networking services such as Facebook, MySpace, LinkedIn, Twitter, and so on—with a history that can be traced back to The Well (1985)—claim to facilitate what Howard Rheingold initially called "virtual community."[20] As if to highlight their communitarian aspects, associated with these services are such ethical issues as privacy and informed consent, which are strongly present in traditional *gemeinschaften*, where individual privacy is often quite limited. But also associated with social networking services are other ethical issues such as trustworthiness, fraud, and misconduct that are much more characteristic of the more anonymous structures of large-scale, disembedded urban *gesellschaften*. As the ease of the use of aliases and misrepresentation suggests, it is questionable whether electronic social networks can accurately be described as "communities." Is it not possible that "Second Life" is more second than life?

To restate this ethical question in political terms: It is not clear that electronic information sharing can yield civil society. As a distinct social formation, civil society became a prominent element of political theory in the eighteenth century as a level of social organization distinct from state, religion, family, tribe, and market. Civil society, as civilian or citizen society, served as the basis of the emergence of the modern (representative) democratic state. But in order to perform this function, civil society had to possess two distinct features that would seem to be denied to associations based on information alone: there must be shared interests that are broader and deeper than cognitive ones, and there must be opportunities for common action. Electronic information sharing can serve as a useful adjunct to already existing civil relationships, but it is arguable whether they can serve as the sole basis of such relationships.

To extend this line of questioning, consider a second and even more telling ethical policy issue that arises for information- and knowledge-based associations. As Marshall Van Alstyne and Erik Brynjolfsson have argued, first in a perspectives article titled "Could the Internet Balkanize Science?" in *Science* and then expanded in an MIT Sloan School report on "Electronic Communities: Global Village or Cyberbalkans?," advances in knowledge production can strain attention so that, in conjunction with the development of internet filtering protocols, networks become increasingly specialized and narrow:

> Working with information requires time and attention. A wealth of information leads to a poverty of attention, so attention must be allocated efficiently. Depending on how this task is managed, the Internet could lead to the fragmentation of research—a [cyber]balkanization of the global village. . . . As quickly as information technology collapses barriers

---

20. Rheingold, *The Virtual Community*.

based on geography, it forces us to build new ones based on interest or time. Ironically, global communications networks can leave intact or even promote partitions based on specialty. . . . Communications that once depended on geography, proximity, and serendipity are screened and filtered for perceived relevance and reputation.[21]

The resulting overspecialization not only leads to the replacement of interdisciplinary interactions and the resulting formation of multi-perspectival cognitive dialogs with much more specialized intradisciplinary interactions that delimit dialog, it turns the thick associations of civil society into thin information exchanges that lack the substance of embeddedness in noncognitive realities. In addition, these intradisciplinary interactions tend to stimulate a positive feedback loop that only increases information production and exacerbates the problem. The possibility is that the formation of information communities whose raison d'etre is to produce more information will lead to a level of information production that outstrips the carrying capacity of embodied communities—resulting at some point in a collapse of knowledge and a collateral information explosion that will affect communities, cognitive and noncognitive alike.

Such balkanization has implications for more than epistemological production and oversaturation of the noosphere. Robert Wright, a political blogger for the *New York Times*, has, for instance, observed that the Internet gives to special interest lobbying a new and insidious strength that tends to undermine reflective democracy. In his words, the Web creates "many 'cocoons'—ideologically homogenous blogs and [W]eb sites—[as] clusters of people who share a political perspective and can convene only because of the nearly frictionless organizing technology that is the Internet."[22] Wright goes on:

> The new information technology doesn't just create [new disembedded] special interests; it arms them with precision-guided munitions. The division of readers and viewers into demographically and ideologically discrete micro-audiences makes it easy for interest groups to get scare stories . . . to the people most likely to be terrified by them. Then pollsters barrage legislators with the views of constituents who, having been barraged by these stories, have little idea what's actually [going on].[23]

Information technology and the communities it makes possible have subverted the idea of republican democracy. Those who drafted the United States Constitution, for instance, explicitly rejected direct democracy—in which citizens vote on every issue—in favor of representative democracy. For Wright, "The idea was that legislators would convene at a safe remove from voters and, thus insulated from the din of narrow interests and widespread but ephemeral passions, do what was in the long-term interest of their constituents and of the nation. Now information technology has stripped away the

---

21. Van Alstyne and Brynjolfsson, "Could the Internet Balkanize Science?," 1479.

22. Wright, "The Internet vs. Obama."

23. Ibid.

insulation that physical distance provided back when information couldn't travel faster than a horse."[24]

Whether political order can survive the stress introduced by the emergence of such non–civil information communities remains an open question. Furthermore, insofar as such "knowledge communities" are based on nonknowledge, their tendency toward irrational politics cannot help but have implications for the noncognitive realities of nature within which humans ultimately live. Epistemic networks may well be the ultimate enemies of natural ecologies.

Bibliography

Ackoff, Russell L. "From Data to Wisdom," *Journal of Applied Systems Analysis* 16 (1989): 3–9.

Alonso, Andoni. *Basque Cyberculture*. Reno: University of Nevada Press, 2003.

Alonso, Andoni and Iñaki Arzoz. *La nueva ciudad de Dios*. Madrid: Siruela, 2002.

———. *La quinta columna digital*. Barcelona: Gedisa, 2005.

Briggle, Adam and Carl Mitcham. "Embedding and Networking: Conceptualizing Experience in a Technosociety." *Technology in Society* 31, no. 4 (2009): 374–83.

Crane, Diana. *Invisible Colleges: Diffusion of Knowledge in Scientific Communities*. Chicago: University of Chicago Press, 1972.

———. *The Production of Culture: Media and the Urban Arts*. London: Sage, 1992.

de Solla Price, Derek J. "Networks of Scientific Papers: The Pattern of Bibliographic References Indicates the Nature of the Scientific Research Front." *Science* 149, no. 3683 (1965): 510–15.

Echeverría, Javier. *Cosmopólitas domésticos*. Barcelona: Anagrama, 1995.

———. *Los señores del aire: Telépolis y el tercer entorno*. Barcelona: Destino, 1999.

———. *Telépolis*. Barcelona, Destino, 1994.

Ellul, Jacques. *Perspectives on Our Age: Jacques Ellul Speaks on His Life and Work*. Edited by William H. Vanderburg. Translated by Joachim Neugroschel. New York: Seabury, 1981.

Galison, Peter. *Image and Logic: A Material Culture of Microphysics*. Chicago: University of Chicago Press, 1997.

Ihde, Don. *Expanding Hermeneutics: Visualism in Science*. Evanston, IL: Northwestern University Press, 1998.

———. *Technology and the Lifeworld: From Garden to Earth*. Bloomington, IN: Indiana University Press, 1990.

---

24. Ibid.

Jaspers, Karl. *Vom ursprung und ziel der geschichte*. Zurich: Artemis-Verlag, 1949. Translated by Michael Bullock as *The Origin and Goal of History*. New Haven, CT: Yale University Press, 1953.

Lessig, Lawrence. *Code: And Other Laws of Cyberspace*. New York: Basic Books, 1999. *Code 2.0*, 2nd ed. New York: Basic Books, 2006.

Lomas, Robert. *The Invisible College: The Royal Society, Freemasonry and the Birth of Modern Science*. London: Headline, 2002.

Müeller-Prothmann, Tobias. "Knowledge Communities, Communities of Practice, and Knowledge Networks." In *Encyclopedia of Communities of Practice in Information and Knowledge Management*, edited by Elyne Coakes and Steve Clarke. Hershey, PA: IGI Publishing, 2006, 264–271.

Polanyi, Karl. *The Great Transformation*. New York: Rinehart, 1944.

Rheingold, Howard. *The Virtual Community: Homesteading on the Electronic Frontier*. Reading, MA: Addison-Wesley, 1993. Revised edition, Cambridge, MA: MIT Press, 2000.

Teilhard de Chardin, Pierre. *Le phénomène humain*. Paris: Seuil, 1955.

Van Alstyne, Marshall and Erik Brynjolfsson. "Could the Internet Balkanize Science?" *Science* 274 (September 29, 1996): 1479–80.

——. "Global Village or Cyberbalkans? Modeling and Measuring the Integration of Electronic Communities." *Management Science* 51, vol. 6 (June 2005): 851–68.

Wagner, Caroline S. *The New Invisible College: Science for Development*. Washington, DC: Brookings Institution Press, 2008.

Wright, Robert. "The Internet vs. Obama," Opinionator: Online Commentary, *New York Times*. Posted February 2, 2010. http://opinionator.blogs.nytimes.com/2010/02/02/obamas-modern-predicament/.

6

System ERROR: Liberate Memory!

Taking into account that the copyright laws sentence us to a delay of seventy years each and every time we want to access the cultural production of our times, the public domain will no longer be contemporary.

When dealing with copyleft and free culture, we generally talk and think strictly about the future. Thus, we tend to project the potential problems and solutions about cultural production toward the future and forget to face these issues when looking at the past. In a similar way that all the present decisions will have their corresponding impact and effect upon the future cultural commons, we need to consider the way some of the decisions taken at a particular time in the past affect the situation today.

Each new modification of the rules governing intellectual property is a new step toward the detriment of the public domain, to the extent that we will never again be able to enjoy a truly contemporary public domain. The dialogue with the space from which our memory feeds, that supplies our imagination or the place where we collect whatever "makes" us enjoy, create, and think, is thus, depending on the country, sentenced to at least a seventy-year delay.

However, the paradigm of free culture and copyleft shows us that there are other alternatives working in other directions such as sharing networks, free licenses, fluid repositories of knowledge, and copyleft files, among others, that actively contribute to the recovery and enrichment of the commons.

> I do not know whether a philosopher has ever dreamed of a company engaged in the home delivery of sensory reality. Of all the arts, music is nearest to this transposition into the

modern mode. Its very nature and the place it occupies in our world mark it as the first to be transformed in its methods of transmission, reproduction and even production.[1]

This text begins with these words of Paul Valery, written in 1928 when he talked about the culture, literature, music, and art in the context that he lived, radically different from ours. Almost a hundred years ago, Valery was able to talk about the changes in human knowledge stimulated by technology. Today, we are still conscious of the importance of the effects of technologies on the way that knowledge is produced, transmitted, and accessed. To some extent, this chapter deals with the changes provoked by new media and resources in our present cultural context, with some contradictions that occur, and the tools at our disposal to overcome "system errors," mainly those related to memory and the circulation of knowledge. These copyleft tools, especially licenses, give us (as users and/or producers) more freedom as well as the ability to collaborate in the enrichment of the public domain.

The system that regulates, preserves, and administers knowledge and its transmission is formed, as any operative system would be, by different components including complex interconnected processes and practices. In our society the elaboration of, circulation of, and access to this knowledge takes place, to a great extent, through images, documents, objects, information, and so forth, and from the uses that emerge from these—for example, in the case of operating-system conflicts, incompatibilities, and errors, in the same way that our personal computer displays an error message to warn us that something is not right in the system. Sometimes, these problems are solved by a gentle thump. Other times, we leave the machine to rest awhile, but finally, often, we have to disconnect the whole system in order to reset it so that everything works again. However, if the problem has not been solved it persists and ends up appearing once more, forcing us irredeemably to change the system configuration and thereby optimize its overall functioning.

In a new context such as that of contemporary cultural production, determined by digital technologies and telematic networks,[2] the allegory of operative systems helps us more than the error metaphor and allows us to address basic questions about knowledge such as memory management, information storage, communication and connections systems, protection methods, and even file administration. These are concepts taken from computer language, but they perfectly fit the terrain of knowledge management, where individual and collective memory, knowledge transmission (communication), the storage and cataloging of content, systems to protect and preserve all this, and different concepts surrounding the notion of the archive are equally essential parts of knowledge—as argued in the introductory statement of this conference on knowledge communities.[3]

---

1. Valery, "The Conquest of Ubiquity," 226

2. See Rodríguez Arkaute, "El contexto ya no es lo que era," 65–71

3. "Introductory Statement," *International Conference on Knowledge Communities*. www.basque.unr.edu/kcc/default.asp.

In this text, some of those system errors and contradictions are addressed when they pertain to knowledge management. These are errors that affect us at different levels, whether as users, authors, or researchers, and that force us to rethink the system. A journey through hegemonic cultural industries such as those of music, cinema, and software allows us to examine right there, in situ, the effects of the digitalization phenomenon, leading us ultimately to the realm of contemporary art, a place where one can encounter all these questions. Finally, I will present a review of the tools at our disposal to reconfigure the system, to reset and optimize it in search of a more coherent functioning within the current context of contemporary cultural production.

The Advent of the Digital

In the current context, shaped by lines of force such as the bursting in of the digital and the increasing prominence of immaterial production, one can see that the influence of the latest new technologies and computer networks has entered into culture, affecting the production of content in multiple layers: the production and creation of artistic works, the distribution and dissemination of these works, and finally, public access. However, the novelty of digital technology dissolves the historically interdependent relationship between a work of art and its physical medium. In this sense, digitalization as a phenomenon offers three new important developments: in the first instance, musical works do not depend on recordable media, photographic imagery travels without material base of any kind, and moving images no longer rely on a tangible medium. In other words, one can confirm the autonomy of content with regard to its base; or as John Perry Barlow ironically puts it, wine has been liberated physically from bottles.

> Thus the rights of invention and authorship adhered to activities in the physical world. One didn't get paid for ideas but for the ability to deliver them into reality. For all practical purposes, the value was in the conveyance and not the thought conveyed. In other words, the bottle was protected, not the wine. Now, as information enters Cyberspace, the native home of Mind, these bottles are vanishing. With the advent of digitization, it is now possible to replace all previous information storage forms with one meta-bottle: complex—and highly liquid—patterns of ones and zeros.

Even the physical/digital bottles to which we've become accustomed, floppy disks, CD-ROMs, and other discrete, shrink-wrappable bit-packages, will disappear as all computers jack in to the global Net. While the Internet may never include every single CPU on the planet, it is more than doubling every year and can be expected to become the principal medium of information conveyance if, eventually, the only one.[4]

Second, the expense of reproducing a work of art, that is, the cost of making copies, is reduced to practically nothing. And finally, digital networks facilitate, to an extent we have previously never known, the immediate and simultaneous distribution of this

---

4. Barlow, "Selling Wine without Bottles."

content. Consequently, a digitalized work of art can be copied and distributed in real time to virtually any connected point on the planet and even, in some cases, beyond it. In such questions the principal issues are based on the challenging of the hegemonic cultural industries of software, music, and cinema, and that, sooner or later, will also apply to the world of art.

These new situations taking place regarding production of, distribution of, and access to culture are viewed by some sections of the industry as serious threats and, in general, they articulate their responses in the form of new restrictions on and harassment of users. The restrictions imposed by the large leisure and entertainment corporations take the form, according to the case in question, of legal reforms, arbitrary charges, measures that criminalize users and even attack freedom of expression. Ultimately they represent a gradual impoverishment of the public domain and a limitation of users' rights. Therefore, clearly those previously mentioned contradictions and system errors posit the economic interests of industry, on the one hand, and the everyday use of technology, on the other, in radically different directions.

The Napster Phenomenon

In many ways, the stormy relationship between industry and the new content use was plainly visible in the case of the Napster phenomenon, the historic computer program dedicated to the massive sharing of music and movie files. Napster, together with the file-sharing networks or P2P networks[5] it helped popularize, are just one demonstration of how access to culture has changed dramatically. More specifically, the question of production, distribution, and consumption of culture in the digital era is most evident in the case of music. Evidently, the example of Napster in the late 1990s and its use of two recently developed technologies (the MP3 audio compression format and the Internet network) did not herald the immediate collapse of all cultural industries. However, it did lead to an upheaval in the field with major consequences for the future of the industry and its models of financial gain. More than anything, Napster served as a warning on the consequences and repercussions that the course of digitalization would have in the production and distribution of cultural content.

Despite what one might think, Napster was not the first, nor was it, in actuality, a so-called P2P sharing program. First of all, this program developed in 1999 in Boston by Northeastern University student Shawn Fanning was not the earliest software of this type, because other software such as Hotline Connect, although less popular, had already been developed in 1996. Moreover, Napster was not strictly a P2P initiative

---

5. Peer-to-peer (P to P or P2P) programs or peer networks, such as Emule, Kazaa, and those making up the Torrent family. P2P programs or networks are those telematic applications and networks that allow users to share and exchange computer files through their own computers—from one computer to another, from one user to another, among equals—without this transfer or exchange of information depending on anyone else, just on the communication between those interested.

because, although file sharing was carried out directly among users, it controlled all the information about these files, the systems used, and the users in centralized servers. Indeed, this was the reason why industry complaints about Napster were successful and it ended up surrendering. Napster achieved unexpected success in a very short time and by February 2001 had twenty-six million users.[6] And in taking the daily routine of users by storm it began a new way of cultural consumption. Digitalized music files circulated by the millions on the net, striking fear into the business strategists of the vast music industry. Yet, far from drawing constructive conclusions from this new situation, it fell back on judicial repression and legal restrictions in an attempt to halt what today we see to be unstoppable.

> In the first instance, they promoted legal measures to control the right to copy on the net; second, they embarked on legal battles against businesses that carried out digital piracy infringement; in the third place, they tried to develop technical protocols to impede the exchange of legal files; and fourth, they developed their own business strategies aimed at concentration and vertical integration.[7]

Such was the importance of this famous file-sharing program, not only at a technical level but in conceptual terms, that authors like José Luis Orihuela spoke of "napsterization" in regard to a return to the roots of the World Wide Web as a means of exchanging knowledge.[8] For José Luis Brea, this "napsterization" even implied changes at a cognitive level, meaning "a fundamental change for the economy of visuality, symbolic practices and cultural production associated with our relationship to it."[9] In general, then, Napster implied a metaphor for the collision of old economic models (production and distribution) and old ways to benefit from cultural production, with new technologies and new uses and users of culture, as well as the clash between digital media and those in favor of obsolete models as a method of trying to prevent these technologies from changing the landscape, bearing in mind, moreover, that music was only the beginning and that what we might term napsterization has continued to this day expanding to other fields of cultural production.

From 2001 on, when a judge ordered the Napster service to be closed to prevent the supposed continual infringement of copyright, to this day, the debate, far from weakening, is more vibrant than ever. The bellicose response of industry has only strengthened alternative options to its knowledge management, based exclusively on optimizing its financial gains. A recent example is the case of The Pirate Bay (thepiratebay.org), one

---

6. "Global Napster Usage Plummets, But New File-Sharing Alternatives Gaining Ground," *EDP Weekly's IT Monitor*, July 23, 2001. At www.allbusiness.com/technology/technology-services/796121-1.html.

7. Buquet, "Música on line," 69. All non-English quotations in this chapter were translated by the author.

8. Orihuela, "Hacia la napsterización del conocimiento." A website, www.napsterization.org was even created by Mary Hodder as a resource to understand the idea of napsterization: the disintermediation by new technologies and digital media of the old economy, incumbent institutions, and analog frameworks.

9. Brea, "Un arte sin materia, sin espacio y sin tiempo."

of the most important Internet spaces dedicated to file sharing that, at the time of first writing and preparing this text, was being prosecuted in the Swedish courts (the home country of its creators) after being threatened and charged by the industry. The judge ruled on the case on April 17, 2009, and finally the four defendants were each sentenced to a year in prison and were also ordered to pay thirty million kronor (about $3.6 million) in damages to leading entertainment companies.[10]

This is not the only example. In France, a recent law obliges Internet service providers (ISPs) to block the accounts of those users who repeatedly download content protected by copyright; all this without even addressing the questionable practice of intercepting private communications between users and arbitrarily censoring communication devices to serve the economic interests of businesses. Apparently the measures adopted by the French government will not be adopted by other European countries, because they have been criticized by the European parliament in Strasbourg and have been the source of yet more problems. In spite of everything, excluding the Swedish trial and a future defined by measures like those in France, it is symptomatic that such attempts and similar initiatives by other pressure groups are met with a rapid response by user groups. Indeed, the Pirate Bay group itself has called attention to the issue through a new initiative: IPREDator. This service, while not the first resource of this kind, makes anonymous communication between users a reality and file-sharing invisible, while leaving no trace except that of exchanging bytes. The fact that there is no record of these transactions in any computer makes intercepting communications and identifying those persons sharing content practically impossible. Thus we see that users are adapting more skillfully to new technological possibilities and clearly, once more, all the industry is doing is delaying the inevitable. It is worth noting, however, that these movements in the community of users are not incompatible with copyright or the existence of viable remunerative models for authors, nor even with the existence of businesses and their profit margins. Everything indicates that if the models of production, distribution, and access regarding cultural creation are changing paradigmatically, business models should do so as well.

In the field of contemporary art, for the moment the situation has not reached the levels it has in other areas of culture. This is most likely because its status as a cultural industry is not as evident and strong as that of other fields like cinema, music, and software. Also, several structural deficits in the art field indicate that it is not geared toward strict financial gain. However, just to note that these issues and problems are not far removed from the art field, one need only observe critically how museums—paradigmatic institutions in the administration, conservation, and diffusion of knowledge in the field of art—manage their cultural activities. It is very significant, as well as typical, to come across texts in museums of the following kind: "All rights reserved. The total or partial

---

10. More information can be found at http://trial.piratebay.org. Although the last update was done on April 15, 2009, complementary information links can be found there.

reproduction of texts and images contained herein is prohibited." The prohibition on taking photographs in a museum, far from being an anecdotal issue, demonstrates a kind of inertia within the structures of art that indicates a certain failure to modernize, and is moreover revealing of a specific model of managing knowledge—in this case within the world of contemporary art. Such notions define very clearly a formula based on the most traditional interpretation of heritage, grounded in an original work of art that must not be reproduced in any form, in the emblematic figure of the individual artist, in the exclusive management of public funds and limiting the rights of users, filtering out any use (even if meant for research or education) through a rigid policy of permission. This is even more the case with many of the recently founded centers dedicated to dealing with contemporary art.

Free Software, Copyleft, and Free Culture

The aforementioned examples of Pirate Bay, French legal measures, and the management of content in museums are merely paradigmatic examples of the conflict (system failure!) between the everyday use of technology and the conservative positioning of industry. Clearly, it is within the field of music where such contradictions are most crudely exposed but, when seeking solutions, the most viable and sustainable responses are found in another industry, the software industry. In fact, although most visibly apparent in regard to music, these conflicts or system failures did not appear there first. For decades, software designers and users have suffered the same problems. Indeed, this has been the case since the early 1970s, when software and hardware took different paths after IBM's decision to sell machines and programs separately, thereby attributing a commercial value to the latter for the first time.

With this change, the first steps were taken in limiting the use and study of computer technology in what subsequently became (to this day) common practice in the form of exclusive software; in other words, software in which the user's possibilities were severely restricted. For example, users had no access to the software code and therefore could not modify or redistribute it, whatever their intention might be. In the early and mid-1980s, however, the term "free software" appeared among various communities, with Richard Stallman serving as the main catalyst of the movement. His decision to leave the Massachusetts Institute of Technology (MIT) for reasons related to limiting the new software panorama, led to the creation of the GNU[11] project.

One of the key questions that concerned Stallman was user freedom to make use of software. He was interested in the idea that, whatever the lifespan of a computer program in the GNU project, it should facilitate as much freedom as possible to whoever used it. In order to guarantee this, he created the General Public License (GPL), from which a

---

11. The GNU Project is a free software, mass collaboration project, announced on September 27, 1983, by Richard Stallman at MIT. It initiated the GNU operating system, software development for which began in January 1984.

number of initiatives and essential documents were developed to form what came to be known as copyleft. As an alternative to the current copyright system, this was intended to loosen the restrictions that limited use of content and to empower the user with certain rights that copyright or the intellectual property laws in Europe limited by default.

Through his project, Stallman argued in favor of a consistent proposal concerning the same notion of freedom, laying the bases for reconsidering the terms "free" and "freedom" in a way that they would be utilized later by a wide community of users. Despite the fact that he developed the idea for the software field, from this time on the philosophical concept of freedom acquired a new value and affected different realms of culture in its widest sense, as well as being extended to more intangible terrain such as the Internet. Discussion of free knowledge and free culture has implied new meaning after Stallman's contributions. It is likewise true that this conceptual extension is not the result of his efforts alone, but rather involves the participation of a whole community, within the parameters he established previously. When speaking about free software, Stallman is very concise and he elevates the issue of individuals' "self-determination" to other conceptual levels. For him, liberty is the foundation of free software as opposed to other ideas such as the concept of gratuity: "Free software is a matter of liberty, not price. To understand the concept, you should think of 'free' as in 'free speech,' not as in 'free beer.'"[12] What he means is the freedom of users to use, copy, study, modify, and improve software—a liberty that can be synthesized into four basic freedoms:

- The freedom to run the program for any purpose (freedom 0);
- The freedom to study how the program works, and adapt it to your needs (freedom 1). Access to the source code is a precondition of this;
- The freedom to redistribute copies so you can help your neighbor (freedom 2); and
- The freedom to improve the program, and release your improvements (and modified versions in general) to the public, so that the whole community benefits (freedom 3). Access to the source code is a precondition for this.

Tools to Reset the System

Having arrived at this point, it is evident that errors and conflicts in the management of knowledge have been detected that have had repercussions for the public domain and collective memory. For this reason, it is necessary to reconfigure the system. In order to do this, the copyleft project offers the necessary tools to efficiently regain the discourse on free culture, the democratic circulation of knowledge, and the creation of horizontal knowledge communities. The resources at our disposal were originated in large part in the world of free software and mark an attempt to transmit its technological and political

---

12. Stallman, *The Free Software Definition.*

discoveries to other areas of cultural production. All this has to do with *open* and *free* formats, file-sharing systems, 2.0 tools, and image repositories.[13] However, without any doubt, the most efficient resources are those of free licenses that have been crucial in the implementation and expansion of copyleft.

These licenses, which are basically contracts between author and user, are based on the rights of the author (rights of reproduction, adaptation, distribution, representation, and public communication) and share various elements that distinguish them from traditional licenses based on copyright. In the final analysis, such licenses, besides their value as legal documents, are essential tools at various levels:

As a *didactic tool*, they have helped initiate into the world of free culture many authors and users who might otherwise have given up, faced with the complex jurisdiction on intellectual property and dense legal terms on which licenses are granted, rights managed, and so on.

As a *distribution tool*, they demonstrate that a system based on copyright has clear limitations in the context of new digital media, and that other systems allow a greater range of possibilities for such distribution. A work that by default allows copying, makes free distribution more accessible, and consequently, reaches more users via channels through which protected works cannot circulate. For example, content published on blogs with free licenses is instantaneously open to being used in other places, thereby contributing exponentially to its free distribution.

They allow for *other models of production*. Ceding some rights to users allows the use of new and previously unknown models of production that have been proven to be sustainable. This therefore favors collaborative, participative, and collective production. It also allows for remixing, sampling, and creative construction based on other people's work.

They allow for *other models of access*. Automatically ceding rights such as, for example, copying makes content more accessible, dissolving filters that typically limit access to culture and clearing the way for more content and intellectual goods accessible in more and better spaces.

When opting for one license over another a question arises that is not as simple as it may at first seem. Even if Creative Commons (CC) licenses appear to be the most widespread and wisely used option, one cannot ignore other initiatives that have been, to some extent, overshadowed by their success.[14] The question of choice is based on two grounds: the demand for a pragmatic focus in a complex terrain like that of intellectual property, and the need to ask oneself about the hegemony of CC licenses and the collateral price that might have to be paid for their wider implementation.

---

13. Recently Creative Commons celebrated the accumulation of a hundred million licensed photos on Flickr: "These photos have been used in hundreds of thousands of Wikipedia articles, blog posts, and even mainstream press pieces; all examples of new works that might not otherwise have been created without our standardized public licenses." Fred Bernstein, "Celebrate 100 million CC Photos on Flickr with Joi Ito's Free Souls," *Creative Commons*, accessed March 23, 2009, http://creativecommons.org/weblog/entry/12540.

14. See http://creativecommons.org.

In addition to these questions there are others, many of them predating the initial concerns but that have been subsequently relegated to a second or third level. When mapping the world of free licenses, and from the perspective of contemporary artistic practices, one inevitably turns to the *Guide to Open Content Licenses* (2004) by Lawrence Liang.[15] It is an indispensable reference for anyone interested in creating or distributing open content through copyleft licenses. Of these licenses, I would highlight the following two in particular, due to their convenience when working with visual or plastic works of art.[16]

The *Free Art License* (the English-language version of the original French *Licence Art Libre*) is one of those most loyal to the spirit of the GPL created by free software and is therefore one of those that most respects the original copyleft concept: "The main rationale for this Free Art License is to promote and protect these creations of the human mind according to the principles of copyleft: freedom to use, copy, distribute, transform, and prohibition of exclusive appropriation."[17]

It allows the user to employ in any way those artistic works licensed to it—even commercial use, so long as it respects the full content of the license and cites the origin of the work in question and any subsequent works that might be licensed in the same way or under any compatible license, granting equivalent rights for the user. The Free Art License explicitly gives permission to any user to copy, or to make reproductions, to distribute and perform the artwork in public, and to modify copies of the originals.

Creative Commons is more than a license in that it is a group of licenses that can be personalized, and is without any doubt the most used of its kind today. Given that not all of these licenses within the CC group comply with the idea of copyleft, I will cite just two. The first (attribution) allows for commercial use and the creation of work derived from protected works, so that it is fully compatible with copyleft.[18] The second (attribution-noncommercial) does not allow commercial use but it does permit derived works.[19] For this reason, some believe that this does not really comply with a copyleft license because it restricts the basic right to enjoy financial gain from these (derived) works. It is important to clarify that those licenses that do not permit commercial use are not strictly copyleft.

However, some people still recommend their use because they leave it to the artists to decide whether their work may be used commercially or not. Furthermore, many

---

15. Liang, *Guide to Open Content Licenses.*

16. Having said that, I would also like to cite the *Aire incondicional* license (http://www.platoniq.net/aireincodicional_licencia.html) that, although of more limited use, deserves mention as part of the Platoniq artists' collective (http://www.platoniq.net). It was created in 2004 by the lawyer Abel Garriaga in collaboration with the collective and within the framework of a project entitled "The Emergence of Community-Based and Migrant E-Strategies in Southern Europe," undertaken at the Shedhalle art center in Zurich, and later traveling to other cities such as Geneva, Basel, and Lucerne. The license permits any use of the works but specifies certain aspects such as what it considers to be lucrative (or commercial) use.

17. *Free Art License 1.3,* http://artlibre.org/licence/lal/en.

18. See http://creativecommons.org/licenses/by/3.0.

19. Ibid.

people involved in artistic creation believe such licenses to be legitimately copyleft without any problem. It is therefore worth underscoring the difference between the freedom of an author to choose one or another license and whether this is a free license or not. Clearly these are different situations. The fact of choosing one or another license does not necessarily imply a copyleft decision.

Through the free licenses and other tools and measures mentioned briefly before, the copyleft project might imply more flexible relations between producer and receiver, as well as establishing other distribution channels and, above all, overcoming elitist stereotypes; not to mention moving away from the growing tendency to concentrate on the spectacular and sensationalistic in the production of contemporary art and culture. It therefore allows the recovery of artistic practices for culture in its most collective sense, freeing them up for the community out of which they undoubtedly emerge, and into which they must necessarily revert. It also turns around the neoliberal tendency toward the spectacular, the lack of criticism, and the use of culture for commercial and political interests. Apart from technical issues of the licenses, thinking in terms of free culture and the free circulation of content facilitates important benefits for knowledge communities, such as:

There is *more freedom for authors*. The authors make the important decisions about their creations, exercising true responsibility over the material they produce and that is put in circulation. These are important decisions that have until now been made and controlled by the industry, legislators, or the managing bodies. These licenses return a freedom to authors that had been previously denied them. One should remember that if nothing is specified to the contrary, all works are protected by the law on intellectual property and all rights to its use are reserved. In other words, nobody can do anything with them. By contrast, copyleft proposes ceding certain rights and allowing certain freedoms to the user or even other authors, without attaining prior permission: one can copy, share, distribute, manipulate, communicate, research, and create based on already existent works.

There is *more freedom for the users*. Users do not have to continually ask permission to make use of other works. They can access more cultural content and intellectual property, in more places, with the understanding that the original author must always be clearly specified. In other words, the user enjoys a freer, more democratic and participative access to culture, with fewer filters, and the access is more immediate and of better quality.

Finally, there is *enrichment of the public domain and common property*. The space of common cultural property is extended, and all citizens are free to enjoy it, to research, create, and communicate, or simply to use it as a means of knowledge or leisure. Copyright and the progressive reforms of the law on industrial property achieve precisely the opposite in that they delay the movement of artistic works into the public domain and make many works inaccessible for years because they do not merit financial exploitation. Nevertheless, they continue to be kept under lock and key for up to seventy years after the death of their authors.

Considering all this, one can reconfigure the system, and today the tools exist to do this. Alternatively, the gradual modification of norms that govern intellectual property and copyright will continue to limit the rights of users, creating specific laws and limits to restrict the everyday use of culture that elsewhere is widely extensive. More errors and conflicts will occur in a system that encourages restriction through the laws on intellectual property and the extension of limits on authors' rights, leading to positions incompatible with the public domain and that progressively hinder the circulation of, distribution of, and access to contemporary cultural production. Indeed, this will take place to such an extent that *the public domain will never again be contemporary,* positing a specific model of restrictive management of knowledge against the creative impoverishment of our memory. This memory needs to be freed up. Finally, there is another key dimension to this reconfiguration of the system—that of the responsibility of the author as a cultural producer when generating knowledge that is subsequently put into circulation.

In the words of Walter Benjamin, "Transmitting an apparatus of production without—as much as possible—transforming it, is a highly debatable procedure even when the content of the apparatus which is transmitted seems to be revolutionary in nature."[20]

The decisions that any cultural producer makes or does not make are crucial for constructing common cultural property as a whole, whether in the past, present, or future. Certain decisions made at the time become methods of control in the present and lead to conflict in the future. This is the principal argument in the 2008 documentary, "Rip: A Remix Manifesto" by the web activist and filmmaker Brett Gaylor.[21] The documentary explores copyright questions and their connections with the remix culture. In one scene, the film establishes four points in favor of a freer society and culture, which, to a large extent, are shared in this text:

1. Culture always builds on the past,
2. The past always tries to control the future,
3. Our future is becoming less free, and
4. To build free societies you must limit the control of the past.

To which one might add, as a summary of this article, that by way of the path opened by free software we can gain several tools to implement all these ideas.

Finally, I would like to turn my gaze on this occasion toward my own context, out of which emerged the words of an important and internationally recognized Basque artist, Eduardo Chillida, who once said: *"Norberarena dena, ia ia ez da inorena."* One might translate this from the Basque language as, "Whatever is only of oneself is almost of no one," in a clear allusion to the artist's need to disseminate and share his/her own work. Chillida was, moreover, the creator of the University of the Basque Country's logo, beneath

---

20. Benjamin, "Author as Producer," 86.

21. Gaylor, *Rip: A Remix Manifesto.*

which the motto of the university where I teach and research reads: *"Eman ta zabal ezazu!"* (Give and disperse). The quote has its origin in a traditional nineteenth-century Basque song, *Gernikako Arbola* (The Tree of Gernika)—a kind of unofficial national anthem for Basques—and is taken from the strophe, *"Eman ta zabal ezazu, munduan frutua"* (Give and disperse your fruits throughout the world). So, the motto of the University of the Basque Country deals with the idea of giving and extending knowledge as one's fruit. If one might, of course, assume that the university is one of the most important focal points for knowledge generation, transmission, and dissemination, it should be necessarily sensitive to these issues, these system errors, and their potential reconfiguration in the form of a potential *"Eman, kopiatu eta zabal ezazu!"* (Give, copy, and disperse!).

Bibliography

Barlow, John Perry. "Selling Wine without Bottles: The Economy of Mind on the Global Net." Electronic Frontier Foundation website. http://w2.eff.org/Misc/Publications/John_Perry_Barlow/HTML/idea_economy_article.html.

Benjamin, Walter. "Author as Producer." In *New Left Review* 1, no. 62 (July–August 1970): 83–96.

Brea, José Luis. "Un arte sin materia, sin espacio y sin tiempo." *El País* (Madrid). October 21, 2006.

Buquet, Gustavo. "Música on line: Batallas por los derechos, lucha por el poder." In *Hacia un nuevo sistema mundial de comunicación: Las industrias culturales en la era digital.* Barcelona: Gedisa, 2003.

Gaylor, Brett. *Rip: A Remix Manifesto.* Produced by EyeSteelFilm in coproduction with the National Film Board, Canada, 2008. www.ripremix.com.

Liang, Lawrence. *Guide to Open Content Licenses. V1.2.* Rotterdam: Piet Zwart Institute, 2004. http://pzwart.wdka.hro.nl/mdr/pubsfolder/opencontent.

Orihuela, José Luis. "Hacia la napsterización del conocimiento." Published June 30, 2003. http://www.ecuaderno.com/2003/01/30/hacia-la-napsterizacion-del-conocimiento.

Rodríguez Arkaute, Natxo. "El contexto ya no es lo que era. Producción artística en el nuevo contexto digital." In *Muestra de Audiovisuales, Facultad de Bellas Artes UPV/EHU.* Bilbao: Facultad de Bellas Artes EHU/UPV-BBVA, 2008.

Stallman, Richard M. *Free Software, Free Society: Selected Essays of Richard M. Stallman.* Edited by Joshua Gay. Boston: GNU Press, 2002.

———. "The Free Software Definition." The Free Software Foundation, Inc. http://www.fsf.org/licensing/essays/free-sw.html.

Valery, Paul. "The Conquest of Ubiquity." In *Aesthetics,* translated by Ralph Manheim, Bollingem Foundation. New York: Pantheum Books; Random House, 1964.

7

Free Software Explains Everything

CHRISTOPHER KELTY

My title is brazen provocation. One might suppose that some kind of theory of knowledge communities (or network societies, or information societies, etc.) is necessary to explain a case like that of free and open source software, in which hackers and software developers collaborate remotely to produce freely available ("copylefted") complex software applications. This chapter argues simply the reverse, that if you want a theory of knowledge communities (or network societies, or information societies, etc.), you should start with the case of free software. I mean this both in the sense that one should start with the empirical and let the theoretical be a refraction thereof, and also in the sense that free software, as such, is in fact the right place to start for any and all explanations of knowledge communities. Such a grandiose claim is undoubtedly not supportable, but I insist on making it in order to jar loose the assumption that every new technology radically changes everything.

Free software is not radically new—it is in my account over forty years old. It does not radically change everything—indeed, it may have changed very few things. However, it possesses within it a concrete set of evolving practices, which are also at the heart of all the technologies for which radical novelty has been claimed throughout the so-called information revolution—starting with the time-shared operating system in the 1960s, through the personal computer, and up to and including devices like the Google Android phone, Facebook, and Twitter, and the even Internet itself. By pulling apart free software and carefully examining what it is, what it is not, what people do in its name, how they argue about it, and what is made and what is not, it is possible to diagnose a large range of issues that frequently appear under the heading of "information society" or "network society" or many permutations thereof.

Free software explains everything because by demystifying this one case, and carefully analyzing it as a set of evolving practices that are not restricted to fiddling with software or hardware, one can begin to ask more precise questions about, for instance, the nature of transaction, exchange, and sharing mediated by computing technologies; the role of intellectual property law; the role of corporate business strategy, consortium-building, and marketing; the techno-managerial organization of intellectual work; and the political import of lived theories of liberalism and techno-utopianism.

As an anthropologist, I want to know what diverse peoples are actually doing in rich, precise detail; and as a historian, I want to know how long they have been doing it and how it has changed. As a philosophically inclined scholar, however, I also want to know what it means. Hence, my work over the last several years has been focused on an empirically grounded, historically specific investigation of the *cultural significance* of free software. But I didn't start out there; like a lot of people I wanted to understand the impact of the *Internet* on our world, not the impact of free software. But it was in the course of asking, "What are people actually doing on the Internet?" and, "How long have they been doing it?" that I came to the topic of free software (a.k.a. open source software) as an essential component of the Internet. They are related as figure and ground—without one, the other makes no sense. What follows is a summary of the book I wrote on this topic, *Two Bits: The Cultural Significance of Free Software*; it concludes with some reflections on how it might be applied to the currently most talked-about "virtual-networked-online-digital-social-community-network," Facebook.

Part 1

Two Bits is both an anthropological and a historical book. The first part is an ethnographic and theoretical introduction that dwells on who *geeks* are, what kind of group they might be, and in what their affinity consists. I didn't start out writing a book about free software, but in the course of working alongside people passionate about it, I slowly started to realize just how important and central it is to so many diverse people. I also don't make strong claims about who geeks (or hackers) are, because I don't think of it as an identity so much as a set of practices and orientations that emerge when one becomes extremely skilled and concerned about how technology and society are organized today: programmers, lawyers, scholars and lots of other kinds of people can be geeks in this sense.[1] One can also be a geek with respect to other things, for instance the Basque language or automobiles, and I think they share some characteristics that I won't go into here.

The second part of the book, therefore, is a detailed history of the various components of free software, stretching back to the early 1960s and covering in detail certain key events in the "making possible" of free software. These include obvious things, like sharing source code and building the Internet around certain ideals of organization; but

---

1. Coleman and Golub, "Hacker Practice."

they also include intellectual property, coordination, and practices of argumentation and proselytism. It is my contention that the five components that I identify as key to the emergence of free software are not only a good way to understand free software, but a toolkit for exploring phenomena that are related to, inspired by, or in reaction to the success of free software.

The third part of the book explores two such "modulations" of the practices of free software—Creative Commons' reconfiguration of free software licenses to cover digital content of all kinds, and Rice University's Connexions project, which has sought to make textbooks open, modifiable, and reusable on the model of free software. The third part was written as a demonstration of the fact that the practices that make up free software are also central to a very large number of activities other than software development occurring on or through the Internet. So in some ways I am suggesting that free software is at the origin of things like Facebook and Wikipedia, social movements like the global justice movement, as well as a new fascination with amateur science and technology, as in the popular magazine *Make* and its associated communities of tinkerers and hackers.[2] But free software is not in itself original; it is made up of a distinct set of empirically identifiable practices which came together in a particular way to give *cultural significance* to free software, and it is my claim that these practices (and perhaps others) are at the heart of our contemporary "knowledge communities" or however one wishes to label them in grand sociological terms.

One way to understand the term *cultural significance* is simply to ask, Why is free software so popular? Why are so many diverse people interested in learning about it, supporting it, transforming it, denouncing it, or responding to it in some way? This is different from asking, as many social scientists have, How is it possible?[3] Rather, it is a way of asking, Why now? and, In response to what? Why is it that free software makes sense to so many people, including many who do not understand software at all?

That significance can be summed up in a couple of ways. First, free software encourages modification. It encourages people to make new things out of free software. Indeed, it gives them a hitherto unrecognized legal right to do so. For those who might never have given free software any thought, the colloquial distinction is: "Free as in speech, not as in beer." This is slightly disingenuous though, because it is also free as in beer, but the distinction is important. Software that is simply free of cost on the Internet may not be free in the sense of freedom. Indeed, it is more likely the opposite, and will instead spy on you, or turn your computer into an undead spam-relaying Zombie. Similarly, the high-quality, feature-rich software that comes free of cost with your fancy new MacBook Air is not free in the sense of freedom, because you cannot, as we say, open the hood and take a look at the internals—the source code.

---

2. Reagle, "In Good Faith"; Stringer, "This is What Democracy Looked Like."

3. See Weber, *Success of Open Source*; Benkler, *Wealth of Networks*; and Feller et al., *Perspectives on Free and Open Source Software*.

So truly free software is free only when it not only allows people to look under the hood, but also to see its source code and tinker with it. Free software gives everyone the legal right to do so, and furthermore, in the best of cases, encourages individuals to help each other modify and redistribute what they make. And this leads to the second aspect of free software's cultural significance: that it *makes things public*. By making possible and encouraging modification, free software creates an opportunity for that software to become public—to become the property of a public who can, at any point in the future, take action to modify, improve, or redefine this software. My own term for what is created in the case of free software is a "recursive public"—which is meant to capture a couple of things: (1) that this kind of public sphere involves not just discussion and debate, but the building of new technologies as well, and (2) that it is "recursively" concerned with the technical conditions of its own existence—online, on the Internet, and through the use of the very software that is thereby created.

So how should one go about studying such a phenomenon? One place to start is by asking, Why do all geeks look alike?

Figure 7.1. Why do all Geeks look alike?
Dennis Ritchie (left) and Kenneth Thompson (right).

It is a serious question: as I traveled the net and the world, I started to wonder: what binds geeks together, what constitutes their affinity? It's not language, or nationality, or race, or even education and training, really. You can find pretty remarkable diversity of all these things among geeks. It might be "culture" that binds them together, but if it is, it is so broad and diverse that it is hopelessly imprecise. As an anthropologist, I am supposed to look for and find cultural difference, even when confronted with a phenomenon that seems to cross nation, language, ethnicity, profession, class, and education. So I started in Boston with MIT geeks—I found a couple who were involved in unusual health-care and IT related work; I traveled to Berlin, where I found a very hip coterie of geeks, organizing meetings and talks in clubs and theaters; I traveled to Bangalore, where I joined a Linux Users Group and network of people called "Friends of Udhay." Then I traveled back to the great nation of Texas, where in my own backyard I found three geeks—Rich Baraniuk, Ross Reedstrom, and Brent Hendricks—hard at work on Connexions, and whom I connected with a group of lawyer-geeks spread around the country, called Creative Commons.

Throughout all these travels, I wondered about the nature of the affinity all these folks had for each other—what constitutes the substance of this "culture," if it can be called that. How was it possible for me to have a conversation about routers, protocols, and standards in Boston with health-care IT professionals, move to Berlin and, in stilted German, continue discussing the Linux Operating system, and then end up in Bangalore and back in English talking about copyright law and Web servers? What kind of group was this? One thing became clear: the affinity that very many of these people showed for one another was mediated at some level by their interest in free software. And so, it turned out, was I. So in true anthropological form, I started to ask: How did I become a geek?

It was at this point that I began a more serious historical investigation of free software, one that would go beyond the surface stories and explanations swirling through this global network of geeks—a more critical history, but also a history that analyzes the phenomenon in order to understand why people are responding to it—and not only geeks, but artists, activists, scientists, and educators as well. I identified five basic practices:

Fomenting a Movement

The place to start is 1998. In 1998, free software blew into national media attention as part of the dot-com boom. That year was the moment at which a very large number of different kinds of geeks started to imagine themselves as part of a movement. It was the year that Netscape released the source code to Netscape Communicator, renaming the project Mozilla, which has now become Firefox. It was also the year the phrase "open source" was coined, at a meeting organized by publisher Tim O'Reilly, leading to an intense set of debates with Richard Stallman, founder of the free software Foundation, about terminology and the commercial success and political goals of free software. It was the year that VA Linux was formed—a company that sold computers with the free software operating system Linux installed on them. When it went public in 1999, at the height of the boom, it was the single largest IPO in history: a 700 percent share price increase in one day.

All of these things fed into the emergence of a movement—and by movement I mean debate, argument, ideology, goals, imaginations of the future, and plans for achieving them. The movement is about discussion, evangelism, and provocation concerning the practices of free software; it's about talk—which is crucial to getting things going in a large-scale distributed project. There are a lot of colorful personalities in this movement.

If you've heard anything about free software, it has probably been about the three main demagogues of the movement: Richard Stallman, Linus Torvalds, and Eric Raymond, all of whom vigorously participated in and fed the creation of this movement. For most people, they represent virulently opposed ideologies: freedom and justice, libertarian deregulationism, radical entrepreneurialism, and so on.

The funny thing about the movement is, even when we consider the endless debates about what to name to use, and all the sound and fury concerning freedom and commercialization and so on, the fact remains that regardless of what hackers say they believe, or the reasons they give, they are all actually doing exactly the same practical things. They use the same tools, they share the same code, they use the same infrastructures and standards, they use the same licenses, and they coordinate and form groups in a handful of ways common to all. Where the debate and discussion makes a difference is in the coherence and understanding of these practices as a single thing, rather than an unintegrated diversity of practices. This is, in fact, what sets it apart from the commercial realm, where corporations work extremely hard to be distinctive in terms of process, product, and message. Free software and open source, by contrast, are unchanged by the very flexible array of ideologies that are claimed in their name: freedom, cost-saving, interoperability, better quality, elitism and populism, anti-microsoftism, and so on. Much of what constitutes the movement therefore is simply the constant reflection on what makes the practices of free and open source software different from what has come before.

Sharing Source Code

Perhaps the most obvious component is the ability to share source code. This might seem intuitive, and not something that needs creating, but it isn't. The story of how source code came to be sharable is also the story of the UNIX operating system, and for that, we need to go back to the two gentlemen in figure 7.1. Kenneth Thompson and Dennis Ritchie created the UNIX operating system and the C programming language in 1969–70 at AT&T Bell Labs. It ran on a PDP-11 and was designed to be as minimalist and modular as possible, helped along by the constraints of a small machine with limited memory and processing power. Thompson learned most of what he put into UNIX from working on a larger project at MIT that Bell Labs and GE had co-funded to create a commercially viable multiuser, time-sharing operating system. UNIX, they joked, was one of whatever Multics had been many of. Or, in that puerile manner endemic to geeks, UNIX (Unics) was a pun, a castrated Multics. Multics has its own colorful history and lore, especially at MIT, but it is UNIX that has gone on too much greater glory. UNIX, however, was a research project, and one that emphasized an elegance of design, a simplicity that many people admired, and one of its key goals was portability—meaning that the software was designed in such a way that it would be easier than normal to get it to run on different kinds of machines.

To facilitate this, Thompson and Ritchie started sending tapes around the world to interested computer scientists. They did something unusual, however: they included the source code. They sent tapes containing both the working operating system and the human-readable source code that would allow someone else, in a different lab and with a different machine, to tweak it and make it work in their own lab. Then another strange thing happened: people who received the system, and changed it (since they had the source code), started to send their changes and new ideas back to Ken and Dennis for release in the next round. The very identity of UNIX as a technical thing started to reflect this proliferation.

One might ask, why did AT&T let them do this? The short answer is that they tried to stop it, but could not, and the reason is that until 1984, AT&T was a regulated monopoly, forbidden by a 1956 consent decree from engaging in any business other than voice telecommunications. Because of this peculiar status, AT&T could not commercialize UNIX, but instead allowed it to be very widely licensed for very low fees (in some cases $150, which was essentially less than the cost of shipping the tapes around the world). This hybrid commercial-academic situation led to a strange proliferation of UNIX all over the world, at the same time that it was deemed a trade secret by AT&T and its circulation policed by the legal department. AT&T was limited in its ability to restrict this novel form of circulation precisely because it was legally prevented from circulating it in a more conventional market.

As a result of its unconventional technical identity and its hybrid corporate-academic identity, UNIX acquired an unconventional pedagogical status as well. John Lions, for instance, an Australian computer scientist, created a book for use in his classes called *Commentary on UNIX 6th Edition, with Source Code*. This book, which is known as the most photocopied document in computer science history, contained the complete source code of UNIX along with elaborate commentary by Lions, which he used in his classes despite AT&T's periodic attempts to restrict this type of use. Lions' commentary was so valuable that it inspired a generation of students. A quotation about his commentary captures what it meant to people:

> We soon came into possession of what looked like a fifth generation photocopy and someone who shall remain nameless spent all night in the copier room spawning a sixth, an act expressly forbidden by a carefully worded disclaimer on the first page. Four remarkable things were happening at the same time. One, we had discovered the first piece of software that would inspire rather than annoy us; two, we had acquired what amounted to a literary criticism of that computer software; three, we were making the single most significant advancement of our education in computer science by actually reading an entire operating system; and four, we were breaking the law.[4]

In the 1980s, Andrew Tanenbaum, a computer science professor in Amsterdam, would create a version of UNIX called MINIX, for similar reasons. Restricted by the trade-secret policing of AT&T and eventually by their decision, after the 1984 divestiture,

---

4. Lions, *Lions' Commentary on UNIX 6th Edition, with Source Code*.

to commercialize UNIX, Tanenbaum created a completely rewritten version of UNIX that he distributed as part of the textbook he had written. What is important to realize here is that this textbook was not called *UNIX Operating Systems*, it was called *Operating Systems*. Full stop. UNIX had become the very paradigm of what an operating system should be. Through sharing and proliferation, in addition to its mere circulation, its design and its availability became part of a moral and technical order that served as a basis for geeks, and formed the core from which free software would grow in the 1980s and 1990s. Hence, at the core of this practice of sharing source code is a story that ignores technical, legal, political, economic, and pedagogical uses of an object, in order to make something seemingly obvious—sharing—come into being.

Imagining Infrastructure

The third component is a definition of an open infrastructure. In 1998, this meant primarily the Internet and the standard PC architecture—but the story that precedes it is a common, albeit underappreciated, one in the annals of information technology: the story of the failed "open systems." Open Systems during the 1980s were supposed to create the ultimate, open, standard architecture based on the UNIX operating system and the Open Systems Interconnection Protocol. Both failed, but the failure revealed an important blind spot that free software advocates would return to in the 1990s: the blind spot of intellectual property.

The story of the attempt to make UNIX the basis of open systems is a story of standardization. The much vaunted portability of UNIX was seen as a major commercial opportunity, not only by AT&T, but by all of the people to whom AT&T had licensed UNIX—and they had licensed it to a lot of people. Everyone agreed about the promise of UNIX and open systems, but none agreed on which version. All these different versions of UNIX were increasingly incompatible with each other. The reason was simple: in order for manufacturers to differentiate their products from each other's, each added its own changes and features; but unlike what occurred in the 1970s, when UNIX users contributed those changes back to Thompson and Ritchie, no corporation had an incentive to give its intellectual property back to AT&T, even if it was based on work AT&T—or some other company—had already done. And so the battles for standardization began. By 1988, there were four competing standards consortia. Curiously, many corporations such as Sun, AT&T, and IBM were simultaneously members of more than one consortium, none of which had any more legitimacy than the others. Rather than competing to offer new products or services, these consortia ended up competing to own the standard. The more they fought, the more they distrusted one another, and the more it became impossible to settle on any one standard.

The unfortunate denouement to this story was the emergence of Windows NT, which took advantage of the cheap PC architecture and of its duopoly partnership with Intel to dominate the market for "networked" computers, by occupying the void created by competing versions of UNIX. By the mid 1990s, the UNIX market was destroyed, even as the standard, known as POSIX, was finally completed.

In the end, the question of how to properly achieve an open infrastructure was never answered—and to a large extent still has not been answered. There are aspects of this story that are repeated in every new attempt to build large infrastructures (like the cyber-infrastructure projects of today). However, what this episode provided was an experience of the failure that turned out to be central to the identities of many of those involved in free and open source software in the 1990s. It pitted two "moral and technical" imagi-nations of order against each other—that of an intellectual property regime intended to reward creativity and risk-taking versus that of a dream of open and free infrastructures that would allow "seamless" integration and efficient data and tool sharing. There is a reason that free software advocates care so much about standards, formats, and things like Digital Rights Management—and the failures of the 1980s IT industry are a key, if ill-understood, cultural reason.

Writing Licenses

The fourth component of free software is the copyright license, associated most closely with Richard Stallman, who created the first such license, called the GNU General Public License, in about 1985. The story of where and why the GPL came about is a story about re-use, permissions and changing copyright laws in the early 1980s, and the EMACS text editor (with its surrounding controversy). The copyleft license, as it came to be called, does a clever thing: when applied to anything, primarily software, it asserts copyright over that software, but then it turns around and gives users the right to copy, redistribute, and modify that software, so long as they give everyone else the same rights. In essence it takes advantage of the rights granted by US copyright law to invert or abro-gate those rights—hence the term "copyleft."

The GPL emerged at a time when copyright law had seen some pretty enormous changes, especially in its 1976 and 1980 amendments, which were designed to deal with threats from complex, hard to understand new forms of high-tech, peer-to-peer content-sharing technologies. The 1976 copyright law changed a number of things, including the requirement to register a copyright and the codification of fair use rules. The 1980 amendment explicitly added software to the definition of copyrightable works. But the changes were relatively slow to percolate into the practices of working programmers. Working out all the details of what can and cannot be copyrighted, what counts as software and what doesn't, and what counts as infringement was not an easy thing to accomplish.

The controversy at the origin of the GPL concerned re-use and permission. Richard Stallman had created a widely used and revered text editor called EMACS, which he distributed to anyone for free. Various new versions started to appear, in much the same fashion as UNIX. The controversy concerns the version for UNIX called GOSMACS, by James Gosling. In 1983, Gosling decided to sell his version to a commercial company, which angered many of the people who had either used it for free, or contributed bits and pieces to it as it evolved. It so angered Stallman that he created a completely new version called GNU EMACS. The problem, however, was that he had used, allegedly with permission, code that was copyrighted by Gosling. The ensuing debate and discussion lasted for months (it is detailed in my book through the use of the USEnet archives), and the ultimate outcome was that Stallman ended up rewriting those portions of the code in order to keep a version for UNIX freely available.

The whole experience confused and angered a number of people, Stallman among them, and it was out of this confusion that the GPL, the copyleft license, was born as a way to legally deal with problems of permission, reuse, and copying in the service of making software more free. It would be another ten years before the GPL was in widespread use, but it grew steadily in an underground fashion, all the time gathering adherents during the era of the UNIX wars and the debate about "open systems." By the end of the 1990s, however, the situation had changed considerably, and today one of the things that most distinguishes free software hackers is their impressive knowledge of intellectual property law.

Coordinating Collaboration

The last component of free software is also the most widely studied and admired: its ability to allow collaboratively created complex technical objects via the voluntary participation of a widely distributed set of contributors. The "wisdom of crowds," "Web 2.0," "social software"—all of these are terms that refer narrowly to this component, by which a large number of people contribute to a goal without being organized hierarchically, or more significantly, without being paid to do so. Though it is mythically referred to as a "self-organizing" dynamic, it is actually a problematic system riddled with questions of leadership and governance. The story of coordinating collaborations is also the story of two of the darlings of free software, Linux and Apache. These two projects were not only central technologies in the rise of the Internet—an operating system and a Web server—but also central experiments in the organization of free software projects. Both were experiments in letting go of hierarchical design in favor of a kind of "generalized adaptability" by which multiple participants could extend and modify a core product to make it do new things. As such both projects implied a new kind of governance of technical development.

Linus Torvalds and his friends transformed Andrew Tanenbaum's MINIX into something far more adaptable to existing uses, and far less useful as a teaching tool. As a result, like UNIX, it was quickly ported to all kinds of architectures, and began to include a large number of additional tools. Apache took the first version of an academic Web server project, called httpd, and similarly turned it into a rapidly evolving framework for new Web-based innovations. Torvalds ruled his group as a charismatic "benevolent dictator" while the oligarchy at Apache followed a more meritocratic process of democratic voting. Both experimented with these forms outside of existing organizations, whether university or corporate, essentially inventing new organizational forms built to suit the technologies and goals of the projects.

A key part of the coordination of collaboration was the combined use of the Internet and tools for managing the collaborative production of software, especially a set of tools known as SourceCode Management systems. SCMs such as subversion, cvs, and rcs achieve something special: they integrate the technical and the social. SCMs manage different versions of a software project so that multiple people can work on it simultaneously without stepping on each other's toes. At the same time, they determine which people have permissions to make which kinds of changes to a project. Hence a kind of socio-technical integration is achieved that allows participants to track and understand the course of a project, and learn who has power and who does not. As the projects grow in size, these tools and their constraints have guided decisions about the management of these projects. A famous example concerns Torvalds' decision to use a commercial version control system called BitKeeper, which resulted in an ideological clash over whether it was possible to create free software using non-free tools. The ultimate answer was no. The collaboration of coordination is thus a central component of free software—one that contains the novel experiments concerning governance and coordination as well as a kind of design philosophy that privileges adaptability over hierarchy.

Recursive Publics

Taken together, these five components tell the story of the historical emergence of free software. It's a story that ends, in many ways, around 2002 or so, but in ending it gives birth to a whole new set of practices that are either directly connected to it, or inspired by its success: Web 2.0, user-generated content, online virtual worlds, Open Access journals, Re-Mix culture, Creative Commons, Open Educational Resources, and so on. All these things have some kind of genealogical or pragmatic relationship to the practices that also make up free software.

Recall that the cultural significance of free software as I've posed it here is that it "makes things public." One should be able to ask of these other kinds of projects, therefore: do they "make things public," are they creating a new form of public sphere, are they changing what it means to participate in governance, and at what levels?

Unfortunately, "the public" as we speak about it these days is a rather domesticated beast, one that is also elusive and constantly sought by those who "want to know what the public thinks." When I say public, however, I do not mean "people out there"—rather I mean *power*, about the ability for people—who are doing little more than simply paying attention to a particular issue—to have the power to control how that issue is dealt with and solved. Such power is rare today, and it is concentrated in the hands of the largest organizations: governments, corporations, NGOs, churches, professional societies, and so on. Publics (or public spheres)—defined as autonomous, independent, powerful spaces of debate that can force change—are hard to find. Indeed most academics would argue that they either no longer exist or have fragmented into interest groups and social movements of diverse forms.

So it should be surprising to suggest that free software brings into being an authentic, independent, and powerful public sphere. Indeed, it does so in a way that, to my knowledge, nobody in the social sciences has recognized: by bringing technology itself into the sphere of discussion—by arguing *through* the creation of technology, not just about it. And the reason it does this is to ensure the continued power of publics to emerge and re-emerge wherever necessary, into the future, in new forms appropriate to changed conditions.

Such an achievement is incredibly *fragile*. There is no essential reason for free software to continue making things public unless the people involved work to do just that. So I think it is important to ask, of things like Web 2.0, Facebook or MySpace, the iPhone, open access or open educational resources, do they, too, seek to make things public? Do they seek to create and enhance the kind of public power that democratic citizens rely on? Do they encourage the kinds of virtues and practices that lead to such public-making? Can we ask this question rigorously and without resigning ourselves to a cynical account of a consumer-driven democracy?

Two Bits was intended to help answer this question: by laying out the five basic components that made it possible for free software to come into existence, one might use those components as a template to ask about whether new modulations of free software practices are also public in this novel sense. *Two Bits* explores in detail the examples of Creative Commons and Connexions. Other projects I have observed include the case of computer scientists analyzing electronic touch-screen voting machines, a case that perhaps more than any other I can think of exemplifies the promise of applying these ideas to some of our most important institutions and the technologies we use to express our political beliefs; another "modulation" is the possibility of "open source nanotechnology"—a project with chemist Vicki Colvin and her student Cafer Yavuz.

In that project we reimagined a way of creating Magnetite Nanocrystals using household items, in order to make it easier to fabricate them for the purpose of removing arsenic from water. That was a clear case of how the creation of publics extends today beyond our national borders to include people—like engineers in Bangladesh where arsenic removal is a pressing concern—who might become directly involved in the direction science and technology takes today. There is also today a burgeoning interest in applying the principles of free software to biology, especially in the case of Synthetic Biology and the attempt to create standardized, openly available biological "parts" for engineering.

Modulation: Facebook

To demonstrate one way of using the tools of *Two Bits* to understand the modulation of the practices of free software, consider the case of Facebook. By early 2009, Facebook had grown to 180 million users. As someone who does not use Facebook, this number made my jaw drop. I started to wonder: what do people like about it, and why it is attracting so many people? At that point in time, two things happened, the first personal, the second very distant. The personal story is that I was contacted by a senior academic in my field—suffice it to say, someone who I would be ill-advised to ignore—via Facebook. I had been sucked into it the way a generation earlier, in the 1990s, we all found ourselves being sucked into the Internet by e-mail. Facebook, it turns out, is hell-bent on replacing the Internet, transforming it from the inside out—and it is doing this by leveraging the cultural and economic relationships we have already created among ourselves. By leveraging those social relationships, it creates the possibility of forcing individuals to use the service: the social relationship of academic hierarchy and opportunity required that I use this service because someone more powerful that I drew me into it. No doubt there are ways I could have refused—but only at the risk of alienating someone socially and professionally important to me.

The more distant event was the global organization of protests in Colombia against FARC (Revolutionary Armed Forces of Colombia); Colombians all over the world came out in protest against violence (though some say it was a global display of support for President Uribe, which is not the same thing). This in itself is not surprising; since the successes of the Zapatistas in the 1990s, such global organization has become de rigeur. What was surprising in this case was the fact that Facebook was the medium of organization, and not simply e-mail, Web sites, or a coordinated media campaign. These two events, then, combined to give Facebook a cultural significance I had not afforded it previously. What's more, it created a certain anxiety. I have characterized free software as a "recursive public," which, though fragile, is an achievement that I argue supports the continued creation and maintenance of a healthy, technologically mediated political culture. Will Facebook do the same? How should we think about this?

The answer is not simple. On the face of it, Facebook is enthusiastically committed to open source software, and its developers say things like "help us keep the web more open and social," as if that were their main goal. Of course, the reality of the situation is that Facebook is a corporation whose goal is to figure out ways to monetize social networking and relationality. This is disturbing, but no more so than capitalism itself. What I want to use *Two Bits* to do here is to pull apart the practices and look at where Facebook is "modulating" the practices refined in free software, and where it is not.

Sharing Source Code, or What Is Being Shared?

There are two kinds of sharing at stake in Facebook: the sharing that users do and the sharing that Facebook developers, both inside and outside Facebook, do.

Facebook Developers Share

In free software, many things are shared, and the focus of the practice is on shared source code. This is the fundamental unit of practice; without it free software makes little sense. But what is important about it is not that it is source code, but that it is *shared*. By innovating ways to circulate and update source code, to share it widely, and to accept and incorporate the changes of others, shared source code provided the basis for large-scale distributed cooperation, beginning in the 1970s and stretching to the present.

This kind of sharing can and is done within corporations—it is in fact a standard practice in software engineering. The differences come with the definition of who is allowed into the group doing the sharing. Amazon, Yahoo, Google, and Facebook run complicated Web-based services for their users; these services are all built inside these corporations and installed on their servers. Many people inside these corporations can share and modify this software, and there is a hierarchy of employees who decide which changes will be included and which will be installed and run on their servers. This is exactly like free software in many respects, but differs because free software lets *anyone* download and modify the source code. Any given project might not accept any change, and there remains a hierarchy of people in charge of that given project and the choice of which changes will be incorporated. However, an individual user can make the changes and install them on his/her own servers/desktops, without needing to ask permission.

Facebook, like Google and other Internet companies, does seek to foster a kind of free software wing among its developers inside and out. The ability to design components, applications, games, and services that interact with Facebook through its API (Application Programming Interface) is fostered and overseen by Facebook, but largely left open to develop as freely or as proprietarily as is necessary. Such an approach makes perfect sense because it is more or less exactly the relationship Facebook and Google have (or had in the past) to the Internet itself, as a core technology that they did not seek to change but merely to extend and add upon. As they have become more powerful, however, they have come to exert far more power and control over the Internet itself. Jonathan Zittrain has recently analyzed the nature of this problem in his work, identifying it as a problem of "tethered" or "generative" platforms.[5] The former are those applications that are completely controlled by a corporation or single source, so that any new ideas or applications have to be approved; the latter are platforms (the Internet being the paradigm case) that allow new ideas to flourish (or die) in a space more openly and freely reconfigurable, without the control of any corporation.

Facebook has created a platform based on the Internet—it is a beneficiary of a "generative" technology; but the platform it has created (currently instantiated in the Facebook API, Facebook Markup Language (fbml), and Facebook "Connect" platform) is tethered in that Facebook retains all rights to determine which applications and uses will be shut down if necessary—the case of Scrabulous (in which developers of a wildly popular Facebook game that infringed Scrabble's trademark were censored by Facebook) being fortunately the only serious one to date. However, it should be clearly stated: *Facebook could have decided to disable the FARC protests if they wanted to.* Because Facebook is not the only game in town, it might not have put a dent in the organizing, but with 200 million users, I suspect that it would have.

---

5. Zittrain, *The Future of the Internet—And How to Stop It.*

Facebook Users Share

Facebook users do, however, share things, much like the analogy with source code. What they share, however, is somewhat less precise than source code: they share actions. They share profiles, status updates, messages, gifts, causes, requests, announcements, and so on. As most users recognize, the power and the peril of Facebook is in the ability to precisely program with whom you share what. If you share everything with everyone, then you run into the "My Boss/Dad/Ex is on Facebook" problem. If you program your privacy precisely, you redefine your online presence in ways that the Internet, e-mail, mailing-lists and blogs could never before afford you. You can control who sees and hears what with a surprising amount of explicit control.

In an even more general sense, what is shared is something like tendencies and beliefs. Facebook allows people to perform themselves in front of multiple and differently constituted (i.e., privacy programming) audiences. These performances are modes of self-fashioning; they strengthen certain ties and weaken others. They are a kind of re-embodiment subsequent to a dis-embodiment that happens with the basic pseudonymity of the Internet. Facebook re-embodies in ways similar to performance on e-mail or a mailing list (e.g., emoticons, vulgarity, formality, and other signals of tendency and belief), and adds a measure of embodiment to a medium that strips away tendencies and beliefs visible on the typing body behind the screen.

The formalization of shared tendencies and beliefs by a system like Facebook is a powerful and possibly frightening development. On the one hand, it resolves a problem that people think they fear in the Internet, which is its radical separation of body and identity. Facebook sutures that separation in new ways—I will insist on re-embodiment here because it emphasizes profiles that tie you to your body, your language, your geographical location, and your network of real-clothes friends and relatives. It does this in a way that is radically different from what games like World of Warcraft or Second Life attempt to achieve. Similarly, free software advocates tend to believe that the only things that matter are your creativity and coding skills, not your body, your friends, your salary, or your degrees.

Infrastructure, or What Is Facebook's Concept of Openness and Standardization?

Facebook is Compuserve for the twenty-first century. I say this with a certain nostalgic fondness for Compuserve—that clunky but friendly walled garden of mostly useless content that, along with AOL, opened up the magic of the Internet to so many people. Facebook, like Compuserve, limits and channels its consumers' experience of technology with the positive benefit that the technology doesn't get in the way, it becomes a tool or platform that more or less functions smoothly and allows people to focus on each other, on what is on the screen, and on interacting for purposes that are not related to the technology that enables that interaction.

However, it is necessary to look behind this user-friendliness, or ease-of-use, to ask how Facebook is standardized, how it is "open," and of what the infrastructure it relies on consist. One aspect of the notion of "recursive publics" is a public that is justly concerned with *all of the layers* that make democratic social organization open to modifiability and reconfiguration. If it is only a public on the surface, then is it still public?

One should ask, therefore, is Facebook an "application" on the Internet similar to the World Wide Web and e-mail? What the Internet has provided, and what has been the engine of creativity for close to twenty years, has been an extensible platform. That means anyone with sufficient time and expertise can propose an application that runs "on" the Internet without having to ask permission from any corporation or government. There are a standards and an engineering society (the ISOC and the IETF), but they are not gatekeepers. This system of extending the Internet by creating applications has worked well enough, though it has created new kinds of problems as it has grown to a massive scale (principally security, spam, and standardization issues that continue to threaten the stability of the global network).

Facebook is not exactly a stand-alone application, though. It is an application that depends on the Web and its standards (html and http), and depends on a new generation of Web-like technologies that transform html and http (ajax and javascript), but it is not an Internet standard that others could use or implement the way one can e-mail, smtp, ftp, and so on. What's more, Facebook's development model is not to be just one application among others, but to become a kind of symbiont (or parasite) on the web by extending its own presence from one site among many to a site on everyone else's site—a parasite. This is the goal of "Facebook Connect," which, when implemented, allows users to log in to other sites as if that site were part of Facebook, and to share one's information (including one's detailed privacy settings, presumably) with that site and its users. Facebook is attempting to achieve what various projects in identity management have tried to achieve (such as OpenID, a project ideologically true to the ideals of free software, but nowhere as widely used as Facebook).

On the one hand, this is undeniably an advantage if it is used to solve the problem of having a hundred different passwords; it would be undeniably good for the human race if we each needed to update and maintain only one "profile." On the other hand, it turns Facebook into an identity management company with tremendous potential control over your actions and relations, to say nothing of what you can and cannot see on the Web. Google pioneered this approach, but Facebook is making it easy to do.

In *Two Bits,* I tell the story of open systems in the 1980s, when large corporations fought to become the next big thing, when they fought over networking and workstations. The "UNIX Wars" brought huge corporations (AT&T, IBM, Sun, etc.) into a war to become the standard for operating systems and networking. It was Microsoft who emerged from this war triumphant, for reasons very similar to Facebook's success: rapid growth meant that huge numbers of users of Windows (especially Windows NT) quickly forced others to adopt it to gain the benefit of being part of the network (more software, more and better technicians, more people in the network/market to sell to). The 1980s open systems story was the story of an attempt to create something like the Internet—a common platform of open systems on which all could fairly compete—but which ended in failure because of a blind spot: the moral injunction to compete based on intellectual property, secrecy, and market dominance. One implication of this story is that a healthy ecology of competing firms has in fact been *less desired* and *less possible to create* than dominance by one: IBM, Microsoft, Google, and Facebook.

The emergence of the Internet is one alternative to this narrative. It is one case where an open platform available to all has generated growth and made people realize the value of this other moral imagination of free and fair competition. It is in many ways pitted against the standard model of big firms dominating markets. Google's success is one strong indicator of the failure to maintain a healthy Internet ecology and instead to create a monopoly system out of the standardized and open Internet. This is not to say that there is no value in that, just as there is much of value in what Facebook provides, but the question to ask is, At what price?

The major concern here, related to the question of "healthy politics," is whether the infrastructure being created by Facebook is open to transformation, critique, modification, and reuse. At first blush, the answer is yes—Facebook's API and Facebook Connect are both ways to make Facebook do whatever we want it to and to leverage that 200-million-person network as a result. But the case of Scrabulous makes the opposite case; it clearly demonstrates that Facebook is built, infrastructurally and legally, to give Facebook ultimate power over what those 200 million people do with Facebook. One needn't entertain fantasies of dark, smoky rooms and conspiratorial theories . . . one only need consider the effect on healthy politics: because it cannot be used for *any* political purpose, it will not be used for some, maybe even many purposes.

The case of the FARC Protests is therefore a signature event. Facebook can be used, and has been used, for the purpose of democratic organization and protest. But an uneasiness remains concerning the tremendous power this seems to leave in Facebook's hands.

Licenses, Contracts, and Terms of Service, or What Role Does the Law Play?

One of the key components of free software and its derivatives has been a general awareness of and concern with intellectual property rights and legal means of control generally. Ever since James Boyle pointed out that the Information Society is structured by Law, and Lawrence Lessig vaguely articulated that "code is law," not only legal scholars but nearly everyone, it seems, has become an expert in IP (Intellectual Property) law.[6] In the case of Facebook there are several complex issues related to IP.

The issue getting the most attention is the terms of service and the de facto rights of Facebook to ownership rights in everything you publish there. This is hardly surprising,

---

6. Boyle, *Shamans, Software, and Spleens*; Lessig, *Code and Other Laws of Cyberspace*.

since it is a corporation, and as they themselves reason, they need that right simply to copy and redistribute what you write to all your friends without having to ask your permission on every status update. In large part, this is a red herring for users, because people don't really use the system to publish copyrightable materials. A more important question is whether you yourself have access to and rights to republish what you write in Facebook. What about exchanges with friends? A curious possibility is that neither you nor any of your friends have a right to *publish elsewhere* a conversation you have on Facebook, but Facebook does.

More generally, this issue might be labeled "Can you take it with you?" In a healthy political sphere, your social "graph" (as they like to say at Facebook) is something neither you nor anyone in it owns, per se. It exists in your collective address books, in your heads, in your actions, and in others' representations of those actions. It is a bit like your reputation, which while unique to you, is not something you can own or control, but something that is entirely created by what others say about you to each other. Facebook owns your reputation on Facebook, and they want (they need) desperately to figure out how to turn it into a stream of revenue. Furthermore, the fact that makes Facebook's social graph valuable is that it is objectified and operationalized. It's a bit like the work of anthropologists in rendering a kinship system into a synoptic representation that can be printed and circulated, occasionally to the people whom it describes. Facebook, like colonial anthropologists, has no intention of giving you the social graph you create with your friends. It might give you access through its API, but it is not going to, and probably cannot, objectify it as something public and available to everyone.

The existence of this social graph, this map of relations created through the sharing of tendencies and beliefs, is the untapped vein of value Facebook is trying to figure out how to mine. But it is also a kind of value for which there is no good legal framework. "Privacy" is the only one Euro-Americans have to work with, and it is a relentlessly individualizing legal framework. Compare this to those notions of collective ownership, responsibility, and liability that exist in communities such as Aboriginal Australia, Papua New Guinea, or Hopi and Zuni culture in Native America, and our system of individual private rights looks hopelessly inadequate.[7] Who owns our collective conversations right now? Well, you own yours, I own mine, and he owns his, and she owns hers. Only Facebook owns them all. Hence the anxiety manifest by users over Facebook's terms of service, which is the only place in which the details of this new legal frontier will be worked out, at least initially. Later, the courts, and perhaps much later the legislatures of the world, will begin to deal with these issues, but the hard work will be done by Facebook users and Facebook lawyers. Indeed, it may already be all over but for the shouting.

---

7. Brown, "Can Culture Be Copyrighted?" and *Who Owns Native Culture?*; Coombe, "Protecting Traditional Environmental Knowledge and New Social Movements in the Americas."

On the developer side, Facebook maintains a commitment to open source software and to certain legal principles of autonomy. If you write software that makes use of the Facebook API, they have the right to determine whether or not your application will be granted access, but you have the right to take it in whatever legal direction you choose. In part this is how Facebook will protect itself. It is how Facebook appeases the developers who tend to have a sharper, if not a precise, sense of the need for a "recursive public."

Coordination, or, the New Permissions

A key practice that emerged with free software was the distributed collaborative creation of software, via the Internet. Linux and Apache are canonical examples, and many of the tools they innovated are also used in projects like Facebook by its developers: source code management tools, bug tracking software, mailing lists, and wikis.

A very important aspect of these tools was the way they organized governance by synthesizing technical tasks and social order. Source code management systems, for instance, coordinate developers' work on a shared document (keeping track of who changed what when), but they also control who has what "permissions" or "rights" to make certain kind of changes. One person might have rights to change everything, while another has rights to change only one file, or only to read, but not to change.

Facebook, in a roundabout way, does the same thing for users: provides a way to manage permissions, that is, who has rights to see what about you and your actions. Facebook is in many ways the opposite of the Web, where everything is visible to everyone, and even more so the opposite of a wiki, where everything is *writable* by everyone. Facebook, by contrast, allows users to restrict who can see what, who can share what with whom, and so forth. It might be seen as an innovation on the permissions systems we have largely seen in place to date: the UNIX-style permissions in which users, groups, and others have read, write, and execute permissions. On analogy with this system, the Facebook permissions systems has you, your friends, friends of friends, and everyone, and can control who reads what you write, what information shows up in a search, what shows up on other people's walls, and so forth. And this to a surprising—but culturally specific—granularity that might include people you went to college with, people you work with, people who live near you, and so on.

Permissions of this sort put the focus on controlling openness and closure in ways that have historically not been possible on the Internet (and which have been highlighted as *advantages* of the Internet). As Kimberly Christen has demonstrated in the case of Australian Aborigines, the "cultural protocols" built into technologies such as the Internet and Facebook are highly culturally specific (witness "college friends" and "work friends" as the key designators of identity—not clan, tribe, or ethnicity), such that groups like the Warumungu, whom Christen works with, must invent ways to work around these technologies in order to make their own cultural protocols stick to them.[8] To some extent we all do this, and Facebook may be an example of a technology that affords the advantages of the Internet, but at least takes the first step toward making these protocols more applicable.

If there is any aspect of Facebook that represents a remarkable innovation, it is this rewiring of permissions. The relationship of sociality and communication has historically concerned only the issue of anonymity and publicity: is the speaker named or not? Is the communication publicly audible/visible or not? Facebook transforms this relation and ramifies it. It makes the hitherto informal and inscrutable channels of *gossip* into a model for all communication.

Ideologies, or Talk about Facebook

Finally, there is the question of ideology. Free software and open source are two names for the same set of practices, divided by a heated argument over why they engage in these practices. Facebook does not suffer from this problem because it is a single corporation; it does not (publicly) question why it is doing what it is doing. However, there is a lot of talk, in and around Facebook, reflecting on what it is and why it is important. There are Facebook-watcher blogs; there are constant reflections of Facebook's actions in the status updates and discussions of users; there are scholars aplenty focused on Facebook and its uses. All these things combine to make of Facebook something important, something more than just a corporation. Will these conversations rise to the level of understanding Facebook's cultural significance? Will this discussion raise the issue of Facebook as a healthy public sphere, or will we turn only to the language of individual privacy and consumer rights? If we turn to the language of "privacy," we forgo the issue of public power that is also at stake in what we make of our new landscape of knowledge. In the end, I think free software, successful or not, is a powerful, detailed, technically and legally precise answer to the question, Who decides?

Conclusion

When *Two Bits* was first drafted in 2005, Facebook was known only to Harvard students. Five years later, it is known to almost four hundred million. Strangely, free software/open source as a phenomenon remains generally unknown by comparison, even though it is safe to say Facebook, Google, MySpace, and every large IT firm to come could not exist without it—and this means without all of its practices, not just the software. One could draw contradictory conclusions about its significance from these facts: that it has had little effect, and that it has had massive effect. These two implications represent something of scholarly import when it comes to the analysis of "knowledge communities" or

---

8. See Christen, "Gone Digital," "Tracking Properness," and *Aboriginal Business*.

"network societies," namely, *what is the appropriate scale of analysis if one wants to make sense of a changing world?*

On the one hand, Facebook cannot change everything (though one might think it does from the rhetoric that surrounds it); on the other, with four hundred million users it can't be insignificant. The question of where to look, and at what scale, concerns the operations of conceptual analysis—the pulling apart of technologies, legal issues, issues of governance and interaction, issues of ideology—in order to become more precise in the analysis of large-scale changes related to the spread of computers, software, and networks among humans on this planet. It will not do to refer casually and without clarity to concepts like "network society" as if that explains everything, even if it is meant as shorthand for something subtle and specific. Such claims fall into the category of "total history" rather than general history as Michel Foucault described it: "A total description draws all phenomena around a single center—a principle, a meaning, a spirit, a worldview, an overall shape; a general history, on the contrary, would deploy the space of a dispersion."[9]

The "dispersion" of free software extends backward into past pathways (the Linux and UNIX operating systems, IP Law and the GPL, Open Systems and corporate standards battles), but it also extends forward as modulations of present practices (new modes of sharing software, new legal battles around terms of service and contracts, new modes of granulated control over privacy). Rather than see every new technology as a sudden shift from one total history to the next, necessitating grandiose claims for the reformulation of human subjectivity with unlikely, perhaps impossible, rapidity, a general history urges one to see the dispersal of series, pathways, and modulations of practice that present no more than temporary and fragile possibilities for the creation of something like recursive publics. Free software may no longer exist, but its reticulate pathways continue to ramify in our near future.

Bibliography

Benkler, Yochai. *The Wealth of Networks: How Social Production Transforms Markets and Freedom.* New Haven, CT: Yale University Press, 2006.

Boyle, James. *Shamans, Software, and Spleens: Law and the Construction of the Information Society.* Cambridge, MA: Harvard University Press, 1996.

Brown, Michael F. "Can Culture Be Copyrighted?" *Current Anthropology* 39, no. 2 (1998): 193–222.

———. *Who Owns Native Culture?* Cambridge, MA: Harvard University Press, 2004.

Christen, Kimberly. *Aboriginal Business: Alliances in a Remote Australian Town.* Santa Fe, NM: School for Advanced Research Press, 2009.

---

9. Foucault, *The Archaeology of Knowledge and the Discourse on Language*, 10.

———. "Gone Digital: Aboriginal Remix and the Cultural Commons." *International Journal of Cultural Property* 12 (2005): 315–45.

———. "Tracking Properness: Repackaging Culture in a Remote Australian Town." *Cultural Anthropology* 21 (2006): 416–46.

Coleman, E. Gabriella and Alex Golub. "Hacker Practice: Moral Genres and the Cultural Articulation of Liberalism." *Anthropological Theory* 8 (2008): 255–77.

Coombe, Rosemary J. "Protecting Traditional Environmental Knowledge and New Social Movements in the Americas: Intellectual Property, Human Right, or Claims to an Alternative Form of Sustainable Development." *Florida Journal of International Law* 17 (2005): 115.

Feller, Joseph, Brian Fitzgerald, Scott A. Hissam, and Karim R. Lakhani, eds. *Perspectives on Free and Open Source Software*. Cambridge, MA: MIT Press, 2005.

Foucault, Michel. *The Archaeology of Knowledge and The Discourse on Language*. Translated by A. M. Sheridan Smith. New York: Pantheon Books, 1972.

Kelty, Christopher M. *Two Bits: The Cultural Significance of Free Software*. Durham, NC: Duke University Press, 2008.

Lessig, Lawrence. *Code and Other Laws of Cyberspace*. New York: Basic Books, 1999.

Lions, John. *Lions' Commentary on UNIX 6th Edition, with Source Code*. 1977; repr., San Jose: Peer to Peer Communications, 1996.

Reagle, Joseph M., Jr. "In Good Faith: Wikipedia Collaboration and the Pursuit of the Universal Encyclopedia." PhD diss., New York University, 2008. http://reagle.org/joseph/2008/03/dsrtn-in-good-faith.

Stringer, Tish. "This is What Democracy Looked Like." In *Transnographies: Ethnography and Activism within Networked Spaces of Transnational Encounter*, edited by J. Juris and Alex Khasnabish. Durham, NC: Duke University Press, forthcoming.

Weber, Steve. *The Success of Open Source*. Cambridge, MA: Harvard University Press, 2004.

Zittrain, Jonathan. *The Future of the Internet—And How to Stop It*. New Haven, CT: Yale University Press, 2009.

8

Right to Know, New Technologies, and New Communities of Citizenship

Antonio Lafuente and Andoni Alonso

Is there a right to know? At first sight it seems so. Very few would deny such a right in our century. Why? Maybe because knowledge is a good with its own distinct features: there is the old idea that truth will make us free. Also, differing from other goods, knowledge is not exhausted when shared: transmitting ideas does not impoverish the giver; knowledge does not wear out when is spread, or represent a loss. Therefore it would be easy to accept that right because it does not imply inequality. Universal education seems to respond to the basic conception that everybody *should have the right to know*. Education therefore allows people to know, and to be able to know. Knowledge could be considered as a vital element for our well-being, as are food, shelter, and security. Those are basic requirements for survival. But the interesting question for our chapter is whether there is a limit—if there is some knowledge that should be kept secret. This would imply the acceptance of a moral and political nature of knowledge. However, this question could be difficult to answer. We understand the need to preserve some personal information in secret; if this secrecy were not upheld, basic elements of human life such as privacy and intimacy would disappear. On the other hand, it is not easy to claim the right to intimacy in the era of computers and networks. Suspicious as we are, we tend to accept the evidence of an extremely invasive revealing of our lives, whether we like it or not.

Following the classical ethical pattern, if knowing is a human activity, then it can be regulated by virtues. Therefore limits could be put in place regarding what to know and how to learn it. Privacy and intimacy are one area, for instance, where the need for boundaries seems clear. Interestingly enough we live in a technological time where such limits are a mirage. According to Tomás Maldonado we live in an era where privacy is humbled.[1] Of course limits are difficult to define, as Roger Shattuck has pointed out.[2] From Francis Bacon on, knowledge has become a means to free humans from all their pains and difficulties. Our knowledge of nature would free us from original sin; we should be able to reconstruct our innocent nature, according to Bacon. This is in clear opposition to Bacon's past, and later brings up the need for boundaries. The Greek *Prometheus* indicates those limits, and also Goethe's *Faust,* but they seem alien to Bacon's position. The difference between *scientia* and *curiositas*, virtue and vice applied to knowledge, begins to blur. Limits to human knowledge also define the nature of what is human, according to the classics.

But now and then various claims are still made as to the need to control and even *forbid* knowledge. This is the spirit behind such bans as those of the Pugash movement of 1970 regarding recombinant DNA, or the ban on human cloning (both are linked).[3] There is a fear of going too far, of transforming that knowledge into hubris: if we do go too far, there may be no going back. Technologies often introduce that kind of moral and political crisis, which requires careful treatment. Also, there is the conviction that certain issues should not be known by the people concerned, but rather managed by the persons in charge. Experts, politicians, leaders can better control the consequences of certain facts if those facts are kept hidden. These issues arise not only from scientific and technological questions but also from political and social ones. Scientific and technological knowledge per se have an unavoidable political and social side. Galileo's defense of the heliocentric theory and Darwin's theory of evolution are classic examples of how scientific knowledge has a deep impact on society, power, and politics: both theories changed the place of human beings in the universe, and those with political and religious power felt threatened. Even today there is disagreement about Darwin's theory.

Nevertheless, here we are not concerned with where to draw the line between what should or should not be known, and how to establish a general ethos on knowledge. Instead, we would like to reflect on how a certain group of people, certain communities, pursue knowledge because they identify themselves as a group. The reason for their view is easy to understand: they see that knowledge as crucial for their progress, they are *concerned* about what that knowledge means. Maybe it can be stated in another way. We depart from the position taken by John Gray in that we consider science in a specific way; science does not refer only to the truth, but also to the needs that human beings have to survive in this world.[4] So in a sense, scientific and technical knowledge are the

---

1. Maldonado, *Crítica de la Ragione Informatica,* 112.

2. Shattuck, *Forbidden Knowledge,* 59.

3. Banning a technology or field of study is a complicated issue. The aim of the Pugwash group was to avoid chemical and biological warfare, having learned the lessons that the nuclear weapons race taught us. However, therapeutical cloning has been shown to be extremely useful for treating various diseases like cancer, Alzheimer's, and others. The Pugwash movement (composed of "pugwashites") still holds conferences on scientific ethics.

4. Gray, *Thoughts on Humans and Other Animals,* 67.

way to cope with facts, dangers, risks, and possibilities. Thus our aim is to show how communities of concerned people seek specific knowledge precisely because they are concerned, because they need to survive and to improve their lives. So the focus is on questions about power and benefit, which adds a political ingredient to knowledge. The right to know *certain* things therefore becomes part of the political agenda. Rephrasing Bacon, power likes to hide and it is a political duty to reveal some of those secrets. Censorship is still active despite the general acceptance of knowledge as a good that should be available to anybody in need of it. Control of information and knowledge is present today in different ways than it was in the past. In the information society, knowledge becomes a scarce good that can be sold; perhaps it is the most valuable good from an economic standpoint. Knowledge, as always, is also a means of control. Both aspects will be considered.

Our chapter consists of a set of examples showing how this right to knowledge was the starting point for creating communities. From environmental to technological developments, such as free software and cryptography, there is an accompanying current relating to restriction of knowledge and the attempt to break restrictions. All of these communities have something in common: the need to generate or gain knowledge because it is important to those communities—sometimes vital, and sometimes seriously affecting basic civil rights. Also, those communities belong to an old tradition, although new communication technologies imply a change in the rules of the game. Therefore, this is not a criticism of science and technology. Many times those knowledge communities are hybrids of experts and laypersons. What joins both types of people, as we said before, is that they have in common a feeling of concern. But our position does not include a criticism of science itself. Science and technology are realities in the world that cannot be denied or suppressed. Rather, it involves criticism of *scientific policy*—the ways in which governments, companies, and interest groups use and conceal knowledge for various reasons: profit, blind faith in progress, patronizing attitudes, and so on. So what we have are different groups of people that ask for, generate, and disperse knowledge as a duty pertaining to citizenship.

Civil Protest and Need for Knowledge

Silent Spring is one of the pivotal books for the present environmental movement; it can be considered as a basis for modern citizens' fight to preserve nature. Its author, Rachel Carson, was a scientist, a biologist worried about the effect of human action upon nature. Post–World War II was a period when industrialization got into full swing and showed its power of destruction. In 1989, Carson's *The Sea Around Us* became a best seller and spurred a change in her career: she retired from her post at the US Fish and Wildlife Service and devoted herself to writing about nature. The use of pesticides and their ecological impact attracted her attention, and she devoted four years to writing the book. Carson began a completely independent study on the effects of DDT, trying to show how this chemical pesticide damaged all forms of life, including humans. The book was a complete success: the public became aware of the perils of using pesticides and began to promote a movement for conservation.

Being a hallmark of the environmental protection movement, *Silent Spring* first became a polemical book *before* publication. Carson confronted various attacks on her work; she was a woman, so an emotional element is assumed in her struggle. As Al Gore writes:

> The attack on Rachel Carson has been compared to the bitter assault on Charles Darwin when he published *The Origin of Species*. Moreover, because Carson was a woman, much of the criticism directed at her played on stereotypes of her sex. Calling her "hysterical" fit the bill exactly. *Time* magazine added the charge that she had used "emotion-fanning words." Her credibility as a scientist was attacked as well: opponents financed the production of propaganda that supposedly refuted her work. It was all part of an intense, well-financed negative campaign, not against a political candidate but against a book and its author.[5]

Interestingly enough, *Time* magazine, which had led a bitter attack against Carson, later named her one of the hundred most influential persons of the twentieth century.[6] Chemical companies like Monsanto, Velsicol, American Cyanamid, and others began a campaign against the book as soon as it was in production. They even circulated pamphlets repudiating its author.[7] Carson's argument was that the chemical industry was misleading the public as well as government officials with false reports on the effects of pesticides. She believed that pesticides should be labeled as biocides because they did not correctly target pests. She was a true scientist and considered knowing as a basic element for surviving and for harmonizing humanity with nature. This conclusion reflects common sense. But Carson's effort was focused on showing how this knowledge about chemicals and technical actions should be taken into account. She was promoting the production of new knowledge that was subsequently dismissed. We recall that the chemist who created DDT was awarded the Nobel Prize, and many of the available pesticides at that time came from the military industry and were developed during the Second World War.

In the second chapter of *Silent Spring*, Carson quotes this sentence by French biologist Jean Rostand: "The obligation to endure gives us the right to know."[8] This sentence precisely frames what this chapter is about: knowledge is a requirement for survival. That is, the right to know beyond for purposes of pleasure or entertainment, which is what scientific popularization offers in many cases. Knowledge of science and technology

---

5. Gore, Foreword to *Silent Spring*, by Carson, xi.

6. Peter Matthiessen considered her among the hundred most influential people of the twentieth century, listed in *Time,* no. 100, 1999, 49.

7. See for instance "The Desolate Year," *Monsanto Magazine*, October 1962, 4–9. This article tries to counter the argument presented in chapter 11, "A Fable for Tomorrow," where Carson depicts a world void of life, including human lives, because of toxic chemicals. This fable is perhaps the most well-known part of her work because of its impressive imagery.

8. Carson, *Silent Spring*, 89.

must become not an amateur hobby but a requirement of citizenship.[9] Our own survival requires us to know and to let others know as well. Useful knowledge is therefore a question of *concerned* knowledge. This is why Carson employs not only well-contrasted scientific data, but also literary elements. What is at stake is bigger than individual concerns; it is, according to her, "a war between human beings and nature." It is clear that, in the final analysis, it is a war against the human race itself and we are required to meet on nature's terms if we want to survive. Her goal is to make that knowledge attractive and well-communicated. Emotions play a substantial role in that concerned knowledge, but this role goes beyond sentimentalism or good feelings.

Interestingly enough, Carson had to suffer attacks that have become topics against activism concerning science and technology. First, as we said, the attacks were against her scientific credibility. Second, as a woman, she was derided for her inclusion of feelings and emotions (seen as a hysterical position); but as a speaker from the Cyanid Corporation pointed out, Carson's proposal would take humanity back to the Dark Ages. Scientific credibility and pursuit of progress became the motto to rebuff criticism arising from civil society. Carson did not condemn all uses of chemical pesticides; rather, she proposed a basic principle of precaution: we do not know enough about these substances and the risk is too high, so what we need is more information. Carson's legacy was to highlight the need to obtain more knowledge in order to prevent disasters. Ecology movements have accepted this proposal; contemporary ecology groups like Greenpeace devote a great deal of effort to acquiring that knowledge. Laboratories for analyzing water, air, chemicals, and other environmental elements are part of many ecology associations' operations. Generating knowledge is a way to obtain the right to know in a society where it is extremely difficult to trust corporations and even government agencies.

Carson was one of the first experts to point out a major conflict of interests: the same agency (USDA) that regulated the use of pesticides was in charge of protecting wildlife. Creation of the EPA (Environment Protection Agency) as a separate division was one of Carson's ideas. Such conflicts of interest have increased, as Peter Barnes shows: chemical corporations hire former officials from the environmental area.[10] The purpose is to solve conflicts of interest using the know-how of the "other side." In this sense it is easy to understand the growing distrust toward government agencies.

Cryptography and Civil Society

The second case we would like to consider is that of cryptography. Cryptography is a special area within Number Theory. Its military applications are obvious and, interestingly enough, its development has also helped the computer industry. Experiences from World War II led to a very restrictive and censorial attitude toward cryptography. As

---

9. See Lafuente, *El carnaval de la tecnociencia*, 27.

10. Barnes, *Capitalism 3.0*, 99–100.

Steven Levy (2001) pointed out, the secrecy surrounding cryptography was extraordinary.[11] Papers on that subject were censored and speakers were not allowed to share
their findings. For instance, Levy recalls how Claude Shannon's contributions were kept
under classified status as late as the sixties, two decades after being formulated. In addition, agencies such as the National Security Agency were kept secret because their task
was the control of cryptography. The reasoning was simple: cryptography belonged to
the government, so no civil effort could be allowed. After three decades and through
many difficulties, Whitfield Diffie was able to develop a new cryptographic protocol
known as the Diffie-Lehman protocol.[12] Diffie confronted many obstacles because his
work was considered a threat to national security. He received pressure from the government to not make his system available. However, distributing his work led to one of the
most fascinating results in Internet technology: PGP, or Pretty Good Privacy.

Philip Zimmerman developed Pretty Good Privacy, which was of great benefit for
private use although at present it is not commonly used. Meanwhile the government
deployed a vast array of countermeasures such as the Clipper Chip—a way of controlling
digital communications—antiterrorist laws, and many other systems of surveillance and
control. The conflict was clear: control over communication—that is, privacy—should
be held by only one side, the government; communication within civil society should
remain transparent. Zimmerman was sued for distributing PGP and accused of "export-
ing weapons to the enemy." The trial lasted three years. Zimmerman soon had the support of various Internet groups such as the Electronic Frontier Foundation, who awarded
Zimmerman a prize during the time of the trial. Writings such as this summarized what
was going on:

> But law enforcement and intelligence officials have a different view of Zimmermann's
> achievement. He is being investigated for possible violation of federal arms-export laws
> because his "cryptography for the masses" has slipped out of America. "The ability of just
> about everybody to encrypt their messages is rapidly outrunning our ability to decode
> them," worries a U.S. intelligence official. "It's a lot harder to eavesdrop on a worldwide
> web than it is to tap a cable," echoes James Kallstrom, assistant director in charge of the
> FBI's New York office: We need balanced public policy because it has unbelievable ramifi-
> cations for business and law enforcement.[13]

According to Lawrence Lessig, "No other technological discovery—from nuclear
weapons (I hope) to the Internet—will have a more significant impact on social and political life. Cryptography will change everything." [14] Lessig's statement may be a bit exagger-
ated but also corresponds to that spirit of secrecy that the US government showed during

---

11. Levy, *How the Code Rebels Beat the Government Saving Privacy in the Digital Age*, 195.

12. For a comprehensive technical summary of Diffie's work, see Diffie, "First Ten Years of Public Cryptography,"
561.

13. Lessig, *Code and Other Laws of Cyberspace*, 35–36.

14. Ibid., 36.

Clinton's administration. In addition, e-government, e-commerce, and many other Internet services require cryptography. Lessig also states that, "Cryptography can be [many] things, both good and bad, because encryption can serve two fundamentally different ends. In its 'confidentiality' function it can be 'used to keep communications secret.' In its 'identification' function it can be 'used to provide forgery-proof digital identities.' It thus enables freedom from regulation (as it enhances confidentiality), but it can also enable regulation (as it enhances identification)."[15] The issue at stake is a basic political right.

As Lessig points out, private cryptography is a basic technological tool needed for democracy; it is required for privacy and intimacy in an era where communications are mainly electronic. Balance of power requires both sides: government and civil society. Diffie and Zimmerman were able to develop a technology *against* the government policy. Reasons to oppose those developments were basically the Real-Politik of a world threatened by terrorism. Somehow the cryptographic movement made theirs this famous statement by Thomas Jefferson: "The man who would choose security over freedom deserves neither." Diffie and Zimmerman's movement brought about the birth during the nineties of a complete Internet movement called "cypherpunk." This group offered technical and political questions for discussion. The basic idea was that individuals need protection in the era of the Internet, just as companies and governments do. In fact companies have taken advantage of users with cryptography programs like cybercash or DRM systems.

Substantial Equivalence and the Right to Suspect

Modern biotechnology has had great success with modified genetic traits, and patenting has become a lucrative source for the biotechnology business. But food implies other aspects apart from nourishment. Cultural diversity, traditions, social ties, among other factors, form a complex network of influences regarding food and eating, beyond purely scientific or objective approaches. Insects are a good source of protein, but it is difficult to convince some cultures of the convenience of eating them. Also, certain foods considered "delicacies" by some—oysters, for instance—can be extremely disgusting for others. So whether something is considered safe or convenient to eat depends on many beliefs that are deeply embedded in cultural and societal facts. There is a fuzzy sense of risk about food that all of us have experienced at times. What is safe? What can be eaten without a sense of danger? In support of our appreciation lies a long tradition, education, and experience that cannot be neglected. It is too easy to leave solutions to the experts, especially with a growing sense of their partiality, of being influenced by other elements such as economy and profit.

Genetically modified (GM) organisms have been under suspicion from the very beginning. The European Community encountered strong resistance among citizens to authorizing the introduction of such food. This differs from the United States, where

---

15. Ibid., 35–36.

70 percent of the GM food of the world is produced. "Substantial equivalence" was a standard proposed to try to resolve that feeling of risk among citizens. Any food has nutrient and antinutrient components; antinutrients are eliminated through cooking or processing of food. Or it might be that the amount of antinutrients is not too high to be a risk. This occurs with very common foods such as tomatoes and potatoes, for instance. So the procedure consists in comparing chemical properties of a modified organism with the properties of what can be considered a "natural" one, a traditional crop (although artificial selection through the centuries makes it difficult to define "natural"). In any case, that was a standard used to try to avoid risks.

The following is a definition of what is considered to be "substantial equivalence": "To date, the safety assessment of genetically engineered and novel foods has been based on the principle that these products can be compared with traditional foods that have an established history of safe use. Furthermore, this comparison can be based on an examination of the same risk factors (i.e., hazards) that have been established for the traditional counterpart."[16] The term was first used in early 1983. In 2000, the OECD (Organisation for Economic Co-Operation and Development) published a report on the issue trying to define and encourage such a protocol to avoid misinformation. It is important to emphasize the goal pursued by the OECD: substantial equivalence was a means to cope with uncertainty and a way to allow free trade of genetically modified organisms. So it was technological expertise in benefit of corporations, a way to introduce GM organisms into the markets quickly.

The question here is how to evaluate that risk. Substantial equivalence has been under attack almost from the time it was formulated. From first being considered a conclusive test, it has since been redefined as a needed but preliminary step complemented by many other tests. This goes directly against corporate interests because it incurs a delay in commercialization of products and requires more expense. However, the question can be defined quite easily. The effects of GM organisms are on the fringes of scientific knowledge. Research progressively clarifies that shadowy zone, and controversies arise not only from industry and consumers but also among scientists themselves. Scientists belong to society and can be on the side of either corporations or consumers. One relevant case is the Pusztai controversy that took place in the United Kingdom.

Arpad Pusztai of the Rowett Institute was appointed as a researcher to study the effects that modified potatoes could have on human health. His study concluded that rats fed with GM food presented a significant reduction in their immune system. That was exactly the opposite result he was appointed to achieve. But Pusztai decided to blow the whistle, and his paper was accepted in the prestigious medical journal *The Lancet*.[17] Richard Horton, director of *The Lancet,* denounced pressures from the Royal

16. Organisation for Economic Co-operation and Development "Substantial Equivalence," at http://stats.oecd.org/glossary/detail.asp?ID=2604.

17. Ewen and Pusztai, "Effect of Diets," 18.

Society to avoid publication of the paper,[18] and it finally appeared in 1999. It was immediately under attack by the Royal Society; the famous institution appointed six independent members to analyze the results, concluding "lack of evidence, bad methodology and miscarried experiments."[19] Rumors maintained that the Rowett Institute was partly financed by Monsanto, the producer of GM potatoes. The controversy spread and reached the general public, and major newspapers, including *the Guardian,* published information on the controversy.[20] Of course this had effects on a technology whose risk assessments have no resonation with specialized NGOs. As a result, there has been an ongoing campaign against genetically modified organisms from diverse points of view.

Ecology organizations like Greenpeace and various consumer associations have claimed the need to apply a cautionary principle with regard to these modified substances. There are three main camps:

1. Those who consider GM organisms harmless, believing they should be marketed as soon as substantial equivalence is demonstrated.

2. Those who consider the need to further explore the issue, who support the right to know, and who want to apply a cautionary principle, using further tests to verify the harmlessness of the organism.

3. Those who consider GM organisms as pollutants that seriously affect not only human health but also the environment.[21]

The second possibility is probably the most interesting one. There is a potential for GM organisms to be used for the benefit of the world's growing population demands for an increased food supply. However, that possibility is not incompatible with the need for more knowledge and the citizens' right to demand and create such knowledge—the right to act in a prudent way. What is dangerous is to allow corporations to use knowledge for mere profit, independently of risks.

The Right to Know and the Right to Be Known: Electro-Sensitivity

Contemporary medicine has experienced unusual growth in the ability to diagnose new illnesses and new syndromes. Suspicions are that pharmaceutical companies are promoting such growth with the aim to make more profit. This seems clear with the growing array of mental diseases where the massive use of medicines is prescribed, especially antidepressants. In this context, a group of people appeared by the end of the last century

---

18. Randerson and Pusztai, "Biological Divide," 11.

19. Correspondence of Pusztai and the Royal Society at www.freenetpages.co.uk/hp/A.Pusztai/RoyalSoc/ReportsAndReplies/RS_referee_reports.txt.

20. Randerson and Pusztai, "Biological Divide," 11.

21. For a complete and very clarifying study on substantial equivalence, see Levidow, Murphy, and Carr, "Recasting Substantial Equivalence."

demanding attention for illnesses not identified in medical books, such as electro-sensitivity. According to these people, their illness can be defined as a sort of allergy to electromagnetic fields. Devices causing these fields are, among others, computers, microwave ovens, cell phone towers, and electric grid stations placed within cities. The question posed was whether it is possible to show a *real* connection between electromagnetic fields and the symptoms supposedly caused by them. If that connection could be proven, it would allow affected people to declare their illness and obtain benefits from public health care or protection from insurance companies. People affected by this allergy tried to call attention to it by informing the general public and specialists, along with a demand more information.

In 1994, a group in Sweden organized their own NGO, the FEB or Swedish Association for the Electro-Sensitive, and compiled a document with more than 350 cases testifying about the illness and the victims' experiences. That book, *Black on White, Voices and Witnesses on Electro-Hypersensitivity,*[22] contains a number of testimonies from those affected, with no further analysis provided. Some media, including the *Independent,* covered the issue and indicated that some forms of childhood cancer, miscarriages, and suicides could be caused by the so-called electric smog (or electrosmog). It is difficult to live far from electric fields in modern societies, so these people lived and suffered and were ignored until the last six years. The World Health Organization (WHO) finally acknowledged the existence of these affected people and gave a technical name to the disease: electrosensitivity, or ES, which was accepted internationally. There is such a thing as electrosmog, and it is a fact. In 2005, the WHO even stated that ES is one of the most common and fastest-growing environmental influences and could be considered a carcinogen.[23]

EMFacts, the blog on ES, gives an idea of the scope of this problem, stating that about 3 to 5 percent of the population suffers from ES.[24] So without being too pessimistic there are about thirteen million sufferers in Europe alone. In Sweden, the first government accepting ES as a work-related illness, there are about 250,000. Doctors and specialists in Germany signed an appeal for preventive measures known as the Freiburger Appeal.[25] By the end of 2005, the United Kingdom, through the Health Protection Agency (HPA), accepted the existence of many people suffering symptoms probably due to electromagnetic radiation. "Probably due" is a formula that tries to satisfy everybody but does not. Concerned people feel they are not being fully recognized and experts claim to be overwhelmed by public pressures. The situation is similar to other cases: for some there is enough scientific evidence, but others believe any step in favor of verification is a risk to the complete democratic system. Being allergic to some elements of modern life threatens the basis of that modern society. Electric fields continue to be created every day.

---

22. Grandung-Ling and Ling, *Black on White*, 23.

23. World Health Organization Media Center, "Electromagnetic Fields and Public Health."

24. See http://www.emfacts.com/weblog/?p=435.

25. IGUMED, "Freiburguer Appeal."

The British medical report *Definition, Epidemiology and Management of Electrical Sensitivity* (HPA, 2005) accepts the existence of affected citizens as patients suffering ES. But the report selects words with extreme care. Its aim is to assess the problem, but it also claims the use of the term electro-sensitivity does not imply the acceptance of a causal chain among symptoms and exposure. It also says that there is inconsistent scientific evidence, and continues by stating the need to consider ES in different parameters than etiological terms because using traditional parameters there is no way to connect the needs of people suffering ES. This has an interesting corollary: ES is a problem that cannot be qualified if a scientific approach is excluded.[26]

Therefore this is a dead end unless the cognitive value given by experience was to provide a solution. If doctors cannot formulate a model of an illness that is able to be generalized, this does not imply the disdaining of personal experiences or placement of that illness under the generic label of "mental disease." If differential tests, diagnostic protocols, clinical routines, and therapeutic practices do not provide relief, a further step should be taken. The ill bodies of those affected people are singular. The existence of some recurrent symptoms—migraine, tiredness, insomnia, facial redness and burning, itching—is actual, but what makes those patients distinct is a peculiar set of symptoms unable to be reduced to stable rules. Doctors do not know how to diagnose the disease, often because health institutions do not agree on the existence of ES as a typified illness. Instead, they listen to the report of a person who knows his or her body and knows what symptoms are occurring, and knows when and why they happen. It is possible that each day we could find different and new problems like electro-sensitivity, impossible to tackle with reductionist procedures. Each body works as a very subtle and complex sensor controlled by a large number of variables that are impossible to regulate.

This complexity leads to a less linear or predictable solution, as modern science used to expect. Perhaps we could confront this issue from a different point of view. There is an idea built up by modern science, but at the same time there is an emergent notion expressed by experienced authorities. The first is technically objective; the second does not seem able, through technology, to measure or qualify nature—it is basically a subjective approach. This alternative provides for multi-naturalism, proposing that illness cannot be reduced to certain parameters following certain laws, or even mere statistics. But patients can be brought together. When that happens, they are validated and are recognized as a group of concerned people. If science cannot give a name to their condition, that means they do not exist as scientific objects (they do not fit into a typified pathology). There is no scientific consensus, but they are still citizens, concerned people mobilized to build a different scientific consensus. So they have generated new knowledge in a very intimate way, through the suffering of their bodies.

---

26. Irvine, "Definition, Epidemiology and Management of Electrical Sensitivity," 5.

The Right to Know What Concerned People Want: The Case of Nuclear Public Discussions

In 2008, at the beginning of the financial apocalypse, one key discussion was where to look for new energy sources. The oil demand (approaching the "oil peak," according to some experts) and high prices created a perceived need to re-launch the nuclear program. Due to this state of affairs, the government of the United Kingdom, after a long period of preventing any new nuclear projects, decided to once again allow them. This brought into the discussion many actors, because the fight against nuclear power is one of the big successes in environmental movements. It was interesting to see that now people like James Lovelock, father of the Gaia theory, defended such an option. Also Patrick Moore, cofounder of Greenpeace, reversed his position against nuclear power that he had sustained for thirty years. Things were moving very quickly, and the threat of an economic catastrophe created a good opportunity to reopen the old debate. However, given former experiences with cases like Chernobyl, Harrisburg, and so on, it was necessary to present the issue in a different way. So a decision was made as an inevitable political choice, scientifically sound, and supported in a truly democratic way.

The main argument was taken from people like Lovelock and Moore: energy—with its CO2 emissions—is causing global climate change, so it is necessary to diversify energy sources, even including nuclear energy. It raises suspicion to see people who previously did not believe in global climate change now use that argument to promote nuclear power. Also, old operative energy systems are part of the problem because it is necessary to guarantee an ongoing energy supply. As a result, there is a need to fuel our high level of consumption and at the same time the need for low-cost production. Thus the British government tried a different approach: the decision to reopen the nuclear program was preceded in the United Kingdom by a poll taken in 2006.

The survey tried to calibrate public opinion on the issue. The government wanted to handle it correctly, so instead of simply choosing a representative sample of citizens to answer the questions, they chose representative individuals from many concerned groups (companies, unions, citizen organizations). Information was provided, groups were formed in various cities, and public debate was organized for several months, in order to obtain a representative opinion. When the survey was complete, the government declared that the citizens supported a nuclear program according to the statistics, but this was not the truth.

Some activist groups, such as Greenpeace, Friends of the Earth, and members of the Green Alliance, objected to the lack of transparency during the process and accused the government of manipulating public opinion. The process impaired one of the most hopeful methods of dialogue between government and the public. In fact, the NGOs involved in the survey sued the government, and the judge, Justice Sullivan, decided in favor of the plaintiffs. The government had to repeat the entire process of surveying the public, this time avoiding bias and the introduction of obscure facts. Judge Sullivan even declared that these kinds of surveys were not a privilege or concession given by the government, but a right of the citizens. Activists pressed further, decrying the wasted time, the discrediting of the government, the crises that erupted among experts, the sabotage of the consultation process, and bad practices in general, calling it a defeat for democracy. In the end, the activist groups accused the government of having a hidden agenda, with the aim of carrying out a sham opinion-gathering process to obtain legitimacy for decisions already made. Eventually, the survey was repeated with a protocol proposed by the BBC, partially improved but equally disputed.

According to those following the new survey, December 8, 2007, was a key date. On that day nine workshops were held in nine different towns and the results confirmed that 43 percent of the participants were in favor of nuclear fission as an energy source. About 1,100 people belonging to various groups and associations were involved in the discussions, and 37 percent rejected nuclear power, with 18 percent remaining unsure. In Newcastle the "no" responses reached 41 percent, two points below "yes." Results at Newcastle showed a rate of opposition to nuclear power higher than the total European rate. But overall results legitimized the government's position, and on January 10, 2008, they finalized the decision to nuclearize the country.

There was no time left to weigh the case if the campaign against global warming was considered valid and, at the same time, if the United Kingdom hoped to remain an international power. Not everyone agreed. Environmental groups created the Nuclear Consultation Working Group to examine ways to proceed, and to scrutinize arguments used by the government. Those involved in this issue agreed that the British decision was crucial, especially if the German alternative—opposition to nuclear power and preference for green power sources, because of global climate change—did not succeed. Criticisms against Gordon Brown's energy policy were not merely tactics but a strategic move. According to Nuclear Spin, many countries would follow the same path if resistance were weak or inconsistent.

Another group of concerned people entered the arena of controversy. The Nuclear Consultation Working Group (NCW), composed of distinguished English scholars who were also activists, opened that year with a quite impressive report: *Nuclear Consultation; Public Trust in Government*. This report gives abundant information regarding obscured facts and misleading arguments that were used by the government. The reason for the obfuscation, according to NCW, was to coerce a public agreement in support of the electric companies' interests rather than favoring scientific objectivity and clarity. However, facts cannot be hidden for long. For instance, there is the basic fact that only 4 percent of CO_2 emissions would be reduced by switching to nuclear power. Also, the argument that states only nuclear power can keep energy costs at bay and secure the United Kingdom's energy independence lacks proof. Other alternate energies would be implemented as well, but in a surprisingly low percentage and without much assurance or speed. These delays give plausibility to the suspicion that the nuclear option was decided beforehand. Advanced economies are extremely dependent on oil. Events of the last several years have shown how fragile those economies can become and how the future is compromised by the model of unsustainable development. But trying to resolve the greenhouse effect with nuclear power plants equals a technological mega-fix, according to Jonathon Porritt, Chief of the Sustainable Development Commission of the UK government. Trying to solve the extreme dependence on cheap energy with more nuclear power is like trying to cure a drug addict with a brain prosthesis. It implies a blind trust of modern technology, independent of any other possibility.

Documents produced by the government do not address other questions, but the *Report on Nuclear Consultation: Public Trust in Government* tries to clarify them. First, it says nothing about the real costs of a nuclear power plant. Building and utilizing a power plant requires many more resources than those previously calculated; these calculations are always deeply underestimated. Also, the argument about not having access to enough solar energy neglects biomass and wind power as other energy alternatives. Lack of serious studies about how to take advantage of these alternate sources is in stark contrast with the evident ease in speaking about radioactive residues and the possible depletion of uranium deposits. In addition, the report mentions nothing about possible accidents, security, efficiency, eventual catastrophes, or terrorism. Competent experts should analyze all these aspects, but there is little discussion about how the results appear, how they were obtained and the variables used with them, and in general the impact of those variables in the decision made by the government. This is an important point because variables that impact and qualify a nuclear option within the energy system (that is, all available energy sources) must be carefully chosen, taking into account technical factors, of course, but also economic, political, and ethical factors.

The Scientists for Global Responsibility report attempts to follow these guidelines: to show the many uncertainties of the nuclear option and to show the relevance of factors that are usually neglected. When decisions are made by unrepresentative committees, when uncertainties such as residuals are hidden, when nobody acknowledges the problems with plutonium and its military applications, when green energy is considered as simply a banner for radical activists or technophobes, then the government commits a clear failure regarding international and intergenerational responsibility. International responsibility requires that problems be resolved without leaving a worse situation for others. Intergenerational responsibility demands the avoidance of future conflicts or irresoluble tensions.

Conclusion

What we have tried to demonstrate is the way that citizens organize themselves around certain issues concerning science and technology. "Concern" is the criteria that allows such organizations the criteria for articulating problems. And science becomes one of the most important issues from a political point of view. What is disputed is basically power and control, or how to achieve power through control. Alliances among experts and laypersons are a basic requirement in order to play this political game. Lack of knowledge leaves those who do not have it out of the game. However, there are exceptions. The case of Rachel Carson shows that experts can be attacked even though they have expertise. The example of cryptography shows that experts can rebel against control and try to avoid the dangers of government pressure through disseminating knowledge, which involves recruiting lay users. The interests of companies can be limited, as in the case of substantial equivalence through the alliance of experts and public opinion. The issue of electro-sensitivity is a good example of people forcing the experts to listen to them. And finally, the nuclear controversy shows how concerned experts, outside the lobbying system, can convey arguments in favor of public concern. All the cases show a similar structure: controversy is a way to limit, to reconsider, and to rethink present and future human needs.

In addition, these cases demonstrate the need to develop and pursue scientific and technical knowledge. Some of these concerned people have made contributions such as new technological devices or new insights into the field of medicine. It is not a question of opposing science and technology; it is a question of understanding it, limiting it, and deciding how it should be used, what decisions we should accept regarding new developments, while maintaining awareness that our actions have an effect on our neighbors and on future generations. So fomenting the production of knowledge becomes a citizen's task, among others. This is because these issues affect something common to all of us: the body, the environment, privacy, and health. These elements belong to the new commons that we share and have a responsibility for, a political responsibility. Thus, the citizen's response attempts to establish a third element between government and corporations, between state and market.

Bibliography

Barnes, Peter. *Capitalism 3.0*. San Francisco: Berret Koheler, 2006.

Carson, Rachel. *Silent Spring*. Boston: Houghton Mifflin, 1994.

Diffie, Will. "First Ten Years of Public Cryptography." *Proceedings of the IEE* 76, no. 5 (1988): 560–67.

Ewen, Stanley and Arpad Pusztai. "Effect of Diets Containing Genetically Modified Potatoes Expressing *Galanthus nivalis lectin* on Rat Small Intestine." *The Lancet*, vol. 354 (1999): 1353.

Gore, Albert. Foreword to *Silent Spring*, by Rachel Carson. Boston: Houghton Mifflin, 1994.

Grandung-Lind, Rigmor and John Lind. *Black on White, Voices and Witnesses about Electro-Hypersensitivity: The Swedish Experience*, 2004. Available at www.feb.se/feb/blackonwhite-complete-book.pdf. [This is an online commented edition of *Svart på vitt—Röster och vittnesmål om elöverkänslighet*, authored by Mimers Brunn Kunskapsförlaget, 20042].

Gray, John. *Thoughts on Humans and Other Animals*. New York: Granta Books, 2002.

IGUMED. "Freiburger Appeal," October 9, 2002. Available at www.feb.se/NEWS/ Appell-021019-englisch.pdf.

Irvine, N. "Definition, Epidemiology and Management of Electrical Sensitivity." Oxfordshire: Health and Public Affairs, 2005.

Lafuente, Antonio. *El carnaval de la tecnociencia*. Madrid: Nadir, 2007.

Lessig, Lawrence. *Code and Other Laws of Cyberspace*. New York: Basic Books, 1999.

Levidow, Les, Joseph Murphy, and Susan Carr. "Recasting Substantial Equivalence: Transatlantic Governance of GM Food." *Science, Technology and Human Values*, no. 32 (2007): 26–64.

Levy, Steven. *How the Code Rebels Beat the Government Saving Privacy in the Digital Age*. Albany, NY: Penguin, 2001.

Maldonado, Tomás. *Critica de la ragione informatica*. Milano: Feltrinelli, 1997.

Organisation for Economic Co-operation and Development (OECD). Agricultural Policies in OECD Countries. "Monitoring and Evaluation 2000: Glossary of Agricultural Policy Terms." Available at http://stats.oecd.org/glossary/detail.asp?ID=2604.

Randerson, James and Arpad Pusztai. "Biological Divide. The Scientist at the Centre of a Storm over GM Foods 10 Years Ago Tells James Randerson He Is Unrepentant." In *The Guardian*. "EducationGuardian" section, January 15, 2008, 11. http://www. guardian.co.uk/education/2008/jan/15/ academicexperts.highereducationprofile.

Shattuck, Roger. *Forbidden Knowledge: From Prometheus to Pornography*. New York: St. Martin's Press, 1996.

World Health Organization Media Center. "Electromagnetic Fields and Public Health." Fact Sheet no. 296. December 2005. Available at www.who.int/mediacentre/factsheets/ fs296/en/index.html.

Part 3

THE ARTS

9

Two Basque Sculptors

PETER SELZ

Jorge Oteiza and Eduardo Chillida were Basque artists whose international acclaim was founded, above all, on their advancement of modernist sculptors' aspiration to penetrate the block, to embrace internal volume, to create sculpture as a dialogue between positive and negative space.

The sculpture of the twentieth century differs markedly from the art of the past by the thinning of mass. Auguste Rodin rendered the effect of movement as vessels of energy in his *Dance Movements* (1910–13) and his dynamic *Nijinsky* (1912), opening the configurations of dancers into receptacles of space and vitalist energetic form. Then, starting with Pablo Picasso's audacious constructions of 1912–14, the potential of making sculpture expanded radically. Prior to the aforementioned breakthrough, sculpture had been either carved from hard materials like stone or wood, or built up with clay or plaster. Now, for the first time, a piece of sculpture could be assembled from a variety of materials.

In Paris before World War I, sculptors such as Alexander Archipenko and Jacques Lipchitz, while still retaining the human body as their theme, pierced their sculptures, working with negative as well as positive forms, thus permitting space to become an integral part of their work. Marcel Duchamp's famous *Bicycle Wheel* of 1913 was not only his first "readymade," it consisted of a rim surrounding empty space intervened by spokes. In Russia, Vladimir Tatlin, having become familiar with Picasso's assembled objects, made even more radical "corner reliefs" that have the appearance of weightlessness and seem to float in mid-air, negating gravity. His *Monument to the Third International* is an open tower, based on the dynamic configuration of the spiral. In the 1920s, Constructivists Naum Gabo (born as Naum Neemia Pevsner) and Antoine Pevsner, his brother, announced that mass was no longer a necessary element in a work of plastic art. Posting their "Realist Manifesto" on the walls of Moscow in the early years of the Revolution, they proclaimed: "We renounce in sculpture the mass as a sculptural element."[1] As Russian artists dispersed from the Soviet Union in the 1920s, they spread the Constructivist aesthetic of making sculpture and in the mid-1930s Alexander Calder, working in Paris, built *Mobiles* in which biomorphic shapes sway and rotate freely in space.

Following a very different tradition, Constantin Brâncuşi fused the work of sculpture with the viewer into a unified space simply by polishing his bronzes to a reflective surface. He also created his *Endless Columns,* which thrust upward into the infinity of space. In England, Henry Moore and Barbara Hepworth pierced their sculptures with holes to allow encircling air to sweep through these cavities, much like water flows through caves in cliffs by the sea. The bodies of these figures are permeated by the space in which they exist and are thus more intensely related to our own environment. In the 1930s, Alberto Giacometti constructed palaces and caves that served as dreamlike ambiences for his figures and objects—all set into spaces of fantasy. In his later work, the void impinges on isolated humans that are protected only by surrounding space.

Jorge Oteiza

Jorge Oteiza was born in 1908 in Orio, in the Basque Country, and started making sculpture in the late 1920s after having abandoned his study of medicine at the University of Madrid. His early pieces, done in cement, show his interest in the forms of early sculptures, especially pre-Columbian art. In 1935, nearly coinciding with Francisco Franco's accession to power, he went to Latin America, where for thirteen years he lived and worked in Argentina, Chile, Colombia, Ecuador, and Peru, keeping in touch with the Popular Front of the Spanish Republic, making, exhibiting, and teaching sculpture, writing about art and aesthetics. He studied not only pre-Columbian art but, going further into the past in his search for the origin of art, he also investigated Neolithic culture and prehistoric artifacts.

Oteiza, like the Basque philosopher Miguel de Unamuno, was brought up in the Catholic faith, and both men had a strong conviction of the necessity of myth. However, in contradistinction to the philosopher, who eventually returned to a strong belief in Christian dogma, the artist, a staunch atheist, felt that it was art that must take the place formerly occupied by religion. Oteiza shared this search for myth with some of his American contemporaries—Adolph Gottlieb, Barnett Newman, and Mark Rothko come to mind.

In 1948 Oteiza returned to Spain, settling in Bilbao. His sculptural work after his return shows an interest in experimenting in various media. He worked in cement, cast stone, aluminum, zinc, and marble. These pieces were in the current style, recalling Jacob Epstein, Henry Moore, and Henri Laurens, but they also reveal an originality of vision.

---

1. Gabo, "The Realist Manifesto," 329.

In 1950, he won a commission for the sculpture for the new basilica of Aranzazu in Oñate, Spain. He created a *Frieze of Apostles* in which figuration and abstraction are fused. The apostles are hollowed figures, emptied of earthy mass. And there are fourteen apostles, presumably because the allotted space called for a sculpture of this size. It was not surprising that the tradition-bound Pontifical Commission censured this modernist work after it was completed in 1953; it was finally installed in 1969. In 1953 Oteiza participated in the international competition for the *Monument for the Unknown Political Prisoner*, which was organized by the Institute of Contemporary Art in London. (Reg Butler received the award, but the monument was never built.)

The emphasis on the void in the *Frieze* later found its theoretical premise in the artist's significant philosophical text, *Quousque Tandem . . . ! Ensayo de interpretación estética del alma vasca* (Essay on aesthetic interpretation of the Basque soul). During his time in San Agustín, Peru, Oteiza had studied the "primitive" anthropomorphic man-jaguar carvings in which he found a synthesis of heroic drama and spiritual content. Analyzing this early culture in the Existentialist context of his time, he wrote, "The history of man from the first people or the first peoples, from the first cultures—like that of San Agustín—clearly manifests the inseparable question of human life and its anguish in the face of death. The fear of space, the fear of nothingness, the cosmic terror, only the most extraordinary of peoples had the resource to overcome it."[2] Oteiza believed that the artist of our time must again have the courage to deal with the Void through an aesthetic transformation because art has become the sacrament, once owned by religion.

In 1957, Oteiza began his investigations of polyhedrons. He made a series of marble pieces with irregular concave or convex openings, followed by sculptures in steel, in which he vacated, or dematerialized, the mass, as exemplified by *Spatial Groupings with Malevich Units* (1957). Kazimir Malevich, Oteiza had observed, signaled the foundation of weightless art. The work of Malevich was, to be sure, also the basis of Minimal Sculpture produced by American artists at the same time, sculptors who, however, emphasized mass rather than renouncing it. For Oteiza and his compatriot Chillida, the Void or *Ma*, as the Japanese called it, became the determining factor of his work. For both artists, it was not simply a matter of vacancy, but an energy-producing element. In the late 1950s, Oteiza produced sculptures, mostly in steel, in which rectangular or curved forms do no more than envelop the void. Oteiza's *Empty Boxes* of 1958 are geometrically composed units with missing "Malevich Units," and they were followed by "Metaphysical Boxes" such as the *Portrait of the Holy Spirit* (1959). These bronze sculptures were almost entirely closed so that space became almost inaccessible. Margit Rowell, in her essay on the artist, written on the occasion of his retrospective at the Guggenheim Museum Bilbao, interprets them as "receptacles or shrines for the eternal life of the soul."[3] Having proclaimed

---

2. Quoted in Arana Cobos, "Jorge Oteiza." This doctoral dissertation is forthcoming from the Center for Basque Studies in 2011.

3. Rowell, "A Sense of Place/A Sense of Space," 345.

the essence of Nothingness, the artist took the consequential step of refraining from making more works of art. His stance can be related to American artists, to Barnett Newman's Zum-Zum sculptures, geometric steel box-like shapes designed for a synagogue, to Mark Rothko's mysterious iconic walls of color and to Ad Reinhardt's black canvases of utter silence.

In 1951, Oteiza had received the Diploma of Honor at the Milan Triennale. In 1957, he exhibited twenty-one sculptures at the Sao Paolo, Brazil Biennial, and was honored with the International Sculpture Prize, and in 1960 his work was introduced to the United States with the Museum of Modern Art's exhibition, "New Spanish Painting and Sculpture," which was curated by Frank O'Hara under my general direction.

During the remaining four decades of his life, Oteiza devoted his time to working on his Experimental Laboratory in Madrid and later in Irun, a studio in which he made small three-dimensional maquettes to examine the effect of light on matter in space. But, except for a small number of steel pieces in 1975, he produced little sculpture in his remaining years. These were the years in which he continued his theoretical writings, such as his philosophical treatise *Quousque Tandem. . . !* mentioned above. In 1963 he originated architectural projects, participated in exhibitions, including a retrospective in Madrid and Bilbao, and assisted in the establishment of the Oteiza Museum by the government of Navarre in Spain.

In 2004, a year after his death, the Guggenheim Museum Bilbao installed a major retrospective, "Oteiza: Mito y modernidad" (Oteiza: Myth and Modernity). In his essay, "Oteiza/Gehry/Guggenheim: Mythographies, Returns, Deferred Actions," Joseba Zulaika asserts the Oteizian quality of Frank Gehry's design: "Gehry was more faithful to Oteiza and to the spirit of radical contemporaneity than the master himself. Oteiza also needed Gehry to bring himself up to date."[4] Richard Serra, the artist who has been the chief occupant of the museum in the Basque Country, published a note in homage to Oteiza in the Guggenheim catalog. There could, however, be no greater contrast in contemporary abstract sculpture than that between the aggressive power of Serra's curving corten steel walls, which cause a strong physical response in the viewer, and Oteiza's spaces of silence.

Eduardo Chillida

Eduardo Chillida, born in 1924, was sixteen years younger than his fellow Basque colleague. There is a great resemblance in their culture—not only in the liberation of space, so basic to their work, but also in choice of materials, be it steel, iron, alabaster, or concrete—which may possibly account for their antagonistic attitude toward each other. It was only in 1997, toward the end of their lives, that reconciliation took place. One signal difference is that most of Oteiza's sculpture was done in a single decade, the 1950s, when

---

4. Zulaika, "Oteiza/Gehry/Guggenheim," 365.

he produced a prodigious amount of sculpture, whereas Chillida's career as a sculptor extended over a half century. Both artists made architectural proposals for sculpture in the public domain, but only Chillida's were executed, whereas Oteiza spent much of his time and intellect in the production of significant theoretical writing.

Chillida studied architecture before turning to sculpture, and one of his first pieces was *Torso* (1948), which was not only informed by his study of Brâncuşi's sculpture but also evokes the image of the cromlech, the Celtic marker which had also occupied Oteiza. By the early 1950s Chillida created sculptural pieces in which the forged iron arms penetrate the air and move freely into space. Released from solid mass, space became the center of the work. These sculptures are certainly similar to Oteiza's work at the same time. It seems likely that the two sculptors, Oteiza, living in Bilbao, and Chillida, having settled in his nearby birthplace of San Sebastián, were familiar with each other's work. Like Oteiza, Chillida was commissioned to work on the new Basilica of Aranzazu for which he created four flat iron doors with relief sculpture.

By the mid-1950s Chillida had received international recognition. The Guggenheim Museum in New York acquired a sculpture, the city of San Sebastián commissioned him to produce his first monument, and in 1958 he received the International Grand Prize for sculpture at the Venice Biennial.

In 1958 Chillida forged a piece which he entitled *Articulated Reverie (Homage to Bachelard)*. This was in honor of his friend, the French poet and philosopher Gaston Bachelard, who considered reverie and imagination, governed by reason, to be elements leading to insight and creation. Similar to this work were a series of iron sculptures called *Rumor of Limits*. Over the years Chillida had given much thought to the concept of limits. According to him, a limit is both an end and a beginning, something which cannot be grasped and is subject to change. It is the moment between past and future. It is in this mysterious realm where the artist does his work, where the sculptor delimits space. The modern concept of space could no longer follow the mechanical and tangible Cartesian model, but postulated that space is relative to time. This idea was of paramount interest to many twentieth-century thinkers: Bachelard, Edmund Husserl, Martin Heidegger, Jean-Paul Sartre, and Maurice Merleau-Ponti. The latter declared that "the shell of space must be shattered"[5]—a precept fundamental to the work of both Basque sculptors. When Heidegger published his treatise, *Die kunst und der raum (Art and Space)*, he postulated, "Emptiness is not nothing. It is also no deficiency. In sculptural embodiment, emptiness plays in the manner of a seeking-projecting instituting of places."[6] In 1969 Heidegger went to St. Gallen to meet Chillida, who illustrated his volume with seven austere collage lithographs.

Between 1960 and 1964 Chillida, wanting to work on a large scale, turned to wood, and he selected Basque oak for this purpose. In the construction of these large sculptures

---

5. Merleau-Ponti, "Eye in the Mind," 180.

6. Heidegger, "Die kunst und der raum."

made of heavy beams, his early training in architecture came to good use. Working along these lines, he built granite sculpture, commissioned by James Johnson Sweeney, for the grounds of the Museum of Fine Arts in Houston, Texas. Soon, however, he felt that these works in wood and stone tended to be too hermetic, that the chambers of the void were too inaccessible, unable to communicate his spatial concerns.

Chillida now turned to alabaster, making beautiful pieces such as *Homage to Kandinsky* (1965) and *Homage to Goethe* (1979), the Olympian genius whose last words are said to have been, "More light." In these sculptures carved of translucent stone, light is able to enter the involuted chambers. The poet Octavio Paz discerned that, "The alabaster sculptures do not enclose inner space; neither do they claim to delimit or define it; they are blocks of transparencies in which form becomes space, and space dissolves in luminous vibrations that are echoes and rhymes thought."[7] The sculptor, who had worked in clay as an art student, returned to using more resistant ceramic clay in the early 1970s. Like Heidegger, he saw the earth as revealing itself in the work of art. Some of his earth pieces, *Lurra* (Earth), are standing stabs or steles with irregular insertions. Most of these silent blocks without edges are rocklike cubes, broken by notches, crevices, and cracks that denote an ineffable and unknown space within. They share the organic quality of the earth and are the artist's closest approach to nature itself.

The predominant material throughout Chillida's career has been metal, and during the 1970s and 1980s he produced an astonishing number of steel sculptures. He liked to call them steles, using the stele motif for Basque tradition and its funerary history for its emotional implications. He dedicated many of them to men he admired, to his friends among sculptors, Alberto Giacometti and Alexander Calder; to the painter Manolo Milares; to poets Novalis, Edgar Allan Poe, and Pablo Neruda; to the philosopher Henri Bergson; the statesman Salvador Allende; and to Agamemnon. Some of these works are audacious in their daring thrust of metal into space. Then, in the 1980s, Chillida fashioned a series of Corten steel tables, which show his concern with problems of levitation and gravitation, with the relationship of weight to space. These horizontal slabs rest close to the ground and are supported by three short legs. The number three is of great importance to Chillida as it has qualities both dynamic and mysterious and, he felt, opens toward new and inaccessible limits. He stated rather arcanely, "The Number Three does not deal with small solutions. One can resolve everything with Two. One can get to the moon with Two. But, you cannot project beyond it. In order to do the impossible, it is necessary to reach for Three."[8]

Eduardo Chillida has arguably produced the finest public sculptures of the twentieth century. The first of these large pieces was simply called *Monument* (1970–71) and was commissioned by the Thyssen Company in Düsseldorf as a gift to the city. It was fabricated of steel and stands five meters high. Also entitled *Rumor of Limits IX*, it is com-

---

7. Paz, "Chillida," 17.

8. Quoted in Esteban, *Chillida*, 59.

posed of a number of cubes and a long diagonal bar that reaches a large arm jutting into space. It combines spatial tension with geometric clarity. Sitting on a lawn in front of a large, undistinguished, late-international style office building, it manages to hold its own with its twisted forms and its daring appearance of instability. It can be seen as Modernist Baroque.

Soon after his return to San Sebastián in 1951, he resolved to create a large environmental sculpture at the edge of the city. It took a long time before his ideas found realization. The *Wind Combs* were finally installed in 1977. In 1968 he had installed a *Wind Comb* at the UNESCO building in Paris, but the San Sebastián site required a different configuration. The site selected by the sculptor and the architects is a ledge of awe-inspiring nature: cliffs of uplifted vertical sandstone, with the termination of the Pyrenees on one side and the waves of the Bay of Biscay on the other. Here, on land and in the sea, Chillida anchored three open steel claws. One comb is set into the cliff, the second sculpture is fastened on a rock in the water and points toward the land, and the third comb is farther out in the sea, silhouetted against the horizon and oriented vertically, opening its arms to the sky. The three seem engaged in a conversation that may be silent or highly animated, depending on the forces of nature. The two horizontal wind combs, the sculptor feels, related to the past, the vertical one to the future, which is unknown. This site, a plaza, has become a destination. It is used as a promenade, as a locale for games and performances, and also a place for silent mediation, for observing the sea, the sky, and the mountains. But on a stormy day at high tide the waves will fill the space with spectacular might and a tempest can even cover the sculptures completely. The *Wind Combs* appear like ramparts defending the city. The sculptor also points at its political ramifications: he affirmed soon after the completion of the work, "Just as the piece of land with its sculpture fights the water and the air to survive and attempts to communicate with the other two pieces nearby, the Basque people are struggling to survive as a distinct culture within Spain."[9]

Chillida's next site-based enterprise, completed in 1980, was the design and building of a new architectural complex for the main square of Vitoria-Gasteiz, in the Basque Country. He collaborated with the Basque architect Peña Ganchegui, who designed the *frontón* wall (Basque handball court) for *jai-alai* games and the court for the *bolatoki*, the ancient Basque ox races. To create a new plaza, Plaza de los Fueros, for the capital of the province of Alava, Chillida decided to dig below ground and in the Baroque tradition; his square is full of involutions, mazes, triangles, and surprises and creates a new coherent space. In its special niche in a deep well and surrounded by protecting walls, there is a fist-like steel stele to symbolize the ancient oak tree in Guernica (Gernika in Basque), which remains the symbol of liberty for the Basque people. It stands in a guarded hub of the Basque capital city and signifies the spirit of independence, metaphorically radiating to all Basque territories in the defense of an ancient culture. In Gernika itself, Chillida

9. Quoted in Schwartz, "Chillida's Silent Music," 71.

erected a large concrete structure entitled *Our Father's House* (1988). Situated two hundred meters from the sacred oak, it resembles a beached ship. The prow is open like a window, open to the world. It conveys a sense of peace; a contrast to the memory of the bombing of the city by Franco and his Fascist allies.

Earlier, in 1986, he built the *House of Goethe* in Frankfurt, the poet's birthplace. A great admirer of the German poet and scientist, Chillida constructed a large sculpture in concrete that is filled with interior mysteries, with interior spaces, which conceal as much as they reveal. The interplay of solids and voids creates a visual tension parallel to the emotion expressed in some of the poet's verse. A year later, addressing the problem of mass in space, he suspended a large and heavy, concrete, claw-like sculpture on the outskirts of Barcelona. This *Eulogy to Water* hovers over a pond that reflects its presence. *Homage to Tolerance*, a concrete sculpture eight hundred meters across that Chillida situated in Seville between the medieval city walls and the river, consists of a wide horizontal curve, meticulously balanced by a vertical arc. Dedicated in 1992, it commemorates the 500th anniversary of the expulsion of the Jews from that city.

In his *Homage to the Horizon* (1990), Eduardo Chillida achieved sublime resolution. Here, classical and geometric simplicity replaces the rich Baroque tension characteristic of the artist's earlier work. This towering form, 1,500 meters high and open to the sky, is placed on a low rise near Gijón, Asturias, where it looks out at the sea. I recall standing under this monument that rises from the earth and elliptically outlines the sky, and gazing at the endless sea in amazement and veneration at a great artist's achievement. His towering sculpture opens the horizon and guides the viewer to experience a unity of form and space, of art and nature.

A few years before Chillida's death he bought and restored an old Basque farmhouse built in 1543, and established the Chillida-Leku Museum and Sculpture Garden in Hernani, not far from San Sebastián.

Bibliography

Arana Cobos, Juan. "Jorge Oteiza: Art as Sacrament, Avant-Garde, and Magic." PhD diss., University of Nevada, Reno, 2008.

Esteban, Claude. *Chillida*. Paris: Maeght Editeur, 1971.

Gabo, Naum. "The Realist Manifesto." In *Theories of Modern Art*, edited by Chipp Herschel, Peter Selz, and Joshua C. Taylor. Berkeley: University of California Press, 1968.

Heidegger, Martin. *Die kunst und der raum*. With seven lithographs by Eduardo Chillida. St. Gallen: Erker-Verlag, 1969. Translated by Charles Siebert as "Art and Space." *Man and World* 6, no. 1 (February 1973): 3–8.

Merleau-Ponty, Maurice. "Eye in the Mind." In *The Primacy of Perception*, edited and with an introduction by James M. Edie. Evanston, IL: Northwestern University Press, 1964.

Oteiza, Jorge. *Quousque Tandem . . . ! Ensayo de interpretación estética del alma vasca.* San Sebastián: Auñamendi, 1964.

Paz, Octavio. "Chillida: From Iron to Light." In *Chillida*, translated by Rachel Phillips. New York: Solomon R. Guggenheim Museum, 1979.

Rowell, Margit. "A Sense of Place/A Sense of Space: The Sculpture of Jorge Oteiza." In *Oteiza: Mito y Modernidad.* Bilbao: Guggenheim Museoa Bilbao, 2004.

Schwartz, Ellen. "Chillida's Silent Music, de Kooning's Eloquent Ambivalence." *ART-News* 79, no. 2 (March 1980): 68–70.

Zulaika, Joseba. "Oteiza/Gehry/Guggenheim: Mythographies, Returns, Deferred Actions." In *Oteiza: Mito y Modernidad.* Bilbao: Guggenheim Museoa Bilbao, 2004.

10

Paris, New York, and the Basque International Art Community

ANNA MARÍA GUASCH and JOSEBA ZULAIKA

At the turn of the nineteenth century, introduction to modernity meant for Basque art-ists the expected trip to Paris. Leaving aside Madrid and Rome, it was in Paris where they discovered the true meaning of modernity. This meant a new way of looking at art and life, including the concrete realities of their Basque society and culture. Joaquín de Zuazagoitia put it in these terms:

> What provided the tone of Basque painting was that our painters, like the Catalans, stopped going to Madrid and Rome and went to Paris. There they vibrated with the con-cerns of impressionist painting, and in Paris, through [James Abbott McNeill] Whistler, [John Singer] Sargent—two Americans—and through [Édouard] Manet, they returned their eyes to the great tradition of Spanish painting. With their eyes educated in Paris, capable of better understanding the Spanish tradition, upon returning they found themselves in a country that was theirs, of such salient traits that it would well deserve to represent it. The naturalism of the painting style then called modern forced them to abandon the great historic topics and to look at the daily life around them with tender eyes. Thus the most notorious characteristics of Basque painting are its capacity to observe the daily life of the Basque Country—that has been at once its power and its limitation—and a return to Span-ish pictorial tradition through the French influence.[1]

Here we have a paradigm of how a new "knowledge community" is created: art-ists needed to go to Paris to discover their own Spanish and Basque reality, much as

---

1. Quoted in Llano Gorostiza, *Pintura vasca,* 30.

archeologists and ethnographers needed to go to European universities to be able to discover their own prehistoric cave paintings and folkloric tradition. The need for a new window with a different perspective, the seductive indirection of a turnaround to discover what is yours, manifests itself in a new type of "knowledge" that transforms and reorders all you previously knew. Hence the pivotal experience of taking the train from Bilbao or San Sebastián and moving to Paris. Paris was Charles Baudelaire, Georges-Eugène "Baron" Haussmann, the commune, the Eiffel Tower, the Seine River. It was above all impressionism and fauvism, later it was cubism; it was everything. But, what did Montmartre, Pigalle, or Les Champs Elysees possess to make a Basque painter fall in love with his town's fishermen or his village's town's bridges? The intoxicating aura of modernity could shift perspectives, touch all perception, and bring about a different subjectivity. Suddenly, in a sort of parallax effect, the artist "knew" something quite different about his own tradition and his autobiography. Nothing was the same, and yet every building and every ruin was still there—only that now the artist was looking through Paris and seemed to be able to see everything anew in the modern glow of its passage and beauty.

The painter Eduardo Zamacois y Zabala (1841–71) was the first to open the way to Paris, soon to be followed by future generations of Basque artists. Anselmo Guinea y Ugalde (1884–1906) was next to jump from paintings of eighteenth-century Spanish historicism and Basque iconography to Parisian impressionism. But the two main figures of that first wave of painters were Adolfo Guiard (1860–1916) and Darío de Regoyos (1875–1913). Guiard, who lived in Paris for seven years and was influenced by Jean Auguste Dominique Ingres and Edgar Degas, broke with the tradition of large paintings dedicated to historical themes for national exhibits and began working on small formats of less than a meter and on topics that were remarkable for their ordinariness and banality: lemons, a man sitting, a landscape with a train, a girl combing her hair.

As to Regoyos, his influence would become decisive among Basque artists both in terms of his audacious techniques (impressionism, fauvism, pointillism, and other styles) and thematic (farmers, pilgrims, dancers, folkloric figures, and farm implements). Still, Regoyos's universe was not imbued in the ideological iconography of a nationalist evocation of Basque rural life; his rural architecture does not portray an ideal organization of the world, nor an epic sense of life; his interest in Basque life had to do basically with aesthetics and light—his preference being not for the harsh light of Castile and Andalusia but the changing tonalities of grey and opaque lights of the Cantabrian landscapes. As Crisanto de Lasterra wrote about him, once he found this universe, "then everything was like a miracle . . . Regoyos would find the salvation of his art touched by the miraculous grace of light."[2] In Brussels *Le Journal de Beaux Arts* had written that Regoyos "was the most audacious" among the painters in a collective exhibit and that "he has thrown him-

---

2. Quoted in Lasterra, *Darío de Regoyos*, 139.

self into complete modernity."[3] His art was not understood by his society, and he became the object of ridicule. His approach to art was a novelty among Basque artists; it could only be seen by eyes struck by European modernity.

The house/workshop of sculptor Paco Durrio in Montmartre became the port of entry for Basque and Spanish artists. His parents were French, and he lived all his life between Bilbao and Paris. As he was a close friend of Paul Gauguin and Pablo Picasso, his art subscribed to modernism.[4] Among Durrio's visitors were relevant names such as Francisco Iturrino (1864–1924) and Juan de Echevarría (1875–1931). Iturrino, who was exhibiting his work with Picasso in 1901, would not select Basque fishermen or local festivals or Bilbao's factories as motifs for his work but would rather paint themes from Spanish folklore such as Andalusian women with mantillas, nudes, gypsies, horses, and gardens; these were more appropriate for the luminosity of his fauve forms in which the line disappears in the light and there are no shadows; they were also more dear to his friend Henri Matisse, with whom he spent the years 1909 and 1910 in Andalusia and Morocco.

Echevarría painted still lifes, flowers, portraits, and Castilian fields; he was not interested in ethnography, but he did have a first romantic period in which he worked in Basque fishing towns, to be followed by more luminous paintings in Granada and more literary ones in Madrid.[5] Among the sculptors, Durrio is the most important name, but Higinio Basterra (1876–1975) deserves mention, for he brought Auguste Rodin's influence after his 1898 visit to Paris, as well as Nemesio Mogrovejo (1875–1910), who went to Paris in 1894 and whose death in 1910 was followed by an exhibit of his work and the creation in Bilbao the following year of the Association of Basque Artists. These painters and sculptors brought from Paris not only aesthetic codes; they embodied new lifestyles and subjectivities. They belonged to another "knowledge community" with its own set of aesthetic and moral values, which would translate into a different sensorial palette and a perspective distanced from nativistic premises. By introducing the basic premises, tastes, techniques, and spirit of modern painting, they were significantly expanding and recreating the local culture.

The ideological divide concerning Basque ethnicity and nationalism was reflected among artists as well. Painters such as Ignacio Zuloaga (1870–1945) and Manuel Losada (1865–1949) focused entirely on the Spanish pictorial tradition. For others, such as Valentín de Zubiaurre (1879–1963), Ramón de Zubiaurre (1882–1969), and the brothers José and Ramiro Arrúe, Basque folkloric and ethnic themes became prominent. The very idea of "Basque art" emerged, to be questioned to this day by some critics. Still others, Aurelio Arteta (1879–1940) most prominently, combined socialist and nationalist sympathies.[6] The artistic community, by bringing together European romantic and

---

3. Quoted in Ibid., 129.

4. See Lasterra, *En Paris con Paco Durrio*.

5. For more elaboration, see Guasch, *Arte e ideología en el País Vasco*, 29–55.

6. See Ibid., 40–55.

modernist styles, as well as local cultural contents, had to blend diverse traditions into a viable aesthetic form.

Architecture was no exception. Eclecticism is perhaps the dominant trait of the early twentieth-century architecture as practiced in Basque cities and towns. One of the best examples is the Teatro Arriaga (Arriaga Theatre, 1890) in Bilbao, by Joaquín de Rucoba, which shows French influences as it is inspired by Paris's Opera house.[7] The group of architects that became known at the turn of the twentieth century was called "the generation of the *ensanche* (enlargement)," the grand urban recreation of Bilbao as an entirely new city on the left bank of the river, across from the old Bilbao of the "seven strccts," needed for the new industrial era. The plan was designed by Pablo de Alzola y Minondo, Ernesto de Hoffmeyer y Zubeldia, and Severino Achúcarro (1873), and implemented mostly by Alzola when he was mayor of the city (1877–79). The influence of the Parisian Gustav Eiffel on Alzola and other architects such as Valentín Gorbeña has been recognized. Many works were projected at the time that never went beyond the design stage; one of them was a large, visionary commercial center (1893) built over the Nervión River in the style of the Haussmannian *passages* of Paris. Its architect was Alberto de Palacio y Elissague, a frequent visitor of Paris and a friend of Eiffel, heavily influenced by the Parisian utopianism of the turn of the nineteenth century,[8] and an enthusiast of the new technologies and the idea of progress.

The Fine Arts Museum

By the time the Association of Basque Artists was formed in 1911, the project of a Fine Arts Museum had been conceived and approved in Bilbao in 1908. It was to be opened by 1914. The building was at the city's old quarter and originally had been a Public Hospital, later turned into the Arts and Crafts School. A second Museum of Modern Art was founded in 1922 and completed by 1924 and was housed in a building owned by the Provincial Council. After the Spanish Civil War, in 1945 the Fine Arts Museum completed its own building next to the park of the *ensanche* where the collections of the two museums were merged. The foundation of the museum during the first two decades of the century marked the artistic interests of a new, prosperous, and cosmopolitan middle class that resulted from the booming industrialization that peaked during the First World War, 1914–18.[9]

In Javier Viar's assessment, these *bilbaínos,* who were mostly "conservative anglophiles . . . facilitated the education of a number of artists, enabling them to visit Impressionist Paris and return with a certain spirit, although tempered, of the revolutionary ideas emanating from the French capital. These artists were essential in the establishment

---

7. B. García de la Torre and F. García de la Torre, *Bilbao,* 86.

8. Basurto Ferro et al., *El Bilbao que pudo ser,* 87.

9. Viar, "The Guggenheim Bilbao," 98–99.

of cultural events and institutions, of which one was the Fine Arts Museum that exists today."[10] Two of those artists, Manuel Losada and Aurelio Arteta, became the directors of the two modern Bilbao museums. A reflection of their artistic overall perspective is that the collection of the joint Museum of Fine Arts that replaced both of them focuses on three main areas: historic or "universal" art (although almost entirely European), contemporary art of the twentieth century, and Basque art.

The Postwar Period

After the 1936–39 Spanish civil war and during the first decades of Francoism, Basque art had no international projection. In 1956 Agustín Ibarrola decided he should try to show his work somewhere outside of his country. Where would he go? To Paris, of course: "I took a bunch of canvases with me with the intention of showing them to the galleries and securing an exhibit. When I saw what they were exhibiting, I didn't dare to show them my Basque workers, fishermen, and farmers. The paintings projected by Parisian galleries were cosmopolitan, de-nationalized, without country, without issues to denounce, nor precise social experiences to transmit."[11] Modernist Paris seemed now too modern and too cosmopolitan for Basque artists suffering under Francisco Franco's dictatorial oppression.

There was, however, one Basque artist who did have an opening in Paris: Eduardo Chillida (1924–2002). He went there in 1948, and the following year had his first exhibit in Paris. In 1950 he had a second exhibit at the Maeght Gallery in Paris. Again in 1954 at the Denise René Gallery and in 1956 at the Maeght Gallery (with a text by Gaston Bachelard for his catalog), Chillida exhibited in Paris. Even if by then New York had "stolen" the idea of modernism from a postwar "Parisian art [that] was now fragmented," and the critic Clement Greenberg had "declared that American art had broken with Paris once and for all,"[12] for Basques, Paris still seemed to be the only place that could grant international recognition. And this was also the case even for New York artists: "Why Paris? Because, notwithstanding the ravages of war, Parisian art still represented Western culture and for New York artists was a taproot of modernist thought."[13]

But there was another artist who, with Chillida, would obtain the greatest international renown and exert unparalleled influence among younger generations of Basque artists: Jorge Oteiza (1908–2003). He travelled a different route; he spent thirteen years (1935–48) in South America, where he became actively involved with the avant-garde movements of several countries. Like no other artist of his generation, Oteiza tried passionately and frequently in a utopian fashion to create a veritable "knowledge

---

10. Ibid., 99.

11. Quoted in Guasch, *Arte e ideología en el País Vasco*, 117.

12. Guilbaut, *How New York Stole the Idea of Modern Art*, 203, 172.

13. Ibid., 4.

community," grounded primarily in aesthetics, that would transform Basque society. He began his artistic work in Madrid in 1929, influenced by the European contemporary movements of Cubism, Russian Constructivism, De Stijl, and the Bauhaus. The stated reason for his trip to South America was to study pre-Columbian statuary in the city of San Agustín.

Oteiza wrote a book-length essay on these statues, theorizing on "art as sacrament,"[14] as well as various essays on aesthetics, and issued "manifestos" for contemporary artists.[15] Upon his return from South America, he settled in Bilbao and by 1950 was awarded a contract to sculpt the statuary for the Basilica of Aranzazu, a project that brought together a group of cutting-edge artists. Oteiza's international recognition would come in 1957 by winning the International Sculpture Prize in the Sao Paulo Biennial with the twenty-nine sculptures of his "Experimental Proposal"—he carried out a deconstruction of the Euclidean forms of the cube, the circle, and the sphere. In the text he wrote for the occasion,[16] Oteiza acknowledges the influences of Wasilly Kandinsky, Piet Mondrian, and particularly Kasimir Malevich. These influences were the knowledge community with which he was truly involved, yet he also referred in that text to the Basque traditional "funerary stela" as a form of religious art he was closest to in his own work. These stelae are three- to five-foot-tall tombstone pillars that express a pre-Copernican world controlled by the premises of circularity, centrality, irradiation, closure, and the internal void; not coincidentally, Chillida named his first abstract sculpture *Ilarik,* meaning in Basque "stela." Oteiza concluded his text with the oracular words: "I return from Death. What we tried to bury grows here." The titanic work of both Chillida and Oteiza in the 1950s can thus be seen as a successful effort at bringing together and confronting the aesthetic practices of contemporary art and the artistic premises of their native culture; valid knowledge had to come from the marriage of the latest European avant-garde and of what had been buried in the unconscious of the traditional aesthetic expressions.[17]

The very year Oteiza won the Sao Paulo Biennial, a group known as Equipo 57 was formed in Paris after a collective exhibit that took place at the Café Rond Point. It was composed of Oteiza, Ángel Duarte, José Duarte, Ibarrola, Juan Serrano, and Néstor Basterretxea—although Oteiza soon broke with the group, to be followed later by Basterretxea. According to Ibarrola, they formed the group in order to help each other make a living while painting and decorating Parisian houses, as well as become a study group "in order to explain to ourselves all of that new aesthetic universe that was falling down on us."[18] Their main interests had to do with the plastic investigation of space as well as with the social and ideological projections of the work of art. It is important to notice that

14. Oteiza, *Interpretación estética de la estatuaria megalítica Americana.*

15. See Oteiza, *Oteiza's Selected Writings,* 2003.

16. Ibid., 220–44.

17. For more on Chillida and Oteiza, see the chapter by Peter Selz in this volume.

18. Quoted in Guasch, *Arte e ideología en el País Vasco,* 122.

they felt the need to work as a "team;" their manifesto declared that they used plastic art as "an investigative tool whose finality is to arrive at practical solutions applicable to objects of daily use, to urbanization."[19] These artists saw themselves as a community of expert knowledge that had to investigate aesthetic issues in order to help express social inequities and solve cultural and urban problems.

In 1958 Chillida won the Grand Sculpture Prize at the XXIX Venice Biennial and the Sculpture Prize granted by the Graham Foundation in Chicago. In 1959 he participated in the Documenta II in Kassel, as well as exhibiting in North Carolina, Canada, New York, Baltimore, Minneapolis, Los Angeles, and Paris.

The 1960s: From Individual Internationalism to Native Collectivist Projects

The same need to work as a team—by linking formal investigations concerning the avant-garde languages with the need to project autochthonous culture beyond local frontiers—was reaffirmed in the collective efforts that took place in 1966 by the groups that formed the so-called Basque School. After the decade of the 1950s, in which Basque artists individually sought their own internationalization following the constructivist and abstract movements of the day (Oteiza, Chillida), in the 1960s the terms were inverted: the search for formal innovation took place under collective interests that looked for clear signs of identity regarding Basque art.

In that context of recovery of historic memory from the perspective of critical nationalism, the various groups of the Basque School emerged, called *Gaur* (Today), *Emen* (Here), and *Orain* (Now).[20] From their provincial territorial bases of Gipuzkoa, Bizkaia, and Araba, these groups tried to renovate the traditional concepts regarding issues such as: How do you build an artistic avant-garde scene in the context of a local community? How do you avoid stagnation, intellectual suffocation, the closure from foreign influences? What kind of relationship should the artists have among themselves to assert their presence vis-à-vis institutional power?

Not all these groups thought alike about the role of the artist.[21] There was a notorious antagonism between *Emen*, the group led by Agustín Ibarrola, which advocated the creation of a cultural front to foment the participation of art in popular expressions (such as cultural weeks, social and sport gatherings), and *Gaur*, which saw its work as

---

19. Quoted in Ibid., 123.

20. According to Pedro Manterola, the creation of these groups was conceived as a wave that could not be resisted: "It all corresponds to the purest Oteiza style. It looks as if it were the outcome of a platonic dream: TODAY, HERE and NOW, and finally in Navarre EVERYONE and everyone together. The creature that Oteiza had baptized prematurely failed to come up to expectations during its gestation filled with difficulties. Like so many others, was it destined to fail?" Manterola, "El arte en Navarra (1960–1979)," 239–40.

21. The groups had the following exhibits: Museum of Fine Arts in Bilbao by *Gaur* and *Emen* (August 1966); Provincial Museum of Araba by *Gaur*, *Emen*, and *Orain* (October 1966); the group *Gaur* also exhibited in various towns in Gipuzkoa, such as Beasain, Villafranca de Ordizia, Tolosa, and Legorreta throughout December of 1966 and January of 1967, accompanied by lectures, the most memorable one being Juan Antonio Sistiaga's "La expression estética como investigación" (Aesthetic Expression as Investigation).

the equivalent of the "Spanish contemporary avant-garde art" on the basis of a "spiritual renaissance" of the Basque artist. This could be gathered from the text that accompanied *Gaur*'s first exhibit in 1966 at the Barandiaran Gallery in San Sebastián: "Our Basque Country has sufficient money, and has sufficient artists of personality and international standing who cannot be unknown and silenced among ourselves; we are not a School of Madrid, we don't accept that two of the Gipuzkoan artists who subscribe this declaration, because they are the only ones in Spain who have won in the exterior the great international prizes in sculpture, that they continue to be treated as if they belonged to the School of Madrid."[22]

The position by *Gaur* toward a "contemporary Basque art" was opposed directly by *Emen*'s more "assambleary" practice, and for whom art was an instrument to take consciousness of an autochthonous culture. Oteiza proposed a more pedagogical role for art; in his *Quousque Tandem . . . !* he emphasized not the production of works of art but the elaboration of an aesthetic sensibility to be transmitted to society through education. It was precisely Oteiza who established the bases for these associations of Basque artists when he wrote of the "discipline of an indivisible intelligence and an indivisible will . . . to bring to an end the deep cultural and material decadence we suffer and the isolation among ourselves and in relation to our country."[23]

Was the contemporary component of modern art what brought an end to the Basque School and the cancelling of a planned great exhibit in Pamplona to include the works of more than a hundred artists? The fact is that the ideological tension within the allegedly unitary project of the Basque School did not allow for the constitution or for an "art of synthesis" between the two aesthetic tendencies: a figurative and realist art propounded by Ibarrola and the group *Emen* that accepted "any aesthetic premise capable of expressing the historic moment of our country," and an abstract art "of triumphal morality and hegemonic spirit" practiced by the members of the group *Gaur* (Amable Arias, Rafael Ruiz Balerdi, Juan Antonio Sistiaga, José Luis Zumeta, Jorge Oteiza, Eduardo Chillida, Néstor Basterrechea, and Remigio Mendiburu).

The 1970s: In Between the European Avant-Garde and Social Realism

During the 1970s the history of Basque art continued to be marked by a series of ideological conflicts. There was no easy reconciliation between "the Basque artist in the European avant-garde" and the languages of popular tradition; nor was there a middle ground between the ahistorical and metaphysical approach by Oteiza, who was trying to eliminate from Basque art any presence of Latin influence to return to the Neolithic period,

22. *Manifiesto del Grupo Gaur.*
23. Ibid.

the "zero cromlech," and the historicist position by Ibarrola who, unlike Oteiza, pointed to more recent events and to nonnative roots in order to advocate social realism.[24]

The Encounters of Pamplona in 1972 provided the first great opportunity to confront the experimental international, national, and Basque avant-gardes as well as a more testimonial and politicized art. As argued by José Díaz Cuyàs: "With the Encounters, the same thing happens as with the carnivals: they can be interpreted as an exercise in liberation, an expression of unofficial culture, an attack against the hierarchy of values, a reinvention of the body, and so on, or else as an inverted reproduction of what is official acting as a safety valve and whose function is ultimately to consolidate the current hierarchy of values. This is the fundamentally ambivalent character of carnival and I believe that this is also the only way to interpret that equivocal festival in Pamplona."[25] The Encounters were in theory sponsored by the Provincial Council of Navarre and the City Hall of Pamplona but in reality were financed by the Huarte family. Their goal was to bring to the public, by means of exhibits, colloquia, and aesthetic experiences developed in the most varied places (streets, plazas, cinemas, and theaters), a plural sample of the latest tendencies in plastic, visual, musical, and theatrical arts, overcoming the barriers between artistic creation and daily life.[26]

About three hundred and fifty people participated in Pamplona—elite musicians, filmmakers, plastic artists, and intellectuals from the Basque Country, Spain, and other countries united in the defense of a concept of an international avant-garde. Among the performances were those of John Cage, the group ZAJ (Juan Hidalgo, Walter Marchetti, Esther Ferrer), conceptual and post-conceptual artists (Vito Acconci, Joseph Kosuth, Dennis Oppenheim, On Kawara), and some of the best known representatives of Spanish conceptual art, such as Isidoro Valcárcel Medina and his installation *Estructuras Modulares* (made of yellow and black scaffolding tubes that were a hundred meters long) and the Catalans Robert Llimos with his *Corredores* and Jordi Benito with his project *24000000 Tm de hulla 3VII*. And next to all of this, the very same day of the opening of the Encounters (June 26, 1972) the exhibit *Current Basque Art* was also inaugurated; it was curated by Santiago Amón, an art critic closely linked to the Huarte family, a fact that generated controversy. Oteiza and Chillida decided not to participate in the Encounters. One of the works at the exhibit by Dionisio Blanco, a militant member of the Communist Party, was censored, which forced Ibarrola and Arri to retire their works in solidarity with Blanco.

---

24. See Serrano, "Arte alavés y arte vasco," 544.

25. Díaz Cuyás and Pardo, "Pamplona era una fiesta," 19.

26. "Una de las notas de los Encuentros quisiéramos que fuese, de un lado, el que el público pueda—casi diríamos deba—intervenir en el hecho artístico de una forma mucho más próxima de la que se tenía por costumbre, habitándolo de una manera distinta; de otro, lógica consecuencia del anterior, el creador va a encontrarse a un público menos pasivo que de ordinario . . . Las razones para ello son muchas. Pamplona es una ciudad de larga tradición cívica, una de las raras en España en las que el pueblo es protagonista de sus fiestas; el tamaño de la ciudad es idóneo . . . Los encuentros se celebran en Pamplona. No se podía pues olvidar ciertos aspectos de la cultura vasca." *Catálogo Alea, Encuentros-72.*

A few months earlier, on April 17, 1972, Basque artists had met in an assembly and signed a manifesto denouncing the partisan use made of the Encounters by the State's cultural apparatus as a policy of international prestige—the very same policy that wanted to show a cultural façade unconnected to the real issues, and particularly to the artistic needs of the Basque Country. There was once again "a clash of cultures" between the elitist character of the organization and the more interventionist aspirations of Basque artists in creative processes to the service of their cultural community.

During this same decade of the 1970s, artists from other parts of Spain expressed their attitude of rejection of Francoism in more open and international fashion. There were events organized by exiled artists in Paris and New York, as in the case of "the Catalans in Paris," particularly in the first generation after Antoni Tàpies (e.g., Antoni Muntadas, Jaume Xifra, Benet Rosell, Joan Rabascall, and Antoni Miralda) and the subsequent case of "the Catalans in New York" (Miralda, Muntadas, Francesc Torres, Eugenia Balsells, and Albert Porta "Zush"—nowadays known as "Evru")—strictly individual experiences outside of any institutional support. Compared to them, Basque artists showed a policy of "behind closed doors" charged with a national ideological project. Even the Basque participation in the Venice Biennial of 1976 entitled *Spain, Artistic Avant-Garde and Social Reality* was marred by controversy among the antithetical positions of Ibarrola on the one hand and Oteiza and Chillida on the other.

A few months after the death of Franco, a group of artists and critics representing the various nationalities of the Spanish state (Ibarrola was the Basque representative) planned an exhibit whose objective was to show what the great aesthetic options had been within Spain during Franco's forty years of rule. The organizing committee set the premises that the work should be art of investigation and art of testimony within the anti-Francoist culture. Ibarrola, who was affiliated with the Communist Party, conceived Basque representation along the premise of the cult of personality and selected the three biggest names of the last decades: Oteiza, Chillida, and himself.[27] Chillida and Oteiza declined to take part in the retrospective.[28]

The scant Basque participation at the Venice Biennial (only Ibarrola attended, and two of Oteiza's sculptures were provided by a collector without the sculptor's authorization) was the expression of the definitive breakup of the more or less tacit agreement among the anti-Francoist opposition forces, namely, between the artists close to the Communist Party and the sympathizers of the Basque nationalist left, the two main ideologies championing the practice of art.[29] In fact, the political parties of the Basque nationalist

---

27. Guasch, *Arte e ideología en el País Vasco*, 171.

28. The refusal to organize a large exhibit of ideologically nationalist Basque artists, as suggested by Chillida under pressure from artists such as Juan Mieg, Carmelo Ortíz de Elguea, Rafael Ruíz Balerdi, and José Luis Zumeta, and the never realized project by Oteiza of organizing a joint pavilion of Northern (French) and Southern (Spanish) Basque countries left the Venetia Biennial without Basque representation. On the absence of Chillida and Oteiza, see "Euskadi alla Biennale," in *Catalogo Generale*.

29. "Euskadi alla Biennale de Venise: Une victoire pour les basques."

left decided to create a Basque Country–Italy committee to organize meetings in Venice under the banner *Aministía Denonzat* (Amnesty for Everyone). In the end, only people from the world of cinema and song took part, in association with roundtables debating issues of amnesty led by lawyers Juan María Bandrés and Miguel Castells. In the opinion of Ibarrola, the events were "a real caricature of what could have been expected from any manifestation of Basque culture."[30]

The Decade of the 1980s: The New Internationalism

A new generation of artists emerged in the 1980s from the recently created Faculty of Arts (1969). Among them are Txomin Badiola, Ángel Bados, Juan Luis Moraza, Darío Urzay, and Pello Irazu. This group brought the end of a large process of crisis and dissolution of the historic avant-gardes in the Basque arena and the beginning of a new postmodern eclecticism. The end result was the formation of an artist with a different profile in which the aesthetic and the political, as well as the local and the international, were resolved not as a dichotomous process, but from a plurality of viewpoints, as well as a given transversality, heterodoxy, and hybridity.

Badiola, Bados, José Ramón Morquillas, Moraza, and others, whose work was cataloged as the New Basque Sculpture, and directly related to the minimal, conceptual, as well as to the post–Anthony Caro British sculpture, began to produce their first works in the years 1978–82. On the other hand, the new realisms of artists such as Vicente Ameztoy, Juan Luis Goenaga, Ramón Zuriarrain, Jesús Mari Lazkano, and Darío Urzay were in tune with the international neo-expressionisms of the day both in the Italian version—the trans-avant-garde—and the German one—the new savages. As explained by Carlos Martínez Gorriarán, Basque art has closely followed the international evolution, without traumas and fissures, yet without renouncing its proper traditional matrix.[31] In this sense, the end of Francoism as well as the end of the modernist project seemed to have liberated the Basque artist from the intense politicization that animated the artists of the 1960s and 1970s when, under the leadership of Oteiza, they believed that art and artists could have a testimonial role, a transformative function in the creation of a new society and culture.

Morquillas is a case in point. Without abandoning his natal Bilbao he works in the deconstruction and alteration of his own environment and daily reality from the standpoint of subversion and resistance as artistic practices. Badiola is also a paradigmatic example of such a *rite du passage* from the profile of the artist of the sixties, ruled over by ideology, to the postmodern artist, given to irony, who, disappointed by the failure of the collectivist aims of the project of the Basque School, decides to initiate a solitary road marked by the same desire of individuality that had characterized the Basque artist of the

30. Angulo, *Agustín Ibarrola*, 314.

31. Martínez Gorriarán, "El arte y los artistas vascos de 1966 a 1993," 121.

1950s. But Badiola in particular embodies the artist who at a certain point of his career decides to leave the Basque Country to reside in one of the great cosmopolitan cities of international art.

After having curated Oteiza's exhibit in Madrid, in 1989 Badiola moved to London first and then in 1990 to New York, where he stayed until 1998. In an interview Badiola explains that the years 1987 and 1988 were particularly intense: "On the one hand, I was teaching at the Faculty of Fine Arts in conditions that deteriorated from day to day . . . On the other hand, there was my own work: 1987 was the year of my first individual exhibit in Madrid. This exhibit had a very positive repercussion . . . In that moment I was somewhat overwhelmed by the alleged success, I had the impression that it was relative, since the reasons that were given to assess the value of my work did not interest me, and just what did interest me was never mentioned."[32]

Like Badiola, in the 1980s other artists felt the need to use the Basque imaginary ironically and without traumas, and to search for constant renegotiations between the issues of proximity and distance. These artists, following the deconstructivist and postmodern fashion of the times, proceeded to dismantle the formalist late modernist principles in which they had been educated. They articulated their creative strategies not so much as a native and referential style (as was the case in the 1960s and 1970s), but to contribute from a self-critical approach to the generalized formula that in the early 1990s came to be known as the New Internationalism—namely, the use of internationalism's lingua franca implemented with local narratives, with metaphors that speak of memory, individual as much as collective, and that do not renounce a certain primordial authenticity. As argued by Jean Fischer, the New Internationalism formula allows artists of different geographic and political areas to tell stories and allegories in need of deciphering, but always with the eyes in *mainstream* that provides the guiding languages.[33]

During these years a new generation of Basque artists began to move to the international capitals of art (New York, London, Amsterdam) to be in tune with the dominant trends in theory (references to authors such as Roland Barthes, Michel Foucault, Jacques Derrida, and Antonin Artaud, Georges Bataille, Slavoj Žižek would be mandatory), as well as formal plastic contributions (Donald Judd, Robert Morris, Bruce Nauman, besides the unavoidable quotes of Oteiza and, to a lesser degree, Chillida). The end result is the formation of languages that can be identified with the international currents of the times but implemented with local narratives immersed in the symbolic history of Basque culture, by taking into account the place of birth and growth of those languages, in a peripheral condition that turns into an artifact of productive differentiation, consciousness of the local beyond any type of "regionalist" limitation.

This new type of art can be seen, at the beginning of the 1990s, in the works of Badiola, Bados, Irazu, Moraza, Urzay, and Marisa Fernández. They "made a respectful

---

32. Power, "Continuando la conversación," 134. See also Eraso, "Txomin Badiola," 143.

33. Fischer, ed., *Global Visions*, x.

step forward in relation to their elders, but without stepping too much beyond the stable and accepted canon, a step forward in which some even viewed an exiled, eccentric form, as well-informed in its drift as it was orphan in its identity."[34] This is how some critics interpreted the first works Badiola presented in Madrid's Soledad Lorenzo Gallery after his stays in London and New York; these were works in which the iron was painted in red, literary elements were added to the image, the epistemological basis of the abstract grammar that characterized the previous decades was put in question, and the very notion that sculpture, now immersed in a process of hybridity by mixing diverse languages (film, video, television, and comics), was subverted.

Some paradigmatic works of these early 1990s were Badiola's *Bañiland* (1990–91) or *Family Complot* (1993)—installations in which modernist mythical figures such as Malevich and Oteiza are deconstructed, as well as designers such as Aalto or Jacobsen and other evidences of failed utopian thinking, and mixed with references to icons of the mass media and other subcultures to provoke with such fortuitous encounter the emergence of the "uncanny" or the "unholy," of what forces in every family situation the formation of deep charges of anxiety, strangeness, and dissolution. As Badiola states in his conversation with Manel Clot: "One of my favorite goals . . . has been to achieve in my work a structure that will allow me to integrate each and every one of the aspects of my life, from the day-to-day events to my political and ideological perplexities, from my affects to the purely aesthetic debates, from my most intimate desires to the chronicling of society."[35]

From the 1990s to the Present: Between the Global and the Local

In this same vein of interaction between mental and subjective ecologies, and echoing the sensibilities of the late 1990s that privileged the micro and the molecular over the high political and ideological discourses, a new generation of artists was formed among Bilbao's students at the Faculty of Fine Arts. Among others, some of the names are Asier Mendizabal, Ibon Aranberri, Inazio Escudero, Mikel Eskauriaza, Jon Mikel Euba, Itziar Okariz, Tsuspo Poyo, Sergio Prego, Francisco Ruiz Infante, and Pepo Salazar. Searching for a combination of the local and the international, the aesthetics and the politics, these artists temporarily left their country to settle in New York (Abigail Lazkok, Itziar Okariz, Segio Prego, Ixone Sádaba), in París (Juan Pérez Agirregoikoa), and in Berlin (Jon Mikel Euba) with the goal of finding new ways to intervene actively in the transmission of "tradition" or cultural heritage (what Homi Bhabha called "to reinstate and reinvent the past"),[36] from the perspective of a renewed dialogue between the international formulas and the shared symbols of a local imaginary.

---

34. "Remix," 30.

35. Ibid., 30–31.

36. Bhabha, *The Location of Culture*, 18.

These artists make extensive use of the new technologies that characterize the current globalized world—its electronic cultural capitalism, its mobility, its utopian promise of breaking down territorial borders. What matters to them is not their "national condition" but what creative strategies are provided by local situations, formally as well as discursively, to be used within the global cultural flows. Vis-a-vis the obvious impact of the Guggenheim Bilbao Museum on the art scene, they recognize its presence but are rather indifferent to its influence: "Up to now the relationship between the Basque artistic community and the Guggenheim institution has been characterized by mutual indifference and each one has functioned in a distinct universe."[37] These artists are regulars in the *Manifesta* exhibits (Euba and Aranberri in *Manifesta 4*, Frankfurt, 2002; Mendizabal in *Manifesta 5*, San Sebastian, 2004); in *Documenta* (Aramberri in *Documenta 12*, Kassel); and in biennials and other exhibits organized by Basque museum institutions. One of these last exhibits was organized by Bilbao's Museum of Fine Arts in 2002, entitled *Gaur, Hemen, Orain,* and later there was the *Chacun à son goût* exhibit in 2007 with which the Guggenheim Bilbao celebrated its tenth anniversary. These exhibits reflected on the ways in which the Basque artist is affected in the global era by the values of proximity and intimacy and on how to negotiate between the local imaginary and the cosmopolitan languages.

The exhibit *Gaur, Hemen, Orain* (Today, Here, Now) recognizes, in the words of Guadalupe Echevarría, the emergence of a new "artistic stage" in the Basque Country: "The history of art provides many artists in the Basque Country, groups and individuals, who have left an enduring mark in the collective imaginary and, at times, tangible signs of their art in its streets, walls, and institutions. But never until now has the network of exchanges and relations among artists been so intense and so branched out."[38] In this new "artistic stage," almost for the first time, Basque artists have socialized with the world by travelling to, settling in, and exhibiting in other countries; they place their works in a global stage in which the "here" and "now" are in New York, London, Paris, Amsterdam, and Madrid as much as in Bilbao, Donostia-San Sebastián, and Vitoria-Gasteiz. This implies that they have to present themselves in front of a public that exceeds their local territory and that they have to question the values of the Basque community by problematizing overused words such as "culture," "tradition," and "people," to the point that even the most familiar shows its uncanny strangeness.

The 2007 exhibit *Chacun à son goût* further demonstrated that Basque artists currently operate far from a nostalgic or traditionalist concept of "locality" while promoting subjective positions within the global visual culture. Its curator, Rosa Martínez, introduced the selected artists as immersed in a debate in between assimilation, rejection, and reconstruction of the historic weight of their specific "locus" as a precondition for creating their own language: "In the synchrony of this concrete present . . . the fundamental

---

37. Jaio, "'Chacun à son goût' at Guggenheim Bilbao."
38. Echevarría, *Gaur, Hemen, Orain.*

issues for a critical debate have to do with the strains and hybridities in between the local and the global, the feelings of individual and social belonging and exclusion, as well as the dialogue between the universalist will of the western artistic modernity and the questioning of its values from multiple postmodern and/or peripheral subjectivities."[39]

Three works that stood out in this exhibit were: Clemente Bernard's photographic series entitled *Crónicas del País Vasco* (Chronicles of the Basque Country, 1987–2001) and generated by the need to look at one's own surroundings "with clean eyes and an open heart"; the video *Irrintzi* (2007) by Itziar Okariz, who lives and works in New York, based on the performance of going through the museum shouting *irrintzis* (a traditional shrill cry used in the past as a way to communicate among valleys); and Ibon Aranberri, who presented at the Guggenheim one of his three installations known as "media trilogy," with which he was trying to activate communitarian situations. The title of Aranberri's installation was *Horizontes* (Horizons, 2001), a work that started from signs and symbols of the institutional and ideological representation of the modernist art movement repeated ad infinitum by the mass media. Previously, in *Gaur Egun (This Is CNN)* (2002) and *G-Pavilion* (2002), Aranberri had worked from the sculpture by Basterrechea that stands before the Basque Parliament, and Picasso's *Guernica*. In *Horizontes* he used the logos by Chillida for diverse purposes, including a reproduction of his *Comb of the Winds*.

Aranberri hung zigzagging rows of Chillida's designs, in 70 by 50 cm. formats, from the ceiling of the Guggenheim's third floor as if they were festive pennants, thus evoking the atmosphere of celebration and political protest that animated the annual festivities of the 1960s and 1970s. In Aranberri's words, "*Horizontes* recreates Chillida's graphic-scupltoric legacy from the perspective of the media. The icons of various cultural and political orders, recycled and altered, lose their original stroke, morphing themselves into more abstract and neutral signs. Set in groups and without any sequential order, they get mixed up and create a forest of graphic lines that can be recognized in the form of a stylistic continuity."[40] Once again symbols and memory obtain new meanings when connected to the context in which they are exhibited.

Postscript

Aranberri and Mendizabal represent the kinds of "artistic knowledge communities" that are operative in the current moment at the interface of local identities and global flows. Many of the allusions of Mendizabal's installations, photographs, videos, and sound pieces include references to his Basque environment—such as to the musical radical rock group Hertzainak (the Basque name for "police force"), the documentary

39. Martínez, "Chacun à son goût," 19. The twelve artists selected by R. Martínez were: Elssie Ansareo, Ibon Aranberri, Manu Arregui, Clemente Bernard, Abigail Lazkoz, Maider López, Asier Mendizabal, Itziar Okariz, Aitor Ortiz, Juan Pérez Agirregoikoa, Sergio Prego, and Ixone Sádaba.

40. "Ibon Aranberri," in *Chacun à son Goüt*, 30.

on the Basque conflict *Hors d'Etat* by Arthur MacCrag (1983), Basque folkloric music such as street bands, or the geography of the country including landscapes of green valleys and views of derelict neighborhoods in Bilbao. In Mendizabal's 16 mm, black-and-white, soundless film *No Time for Love* (2000), two overarching poles get condensed: the recourse to a formalist-constructivist pole and the need to overcome it through sociopolitical references. The title itself is borrowed from a song by Hertzainak in reference to the impossibility of making compatible such concepts as love and revolution, desire and militancy.

What is intriguing in Mendizabal is his capacity for camouflage, his constant references to the radical nationalist left, concretely to the 1960s with allusions to the Brigata Rossa, the Baader-Meinhof Gang, Jean-Luc Godard, Gilles Deleuze, and Félix Guattari, and punk-rock groups such as The Clash and Dead Kennedys. The references are superimposed on a peculiar mix of the vernacular, the popular, and the communitarian. He is interested in the notion of "multitude," rather than "people," much as Paolo Virno is. All of this explains Mendizabal's inclusion of other artists' works, such as the video *Zer eskatzen du herriak!?* (What are the people asking for?), in which a band of street musicians interprets a festive theme, the photographs of the series *Bilbao* (2002–03), documents regarding the construction of *txoznas* or marquees for popular festivities, or *Pabilioia* (2002–03), on people hanging around carnival floats.

After the failure of modernity's universalizing project, the artist seems to be suggesting that it is the moment to return to the vernacular, the popular, the youth cultures and subcultures, particularly the musical ones, mixing political signs with punk, rock, and hardcore. For artists of Aranberri and Mendizabal's generation the local constitutes a major source of inquiry combined with a new understanding of the relationship between history and social agency, between the field of emotions and that of politics, the grand scale factors and the vernacular factors—in short, their challenge is to create a knowledge community in which the global cultural flows and the specific local realities collide and crossbreed each other.

Bibliography

Angulo, Javier. *Agustín Ibarrola, ¿un pintor maldito? Arte vasco de postguerra 1950–1977*. San Sebastián: L. Haranburu, 1978.

Aranberri, Ibon. "Horizontes," in Miren Jaio, *'Chacun à son goût' at Guggenheim Bilbao*. Available at the Web site of Afterall Online (London), www.afterall.org/online/chacun..son.got.at.guggenheim.bilbao.

Basurto Ferro, Nieves, Paloma Rodríguez-Escudero Sánchez, and Jaione Velilla Iriondo. *El Bilbao que pudo ser: Proyecto para una ciudad, 1800-1940*. Bilbao: Diputación Foral de Bizkaia, 1999.

Bhabha, Homi. *The Location of Culture*. London: Routledge, 2004.

Catálogo Alea. Encuentros-72. Pamplona, 1972.

Díaz Cuyás, José and Carmen Pardo. "Pamplona era una fiesta: Tragicomedia del arte español." In *Desacuerdos 1, Sobre arte, políticas y esfera pública en el Estado español*. Barcelona: Macba, 2003.

Echevarría, Guadalupe. *Gaur, Hemen, Orain*. Bilbao: Museo de Bellas Artes de Bilbao, 2002.

Eraso, Miren. "Txomin Badiola. El otro, el mismo." In *Malas formas: Txomin Badiola, 1990–2002*. Barcelona: Museo de Arte Contemporáneo, 2002.

"Euskadi alla biennale." In *Catalogo Generale*. Venecia: La Biennale de Venecia, 1976.

"Euskadi alla Biennale de Venise: Une victoire pour les basques." *Enbata* 429 (November 1976).

Fischer, Jean, ed. *Global Visions. Towards a New Internationalism in the Visual Arts*. London: Kala Press, 1994.

García de la Torre, Bernardo I. and Francisco Javier García de la Torre. *Bilbao: Guía de arquitectura*. Bilbao: COAVN, 1993.

Guasch, Anna Maria. *Arte e ideología en el País Vasco: 1940–1980*. Madrid: Akal, 1985.

Guilbaut, Serge. *How New York Stole the Idea of Modern Art: Abstract Expressionism, Freedom, and the Cold War*. Chicago: University of Chicago Press, 1983.

Jaio, Miren. "'Chacun à son goût' at Guggenheim Bilbao," on Web site of Afterall Online (London), www.afterall.org/online/chacun.son.got.at.guggenheim.bilbao.

Lasterra, Crisanto de. *Darío de Regoyos: Poesía del color y de la luz*. Bilbao: T. G. Arte, 1966.

———. *En Paris con Paco Durrio*. Bilbao: T. G. Arte, 1966.

Llano Gorostiza, Manuel. *Pintura vasca*. Bilbao: Grijelmo, 1965.

Manifiesto del Grupo Gaur. San Sebastián: Galería Barandiarán, April–May 1966.

Manterola, Pedro. "El arte en Navarra (1960–1979). Algunos recuerdos en torno a una década crucial." In *Arte y artistas vascos de los años 60*. San Sebastián: Diputación Foral de Guipúzcoa, 1995.

Martínez, Rosa. "Chacun à son goût." In *Chacun à son goût*. Bilbao: Guggenheim Bilbao Museoa, 2007.

Martínez Gorriarán, Carlos. "El arte y los artistas vascos de 1966 a 1993." In *Nosotros los vascos. Arte V. Vanguardias en arte, arquitectura y cine*. San Sebastián: Lur, 1994.

Oteiza, Jorge. *Interpretación estética de la estatuaria megalítica Americana*. Madrid: Ediciones de Cultura Hispánica, 1952.

———. *Oteiza's Selected Writings*. Reno: Center for Basque Studies, University of Nevada, Reno, 2003.

———. *Quousque Tandem . . . ! Ensayo de interpretación estética del alma vasca.* San Sebastián: Colección Azkue, 1963.

Power, Kevin. "Continuando la conversación." In *Malas formas: Txomin Badiola, 1990–2002.* Barcelona: Museo de Arte Contemporáneo, 2002.

"Remix." In *Malas formas. Txomin Badiola, 1990–2002.* Barcelona: Museo de Arte Contemporáneo, 2002.

Serrano, Javier. "Arte alavés y arte vasco. Escuela de Arte Vasco." In *Arte y artistas vascos en los años 60.* San Sebastián: Diputación Foral de Guipúzcoa, 1995.

Viar, Javier. "The Guggenheim Bilbao, Partner in the Arts: A View from the Fine Arts Museum of Bilbao." In *Learning from the Bilbao Guggenheim*, edited by Anna María Guasch and Joseba Zulaika. Reno: Center for Basque Studies, University of Nevada, Reno, 2005.

Part 4

ONLINE

11

Online Knowledge Crowds and Communities

Caroline Haythornthwaite

Since the emergence of the Internet, there has been debate about the nature and quality of online communities, with concern that the lean, text-based media that support online discussion provide a pale alternative to the richness of face-to-face interaction. Nevertheless, social connection has found a way, with online participants developing norms and standards for online interaction that reflect and extend offline practices, with the Internet now supporting vibrant, geographically-distributed knowledge communities. The technologies have also evolved. While still heavily text-dependent, online interaction now extends to the use of images, audio, and video, and linear text has given way to more comprehensive and personal use of screen space for the presentation of self, knowledge, and work. Diversity in the ways and means of presentation of the individual are equally matched in presentations of the collective, and in ways of organizing collectives. Simple, e-mail-based listservs, and web sites modifiable only by designated webmasters, are giving way to collective, participatory methods and forums such as online discussion boards, blogging and commentaries, and collective definition and editing through wikis.

These means contribute to the emergence of *distributed knowledge communities* that coalesce around topics of interest. As Lee Sproull and Sara Kiesler predicted in 1991, communities have been arising around shared interests rather than shared geography or employer.[1] To be sure, such communities have existed for centuries among distributed scholars, from the letter-writing of the seventeenth century among members of the

---

1. Sproull and Kiesler, *Connections*.

science and philosophy community[2] to the pre-Internet invisible colleges of academia.[3] Yet, as in many areas affected by the Internet, quantitative change leads to qualitative difference.

Quantitative change in access has led to qualitative difference in social practices: in who we interact with, from where, how often, and for what purposes. Internet structures make it much easier to start a new platform for a knowledge initiative, be found online, and gain participation. Internet connectivity permits frequent engagement, from anywhere at any time, shrinking the turnaround cycle of communication and thereby creating a sense of connection and community with others. Further, as Internet connectivity becomes commonplace, it also becomes legitimated. Thus, an online interaction, information retrieval, knowledge exchange, or community is accepted as a legitimate venue, with the knowledge and interpersonal ties gained there considered as legitimate as any found offline.

Although this all seems self-evident, even as little as three years ago, the Modern Languages Association was just forming recommendations about online publication and tenure consideration.[4] Although rapidly adopted in physics, online publication of drafts, pre-prints, and peer-reviewed articles have been a hard sell over the last ten years in many knowledge communities. Surprisingly, two arms of the university have been at odds about these standards: while tenure committees have held to the standard of traditional peer-reviewed, print-based journals and books,[5] libraries have been facing the rising costs of journals, particularly in the sciences, and the unenviable position of buying back the work of the university's own employees. University libraries have thus become the leaders in creating online institutional repositories as long-term storage facilities for the work of their own university faculty, students, and staff (e.g., the Association of Research Libraries' Scholarly Publishing and Academic Resources Coalition–SPARC). As we will return to below, the whole notion of online academic publishing is tied to the larger issue of what motivates academics in their profession, and how an orientation to the ideals of open science merges with ideas of open access and the legal platform of creative commons licensing to provide the underpinning for change.

Strong adherence to existing practices may be one reason that online communities were greeted with such suspicion when they first arrived on the scene. The debate about whether online communities are "real" communities has centered on whether these initiatives can sustain the kind of multi-threaded, interpersonal ties that lead to commitment

---

2. Shapin, "Here and Everywhere"; Willinsky, "The Unacknowledged Convergence of Open Source, Open Access, and Open Science."

3. D. Crane, *Invisible Colleges.*

4. Inside Higher Ed, "Radical Change for Tenure"; American Historical Association, "Suggested Guidelines for Evaluating Digital Media Activities."

5. Estabrook, with B. Warner, "The Book as the Gold Standard for Tenure and Promotion in the Humanistic Disciplines."

to community goals and values.[6] While some still question the application of the term "community" to online venues, there has also been much work substantiating their place as suitable environments for collaboration, knowledge co-construction, and communities of practice.[7] This work has given insight into what it takes to build a community online, and many examples now provide evidence and models of sustained commitment to communal goals (e.g., Howard Rheingold's descriptions of the Well; Nancy Baym's description of soap opera fans; or Christina Preston's description of Mirandanet, a knowledge community for learning about educational technology, http://www.mirandanet.ac.uk/home.php[8]).

The debate about the legitimacy of online communities carries over to knowledge communities where the challenge is to the legitimacy of online knowledge activity. Not only is the knowledge that is posted online suspect, so too are people's commitments to collaborative activity. What kind of trust can be placed in an online relationship? What hold or expectation can we have that the individuals involved will contribute their part of the work, maintain civil discourse online, and not steal the ideas and sell them for profit? Indeed, many of these cautionary notes are necessary, but they are not unique to online venues. But our measures of trust and relationships have had to be transformed for the online world. Thus, it is of importance to consider what motivates and sustains commitment in online venues where the supposed social controls of traditional face-to-face interaction and community are seemingly absent.

Meantime, while we've been grappling with the question of how to gain strong, long-term, high overhead commitment to knowledge communities, another form of collaborative activity has arisen premised on exactly the opposite set of principles—weak, short-term, low overhead contributions to knowledge. *Crowdsourcing* has become a new form of knowledge activity, particularly notable in the creation of Wikipedia, but also prevalent in blogging and commentaries associated with blogs, and collaborative writing projects that encourage reader contributions.[9]

At one level, the promise of online knowledge crowds is the promise of participatory democracy,[10] newly minted as the promise of citizen journalism and participatory culture.[11] This view sees the Internet as providing a platform for "netizens" to voice

6. For a review, see Haythornthwaite, "Social Networks and Online Community."

7. For example, Wellman, Salaff et al., "Computer Networks as Social Networks"; Wellman, ed., *Networks in the Global Village*; Preece, *Online Communities*; Haythornthwaite, Kanfer et al., "Modeling Distributed Knowledge Processes in Next Generation Multidisciplinary Alliances"; Haythornthwaite, Kazmer et al., "Community Development among Distance Learners"; Wellman, "Physical Place and Cyber Place"; Orlikowski, "Knowing in Practice"; Renninger and Shumar, eds., *Building Virtual Communities*; Wellman and Haythornthwaite, eds., *The Internet in Everyday Life*; Haythornthwaite and Bregman, "Affordances of Persistent Conversation"; Preece and Maloney-Krichmar, eds., "Online Communities"; and Andrews and Haythornthwaite, *The Sage Handbook of E-learning Research*.

8. Rheingold, *The Virtual Community*; Baym *Tune In, Log On*; and Preston, "Braided Learning."

9. Howe, "The Rise of Crowdsourcing."

10. Hauben and Hauben, *Netizens*.

11. Jenkins et al., *Confronting the Challenges of Participatory Culture*.

their opinions and create an alternate structure for engaged citizenry[12]—an alternative, complement or watchdog to government or to the media depending on the particular discussion. In this case, crowdsourcing is the beginning of some larger change or action, with an idea of continued attention and action around the topic of interest. Although this crowd is not a community, it is assembled *in the interests of community*, that is, of society, and members of this crowd are likely to pay attention to the actions of other members of this crowd even while not interacting with them directly.

This crowd of concerned netizens sits somewhere between notions of a virtual community and the leaner, more independent, and often commercial perspectives on crowdsourcing. This kind of crowdsourcing looks to individuals as independent contributors to a collective enterprise, but not a collaborative one. Individuals contribute information to a computer program, but have little or no need to engage with fellow contributors. Whether for commercial or scientific purposes, the collective end result belongs to and is made use of by an *authority* outside the contributor pool (e.g., SETI@home, GalaxyZoo, AfricaMap, NASA clickworkers, 23andMe). This contrasts with a richer type of crowdsourcing that generates modifiable and updatable content, such as the encyclopedic knowledge brought together on Wikipedia, or the geographic information on OpenStreetMap, and puts these kinds of enterprises closer to the netizens than to the independent contributor crowds.

Borrowing the idea of rich and lean media first described by Richard Daft and R. H. Lengel in 1986, *richer media environments* contain more opportunities and means for discussion, evaluation, and correction than *leaner* media environments.[13] Daft and Lengel described rich media as better communication means for discussion, negotiation, and interaction. They are better means for dealing with problems of equivocality where even the questions to be asked must be negotiated. Lean media are best used for known data exchange, that is, for dealing with problems of uncertainty where the questions are clear but data must be found to answer them.[14] As will be discussed further below, richer collective environments, online or off, contain structures for internal self-governance that allow for negotiation and adjustment of goals, whereas lean environments support more authoritative control on information use and goals.

Knowledge crowds provide an interesting contrast to knowledge communities and one that helps tease out the motivations of contributors to each. Questions we can ask are: How are these different kinds of knowledge initiatives organized? What distinguishes a successful, free-wheeling, online, crowdsourced knowledge collective from the formal dynamics of a knowledge community? How does each support knowledge processes of learning, debate, data collection, analysis, dissemination, and evaluation? To explore

---

12. Hauben and Hauben, *Netizens*.

13. Daft and Lengel, "Organizational Information Requirements, Media Richness and Structural Design."

14. Perrow, *Organizational Analysis*; Daft and Lengel, "Organizational Information Requirements, Media Richness and Structural Design."

this, we turn to some examples of these forms of organizing, examining the features that distinguish them, and how these facilitate contribution and participation in these different knowledge systems.

Modes of Contribution and Participation

Crowds and communities may be considered at two ends of a spectrum of organizing. At one end are efforts that harness the knowledge and talents of many (relatively) anonymous individuals through online systems that aggregate discrete contributions into a whole. At the other end are communities, which meld, form, and define knowledge through the continued efforts of those among a set of known participants. Each has different patterns of contribution, participation, aggregation, and evaluation in their organizational structures.

Knowledge Communities

At the community end of the spectrum is a mode of contribution and participation I will describe as *heavyweight*.[15] "Weight" in this case is used to refer to the commitment an individual has to the collective enterprise, not to the significance of it. Commitment to a knowledge community entails the heavy burden of learning about the topic, equipment, methods, and norms of production around this domain of knowledge.[16] To this I would add the need to learn about the *networks of knowledge and expertise*.[17] This entails learning about the *knowledge structure*: How are knowledge concepts related? What references are most used? What standards exist for comparing references? It entails learning about the *actors* and their place in the knowledge network: Who is a novice, and who the expert? How are novices and experts tied? What relationships exist among actors? Who performs what roles: instructor, researcher, writer, editor, gatekeeper, guru? And it entails learning about *network practices* around these networks, for example, how are relationships to others signaled (university affiliations, association memberships, review committee memberships) and to others' ideas signaled (e.g., citations, weblinks, RSS feeds)? How are contributions evaluated and contributors rewarded for their work?

A prime example of a heavyweight knowledge community is academia. It should not be a surprise given the kinds of overhead listed above that it takes so long to become a member of an academic community (earning a doctorate and academic tenure), and also why such a community can be expected to cling to its existing recognition and reward practices (peer review, tenure review, book and print productions). As noted above, it has been a strain for tenure committees to adopt new online publication practices, and,

---

15. Haythornthwaite, "Crowds and Communities."

16. Latour, *Science in Action*; Knorr-Cetina, *Epistemic Cultures*; and Hjørland and Albrechtsen, "Toward a New Horizon in Information Science."

17. Haythornthwaite, "Articulating Divides in Distributed Knowledge Practice."

at present, that change accepts only the change in medium rather than any substantive change in practice. The peer-reviewed online journal is now (generally) accepted, but the place of a website, blog, or wiki is undetermined. How then is a tenure committee to deal with an island in Second Life, software of any kind (outside engineering and computer science), collaborative publishing ventures (e.g., a crowdsourced, wiki-produced paper), or products with no fixed state (an ongoing wiki site)?

So, why do academics place their work online? What motivates the individual to distribute their ideas freely and openly, and to create platforms for others to do the same (e.g., the Public Knowledge Project, http://pkp.sfu.ca/)? What is the relationship between individual practices in dissemination of personal work products and their knowledge community?

I suggest that the concept of co-orientation to a community's values provides a strong and enduring base for community behavior. Individuals spend time, energy, and personal commitment to the working of a community. Hence it is not surprising that it endures beyond day-to-day activity. During times of change, we may get a rare insight into the enduring principles that underpin a community.

Academic response to the Internet in relation to academic publishing seems to be just such an opportunity. For the academic case, I suggest the answer to the questions above can be found in the "academic calculus" performed by each academic as they consider where, how, and when to publish. One part of the calculus equation is the extent to which the individual adheres to principles of *open science and open access*—that is, their personal stance on whether information should be free. "Free" is interpreted both in Richard Stallman's open source sense of "free as in free speech," that is, free to use, reuse, modify, and transfer, and in the academic, education, and library sense of "free as in free beer," that is, available easily, universally, and without cost to readers. John Willinsky articulates well how the confluence of open source, open access, and open science sets the stage for the use of the Internet as an open platform for publishing.[18] Relevant to our discussion of communities, we owe another debt to seventeenth-century science for our orientations to open source. In a recent article, Steve Shapin describes how the habit of the seventeenth-century scientist was to work with a community of interest rather than a set of coworkers.[19] This we see living on in contemporary academic practices—cross-university disciplinary associations and participation in peer review—and attitudes—the loyalty, orientation, and *co-orientation* to providing open access to work products, whether these are ideas, theories, experimental results, software, data, or courses, and whether wrapped in book covers or web frames.

Until very recently, publishing companies and print media were that access point. They took on the burden of collecting, editing, printing, promoting, and disseminating

---

18. Willinsky, "The Unacknowledged Convergence of Open Source, Open Access, and Open Science"; See also Willinsky, "The Access Principle and Toward the Design of an Open Monograph Press."

19. Shapin, "The Scientist in 2008."

academic texts. But somewhere recently they took a wrong turn. First, journals became more expensive. Then, when journals went online, pricing schemes changed for academic libraries from one-time payment for a permanent resource to yearly payments for ephemeral resources (as a response to the ephemeral part, see the LOCKSS initiative (Lots of Copies Keep Stuff Safe, http://www.lockss.org/lockss/home). To protect budgets, libraries looked to cut subscriptions. However, to protect their stakeholders, they were obliged to keep them. This dilemma created a movement among librarians to make their stakeholders aware of the costs of publishing in particular journals, and initiated the developing practice of maintaining institutional repositories (see the SPARC site, http://www.arl.org/sparc/about/index.shtml, and in particular the copyright addendum form for amending authors' rights in keeping with principles of open access, http://www.arl.org/sparc/author/addendum.shtml). Now academics pause in their calculus to consider what a publication choice costs their institution, and the copyright arrangement they are signing.

Another factor in the equation is the competition from all those newbies and nonacademics who can create websites, journals, and diaries online at the drop of a hat, while academics wait through the cycle of peer review and publication (online or off). Why not just post it online in the first place and be done with it? The development of the creative commons licensing scheme has been highly important for overcoming a key reason not to post in this way, that is, that someone would steal the idea.[20] The creative commons licensing provides a way to say just how free you want your newly posted online text to be, and is a highly important development that promotes online dissemination of works.

All this online posting has actually created another change in the publishing landscape, and thus in the academic landscape. With peer review, only those who pass review can be published, hence publication alone indicates acceptance into the community and recognition by the community. But, when anyone can post to the web, the scales tip to make *retrieval* the important dimension. Information does not so much want to be free as it wants to be found, cited, linked to, referenced, and indexed. And thus, the online venues again become more valuable in an academic calculus as papers and information reach others earlier and more easily when online, are retrievable by search engines, and gain visible popularity through use.

The long investment in joining a community—including, for academics, an understanding of the nuances of publishing calculus—also highlights the amount of work that goes into defining the boundaries and practices of knowledge domains, and thus how knowledge communities face yet another contemporary challenge, that of multi- and interdisciplinary work, and the merging and combining of knowledge across disciplines.[21] Treating this topic in depth is beyond the scope of this chapter, but it is interesting to observe that while "the world is [becoming] flat," it is also becoming closer—we have

20. Lessig, *Code* and *Code: Version 2.0.*

21. Haythornthwaite, "Articulating Divides in Distributed Knowledge Practice"; Haythornthwaite, Lunsford et al., "Challenges for Research and Practice in Distributed, Interdisciplinary, Collaboration."

more frequent contact, interaction, and engagement with different places, cultures, and disciplines. And frequency affects attention. It drives our "attention structures," that is, that which we observe, value, and count as outcomes, and it builds stronger ties between people, places, and discipline.[22]

In academic communities, we are not only more tied to other disciplines directly in interdisciplinary endeavors, particularly with computing—and even the humanities are joining up with new cyber-infrastructure initiatives directly related to issues of "what to do with a million books"[23]—we are also tied by exposure to the practices of other disciplines. When physicists easily accept publication of preprints and online papers and computer scientists consider the conference paper as the finished product, social science researchers take notice and ask, Why do we have to keep our papers offline, unpublished, uncirculated before, during, and after publication in traditional venues? And humanities scholars notice that when books cannot get published within the timeframe for getting tenure at a university, other forms of evaluation must step in, such as journal articles. How long will it be before the practice of accepting journal articles turns to the practice of accepting online publishing? Probably not long. It is not that online venues do not already exist if individuals chose to use them. What is at issue in a *community* is not that other forms of expression and products are not possible, but that only *certain* choices among them are deemed *acceptable*.

Knowledge Crowds

At the other end of the spectrum of contribution and participation is a mode I will refer to as *lightweight*. This is best demonstrated in the restricted contributory behavior associated with lean crowdsourcing projects. These forums exist to draw in contributions, responses, and comments, but are configured by site owners to limit the types of input and the visibility of individual contributors and contributions. At their leanest, they ask for a contributor's action, but not their opinions—for example, as in clicking on surveys, identifying objects (NASA clickworkers), verifying spellings (Distributed Proofreaders, http://www.pgdp.net/c/)—and return only quantitative measures of participation or aggregate summaries of responses. In these highly lean forms, individuals interact with the computer, not with each other, and the site owners retain authority and control over the acceptance or rejection of submissions, and what is done with them.

But crowdsourcing also covers a spectrum from impersonal lean data collection environments to ones that begin to take on the look and feel of communities. Crowdsourcing ranges from applications that appeal for isolated, minimal, discrete, objective, and often anonymous contributions to versions that include more personal and social presence. Crowdsourced initiatives include opportunities to contribute in many forms, from the

---

22. Scott, *Organizations*; Goldhaber, "The Attention Economy and the Net"; Davenport and Beck, *The Attention Economy*; and Monge and Contractor, *Theories of Communication Networks*.

23. G. Crane, "What Do You Do with a Million Books?"

lean clickworkers contribution to the richness of Wikipedia. Through these initiatives, contributors can:

- Provide access to idle computer cycles (BOINC)

- Identify objects (NASA clickworkers; GalaxyZoo)

- Add annotations, and tags to others' content (The Commons on Flickr, http://www.flickr.com/commons, including photos from the Library of Congress[24]; Steve: the Museum Social Tagging Project, http://steve.museum/index.php)

- Contribute commentary for the owner of the site or poster of material (books put online for comment before publication; blog commentaries)

- Contribute corrections to others' content (e.g., in Wikipedia; open source projects)

- Provide original data for inclusion in online applications (e.g., OpenStreetMap; Google Earth)

- Provide original comments, reviews of online content that address the owner/original poster and other participants (e.g., blog communities)

- Contribute original designs that are voted on for production by visitors to the site (t-shirts, http://www.threadless.com/submit; shoes, http://ryzwear.com/; comics, http://zudacomics.com/)[25]

- Contribute original contributions for commentary and/or amendment by other visitors to the site (new entries in Wikipedia; original code for Open Source initiatives)

---

24. Raymond, "My Friend Flickr."

25. A more commercial crowdsourcing of design entails competitions with the company deciding on the winning entry. This is indeed a crowdsourcing way of acquiring input, but one that follows long-standing ideas of open competitions. For example, see the call for redesign of everyday objects by *Dwell* magazine (accessed March 26, 2009, from http://www.dwell.com/contests/innovate-it.html). What at first looks like the crowdsourcing initiative—a call to anyone with access to the Internet to submit a design—reveals itself as a traditional sort of corporate competition. Note first that the review of the entries is not crowdsourced as in the examples given above: "Entries will be judged by a panel of *Dwell* editors, who will select what they believe to be the three most intriguing ideas for objects needing re-innovation." Moreover, note that the ownership of the ideas submitted follows a traditional commercial model—ownership by the company: "By submitting an entry, you grant to Sponsors and their respective successors and assigns an unlimited, worldwide, perpetual license to publish, display, use, exploit, edit the text, adapt, modify, copy, disseminate, post, or dispose of the design, text and other submitted materials online, in print, film, television, or in any other media for editorial, advertising, promotional or other purposes without compensation or notification of any kind to you, except as prohibited by law." It would be unfortunate if these kinds of "old models now posted to the web" were held up as great examples of Web 2.0 practice. They are not. They have missed the opportunity to engage collaboratively with their participants and readers. They have missed the boat on creative commons licensing. For a site and organization that "gets" the idea of crowdsourcing from a Web 2.0 perspective, see http://www.burdastyle.com. On this "open sewing site," patterns have been made available online, copyright-free. For their take on "open source sewing" see http://www.burdastyle.com/help/index/66#entry-2. From the site: "You've arrived to your kind of 'candy' store. All patterns, accompanied by instructions and related creations are copyright-free and easy to download. If you have a pattern you are proud of, please share." (http://www.burdastyle.com/patterns). And, "Our pattern catalogue is growing larger by the month. BurdaStyle and our members are diligently adding to the variety of trends, basics and accessories available on our site, all of which are open source (copyright-free)." (http://www.burdastyle.com/help/index/60#entry-1, accessed March 25, 2009)

• Acknowledge and interact with others about the site, topic of interest, or collective of interest (e.g., on the Talk pages of a wiki).

At their richest, crowdsourced knowledge communities build on distributed, individually held knowledge and act as a portal through which distributed knowledge can be accumulated into a whole. As well as the well-known example of Wikipedia, there are sites for volunteered geographic information (VGI), where individuals contribute mapping information, corrections, and images to such sites as OpenStreetMap,[26] and the collaborative world building that takes place in Second Life. Contributors are distinguished by taking charge of different parts of a knowledge, geographical, or virtual world. Specialized or local knowledge that otherwise would be very difficult for an individual or an organization to gather is brought together in these crowdsourced initiatives.

Contrasting Crowds and Communities

By contrast with virtual communities, crowdsourcing enterprises are distinguished by low barriers to entry, low need for commitment, and an appeal to everyone to contribute what they can. For example, the Distributed Proofreaders site specifically asks for a little at a time:

> Remember that there is no commitment expected on this site beyond the understanding that you do your best. Proofread as often or as seldom as you like, and as many or as few pages as you like. We encourage people to do "a page a day," but it's entirely up to you! We hope you will join us in our mission of "preserving the literary history of the world in a freely available form for everyone to use.[27]

And Wikipedia takes a moment to assure the nervous contributor:

> Be bold in updating articles and do not worry about making mistakes. Your efforts do not need to be perfect; prior versions are saved, so no damage is irreparable.[28]

In online communities, members often participate in ways that are similar to those for crowdsourcing, that is, editing, annotating, adding commentary, entering content, uploading pictures, and so on. The difference is that *in communities*, individuals contribute with *full attention to the other members of the community*, with full expectation of timely entry and response, commitment to a contribution that reflects on their status in the community, and a continued expectation of interaction with community members. They add to

---

26. Goodchild, "Citizens as Sensors," 211–21; Haklay and Weber, "Open Street Map," 12–18; and Budhathoki, Bruce, and Nedovic-Budic, "Reconceptualizing the Role of the User of Spatial Data Infrastructure," 149–60.

27. Distributed Proofreaders, last updated September 30, 2010, http://www.pgdp.net/c/.

28. "Wikipedia: 5 pillars," Wikipedia, last updated October 3, 2010, http://en.wikipedia.org/wiki/wikipedia:5P.

and engage in discussion that concerns the community, covering both the topic and the development and adherence to internal group practices.[29]

Overall, the difference between a crowd and a community is not in what the collective does, but in how—or indeed, whether—its participants need to pay attention to each other in order for the enterprise to succeed. *Knowledge creating communities* need to be designed to accommodate participants' attention to each other, since they are working through ideas, plans, and outcomes in consultation and debate with others; *knowledge aggregating sites* do not need individuals to engage directly with each other, but do need adherence to site norms and practices, for example, doing their best to contribute in a responsible and trustworthy way. Co-orientation becomes important again, and perhaps more important for knowledge crowds. Where there is no interpersonal element as a reason for participation and as a sanction on nonconformity, commitment to the overall goal of the site may be the only motivator for contribution and the only control on appropriate contribution. Thus, an interest in astronomy, design, or software development, or a commitment to open source, open science, or open access, may be key for understanding how and why crowds participate in lean initiatives.

Discussion lists, collaborative learning, and many game-oriented settings exemplify knowledge-creating communities, whether oriented to academic or serious leisure pursuits (such as geo-caching, www.geocaching.com/; music, www.last.fm[30]). Sites that accumulate contributions from many individuals or many individual points exemplify the knowledge aggregators, such as the clicks on pictures of Mars craters (NASA clickworkers), pictures and other information on local places (Open Street Map, Google Earth), and individuals' genomic information (23andMe[31]). The collective becomes a knowledge resource by its accumulated, crowdsourced content. Note again how impersonal crowd behavior is, to the point where contribution can be reduced to actions (clicks, photos, GIS coordinates), not personalities. There are no network stars in a crowd, and indeed, the emergence and recognition of a star signifies a move to a community orientation. For example, Wikipedia contains an acknowledgement of the substantial contributions of Simon Pulsifer.[32] The posting of this as an entry on a site that otherwise does not attribute contributions to individuals (although this may be discoverable via the talk pages, it is not a feature of the encyclopedia entries), marks a change from topic goals to personalities, and thus to the human element in the production.

While these examples refer to contribution of content, another layer of knowledge can also be crowdsourced—that of critique. An example of this is the accumulation of commentaries posted on Digg that provide thumbs-up or thumbs-down rating of sites

---

29. Poole and DeSanctis, "Understanding the Use of Group Decision Support Systems"; DeSanctis and Scott and Poole, "Capturing the Complexity in Advanced Technology Use," 121–47.

30. Baym and Ledbetter, "Tunes That Bind?"

31. Scola, "Crowdsourcing the Genome."

32. "Simon Pulsifer," Wikipedia, last updated May 6, 2010, http://en.wikipedia.org/wiki/Simon_Pulsifer.

identified as of interest by other Digg members.[33] Also, in the design examples given above, each case uses ratings from site visitors to evaluate entries for production. Open online publishing is "critiqued" by the crowd as Google pagerank or YouTube ratings rise, or as academic articles appear on lists such as CitesULike. Contrast this with academic peer review—an invitation only, private, and anonymous practice. An exception is—or was—Stevan Harnad's open access journal *Psycholoquy,* which published articles with open peer commentary; however, publication of the journal is currently suspended.

In considering internal focus (and design for internal focus) as a distinguishing factor between crowd and community collectives, it is relevant to note that it is often hard to keep a crowd from pushing to become a community, and sometimes vice versa. For example, even the simplest count of computer cycles donated to a distributed computing effort have been used to generate competition across individuals, teams, and regions of participants. Aggregator sites give totals across various distributed computing applications, providing a visible sign that has been adopted by contributors to view and engage with the contributions of others. As described on the DC-Vault site:

> The DC [Distributed Computing] Vault is the place to compare your team's performance against others, the place to look out for when you plan your next taunting fest, the place you can refer others to and brag about how devilishly high ranked your team is . . . or not.[34]

Similarly, while it appears that membership in online communities sets individuals free from the constraints of synchronous, co-located interaction, opening the door for full participation from anywhere, anytime, such participation is often illusory. Individuals can participate in any of these venues in a lightweight manner, dropping in and out as lurkers, peripheral contributors, or intermittent participants. With the increase in types of online knowledge communities, this kind of partial, rotating commitment may be commonplace as a means of managing multiple memberships. Even without rotation, the communities themselves depend on a steady flow of new voices to maintain and promote community knowledge. Thus, existing virtual communities already manage lightweight contributors who are coming to know the topic and to join the community.

Summary

In this chapter I have walked through some key distinguishing features of online crowds and communities, describing what differentiates these forms of organization in a knowledge context, with particular attention to the impact on academic knowledge communities. My investigation of the differentiating factors of crowds and communities is a work in progress, developing as more sites and more kinds of online collectives appear and

---

33. Halavais, "Do Dugg Diggers Digg Diligently?"

34. Distributed Computing, http://www.dc-vault.com.

are identified. The current chapter builds on my recent presentations and work articulating the dimensions of collaborative activity along which lightweight, crowdsourced and heavyweight, community-based collectives vary.[35] Although it has not been possible within the scope of this chapter to indicate all the background, this work also builds on the significant literature about the nature of community both online and off, social networks, epistemic communities, distributed knowledge, group processes, collaboration and collaborative learning, adult and expert learning, online learning, computer-mediated communication, and the Internet.

While two forms of online knowledge organization—crowds and communities—have been highlighted in this discussion, the goal has been to articulate the underlying dimensions that define the continuum from crowds to communities rather than to classify any particular venture as one or the other. While individuals may consider themselves to be a strong community member of a knowledge crowd, or just a lurker in a virtual community, what differentiates these collectives is not an individual's actions or perceptions, but rather the extent to which either environment provides the means for a more or less engaged knowledge collective. To summarize, three dimensions of activity emerge from this work that distinguish knowledge crowds and communities:

- *Contribution type, granularity, and authentication.* At the leanest end of the lightweight collectives, the contribution is straightforward, with easy to learn rules, coordinated by pooled interdependence of similar contributions; for heavyweight collectives, greater learning is required for contribution, with contributions evaluated by other participants in a peer-review process, and the overall collective coordinated through reciprocal interdependence.

- *Individual to group focus.* Lightweight collectives are individually oriented, often anonymous, with no tie needed between contributors. Heavyweight collectives require contributors to pay attention to others for coordination, collaboration, and evaluation.

- *Recognition, reputation, and reward.* The previous two dimensions provide the framework for understanding individual motivation, reputation, and reward systems, and thus also for design to support the aims of light and heavyweight initiatives. The leanest of lightweight collectives can assess contributions only through quantitative measures of contributions and statistical aggregation. Heavyweight collectives require qualitative judgments of contributions, contributors, and internal practices, increasing the attention and adherence to internal standards.

These dimensions help distinguish among current forms of organizing, both in terms of site and project design, and of collective knowledge processes. Attention to these dimensions may help in the design of new knowledge projects, as well as in the appropriate matching of incentives to organizational form.

---

35. Haythornthwaite, "Crowds and Communities."

Conclusion

This chapter has described in brief some basic differences in structures and individual motivations for engaging in knowledge crowds and communities. The Internet has opened up a vast new space for the formation of knowledge collectives. To date, the emphasis has been on online communities, virtual associations of like-minded individuals with common interests in a knowledge domain. However, recent successful ventures, from NASA's clickworkers to Wikipedia, have shown important new ways of harnessing the knowledge of individuals into a crowdsourced whole. As we look to future knowledge collectives, both lean, lightweight collectives and richly nuanced, heavyweight communities will offer new and different means and options for knowledge aggregation, evaluation, collaboration, and dissemination.

Acknowledgments

Earlier versions of ideas about the organization of crowd and community-based enterprises were presented at the Annual Conference for Print, Internet and Community, Tel Aviv, Israel, June 2006; the Southern Illinois-Edwardsville University Library and Information Services Spring Symposium, Edwardsville, IL, April 2008; and at the Hawaii International Conference on System Sciences, January 2009.

Bibliography

American Historical Association. "Suggested Guidelines for Evaluating Digital Media Activities in Tenure, Review, and Promotion—An AAHC Document." American Historical Association, 2001. Accessed March 24, 2009. http:www.historians.org/perspectives/issues/2001/0110/0110pro1.cfm.

Andrews, Richard and Caroline Haythornthwaite. *The Sage Handbook of E-learning Research*. London: Sage, 2007.

Baym, Nancy. *Tune In, Log On: Soaps, Fandom and Online Community*. Thousand Oaks, CA: Sage, 2000.

Baym, Nancy and Andrew Ledbetter. "Tunes That Bind? Predicting Friendship Strength in a Music-Based Social Network." *Information, Communication and Society* 12, no. 3 (2009): 408–27.

Budhathoki, N. R., B. C. Bruce, and Z. Nedovic-Budic. "Reconceptualizing the Role of the User of Spatial Data Infrastructure." *GeoJournal* 72, no. 3–4 (2008): 149–60.

Crane, Diana. *Invisible Colleges: Diffusion of Knowledge in Scientific Communities*. Chicago: University of Chicago Press, 1972.

Crane, Gregory. "What Do You Do with a Million Books?" *D-Lib Magazine* 12, no. 3 (2006). www.dlib.org/dlib/march06/crane/03crane.html.

Daft, Richard L. and R. H. Lengel. "Organizational Information Requirements, Media Richness and Structural Design." *Management Science* 32, no. 5 (1986): 554–71.

Davenport, Thomas H. and John C. Beck. *The Attention Economy: Understanding the New Currency of Business*. Boston: Harvard Business School Press, 2001.

DeSanctis, G. and M. S. Poole. "Capturing the Complexity in Advanced Technology Use: Adaptive Structuration Theory." *Organization Science* 5, no. 2 (1994): 121–47.

Estabrook, Leigh and Bijan Warner. "The Book as the Gold Standard for Tenure and Promotion in the Humanistic Disciplines." Committee for Institutional Cooperation, IL, 2003. Accessed March 24, 2009. http://www.cic.net/Libraries/Reports/ScholarlyCommunicationsSummitReport_Dec03.sflb.

Goldhaber, Michael H. "The Attention Economy and the Net." *First Monday* 2, no. 4 (1997). http://firstmonday.org/htbin/cgiwrap/bin/ojs/index.php/fm/article/view/519/440.

Goodchild, M. F. "Citizens as Sensors: the World of Volunteered Geography." *GeoJournal* 69 (2007): 211–21.

Haklay, M. and P. Weber. "Open Street Map: User-Generated Street Maps." *IEEE Pervasive Computing* 7, no. 4 (2008): 12–18.

Halavais, A. "Do Dugg Diggers Digg Diligently? Feedback as Motivation in Collaborative Moderation Systems." *Information, Communication and Society* 12, no. 3 (2009): 444–59.

Hauben, Michael and Ronda Hauben. *Netizens: On the History and Impact of Usenet and the Internet*. Los Alamitos, CA: IEEE Computer Society, 1997.

Haythornthwaite, Caroline. "Articulating Divides in Distributed Knowledge Practice." *Information, Communication & Society* 9, no. 6 (2006): 761–80.

———. "Crowds and Communities: Light and Heavyweight Models of Peer Production." Chapter in an Edited Book. Los Alamitos, CA: IEEE Computer Society, 2009. http://www.ideals.uiuc.edu/ handle/2142/9457.

———. "Social Networks and Online Community." In *Oxford Handbook of Internet Psychology*, edited by Adam Joinson, Katelyn McKenna, Ulf Reips, and Tom Postmes. Oxford, UK: Oxford University Press, 2007.

Haythornthwaite, Caroline and Alvan Bregman. "Affordances of Persistent Conversation: Promoting Communities that Work." In *Learning, Culture and Community in Online Education: Research and Practice*, edited by Caroline Haythornthwaite and Michelle M. Kazmer. New York: Peter Lang, 2004.

Haythornthwaite, Caroline, Michelle M. Kazmer, Jennifer Robins, and Susan Shoemaker. "Community Development among Distance Learners: Temporal and Technological Dimensions." *Journal of Computer-Mediated Communication* 6, no. 1 (2000). http://jcmc.indiana.edu/vol6/issue1/haythornthwaite.html.

Haythornthwaite, Caroline, K. J. Lunsford, G. C. Bowker, and B. Bruce. "Challenges for Research and Practice in Distributed, Interdisciplinary, Collaboration." In *New Infrastructures for Knowledge Production: Understanding E-Science,* edited by Christine Hine. Hershey, PA: Idea Group, 2006.

Hjørland, Birger and Hanne Albrechtsen. "Toward a New Horizon in Information Science: Domain Analysis." *Journal of the American Society for Information Science* 46, no. 6, (1995): 400–25.

Howe, Jeff. "The Rise of Crowdsourcing." *Wired* 14.06 (June 2006). http://www.wired.com/wired/archive/14.06/crowds.html.

Inside Higher Ed. "Radical Change for Tenure." (Published December 30, 2005). http://www.insidehighered.com/news/2005/12/30/tenure.

Jenkins, H., K. Clinton, R. Purushotma, A. J. Robinson, and M. Weigel. "*Confronting the Challenges of Participatory Culture: Media Education for the 21st Century.*" Chicago, IL: MacArthur Foundation Reports on Digital Media and Learning, 2006.

Kanfer, Alaina, Caroline Haythornthwaite, Bertram C. Bruce, Geoffrey Bowker, N. Burbules, J. Porac, and James Wade. "Modeling Distributed Knowledge Processes in Next Generation Multidisciplinary Alliances." *Information Systems Frontiers* 2, no. 3/4 (2000): 317–31.

Knorr-Cetina, Karin. *Epistemic Cultures: How the Sciences Make Knowledge.* Cambridge, MA: Harvard University Press, 1999.

Latour, Bruno. *Science in Action: How to Follow Scientists and Engineers Through Society.* Philadelphia, PA: Open University Press, 1987.

Lessig, Lawrence. *Code: and Other Laws of Cyberspace.* New York: Basic Books, 1999.

———. *Code: Version 2.0.* New York: Basic Books, 2006.

Monge, Peter R. and Noshir S. Contractor. *Theories of Communication Networks.* Oxford, UK: Oxford University Press, 2003.

Orlikowski, Wanda J. "Knowing in Practice: Enacting a Collective Capability in Distributed Organizing." *Organization Science,* 13, no. 3 (2002): 249–73.

Perrow, Charles. *Organizational Analysis: A Sociological View.* Monterey, CA: Wadsworth, 1970.

Poole, M. S. and G. DeSanctis. "Understanding the Use of Group Decision Support Systems: The Theory of Adaptive Structuration." In *Organizations and Communication Technology,* edited by Janet Fulk and Charles W. Steinfield. Newbury Park, CA: Sage, 1990.

Preece, Jenny. *Online Communities: Designing Usability, Supporting Sociability.* New York: John Wiley & Sons, 2000.

Preece, Jenny and Diane Maloney-Krichmar, eds. "Online Communities: Design, Theory, and Practice." (Articles 1–10) *Journal of Computer-Mediated Communication* 10, no. 4 (2005). http://jcmc.indiana.edu/vol10/issue4/.

Preston, C. J. "Braided Learning: An Emerging Process Observed in E-communities of Practice." *International Journal of Web Based Communities* 4, no. 2 (2008): 220–43.

Raymond, Matt. "My Friend Flickr: A Match Made in Photo Heaven." *Library of Congress Blog.* Posted January 16, 2008. http://www.loc.gov/blog/?p=233.

Renninger, K. Ann and Wesley Shumar, eds. *Building Virtual Communities: Learning and Change in Cyberspace.* Cambridge, UK and New York: Cambridge University Press, 2002.

Rheingold, Howard. *The Virtual Community: Homesteading on the Electronic Frontier.* Rev. ed. Cambridge, MA: MIT Press, 2000.

Scola, Nancy. "Crowdsourcing the Genome." *Seed.* February 27, 2009. http://seedmagazine.com/content/article/crowdsourcing_the_genome.

Scott, W. Richard. *Organizations: Rational, Natural, and Open Systems.* Toronto: Prentice-Hall, 1992.

Shapin, Steven. "Here and Everywhere: Sociology of Scientific Knowledge." *Annual Review of Sociology* 21 (1995): 289–321.

———. "The Scientist in 2008." *Seed.* November 20, 2008. http://seedmagazine.com/stateofscience/sos_feature_shapin_p1.html.

Sproull, Lee and Sara Kiesler. *Connections: New Ways of Working in the Networked Organization.* Cambridge, MA: MIT Press, 1991.

Wellman, Barry. "Physical Place and Cyber Place: The Rise of Personal Networking." *International Journal of Urban and Regional Planning* 25, no. 2 (2001): 227–252.

Wellman, Barry, ed. *Networks in the Global Village.* Boulder, CO: Westview Press, 1999.

Wellman, Barry and Caroline Haythornthwaite, eds. *The Internet in Everyday Life.* Oxford, UK: Blackwell Publishers, 2002.

Wellman, Barry, Janet Salaff, D. Dimitrova, L. Garton, M. Gulia, and Caroline Haythornthwaite. "Computer Networks as Social Networks: Collaborative Work, Telework, and Virtual Community." *Annual Review of Sociology* 22 (1996): 213–38.

Willinsky, John. *The Access Principle: The Case for Open Access to Research and Scholarship.* Cambridge, MA: MIT Press, 2006.

———. "The Unacknowledged Convergence of Open Source, Open Access, and Open Science." *First Monday* 10, no. 8 (Aug. 2005). http://firstmonday.org/htbin/cgiwrap/bin/ojs/index.php/fm/article/view/1265/1185.

———. "Toward the Design of an Open Monograph Press." *The Journal of Electronic Publishing* 12, no. 1 (2009). doi: 10.3998/3336451.0012.103.

12

The Online Social Networks of the Basque Diaspora: Fast Forwarded, 2005–2009

Pedro J. Oiarzabal

Networks: International Migration, Diaspora, and the Internet

The framework of this chapter[1] lies in the understanding of international migration as a network; the formation and maintenance of diasporas as transnational networks of migrants, their descendants, and their communities; and the fact that the Internet is a global network of individuals and computers or electronic nodes that tend to reinforce, facilitate, and cultivate social networks that individuals and groups may maintain in the offline world.[2] Networks are traditionally described as a set of actors or nodes connected by a particular type of relationship.[3]

A growing body of literature analyzes the causes of contemporary international migration as well as its persistence over space and time by exploring inter-personal decision-making processes and the social relations and networks that influence migrants.[4]

---

1. The author would like to thank Dr. Caroline Haythornthwaite of the University of Illinois, Urbana-Champaign (US), and Dr. Andoni Alonso of the University of Extremadura, Cáceres (Spain), for reviewing previous drafts of this chapter.

2. See Boase et al., "The Strength of Internet Ties."

3. See for example, Wellman and Berkowitz, eds., *Social Structures*; Garton, Haythornthwaite, and Wellman, "Studying Online Social Networks"; and Haythornthwaite, "Social Networks and Online Community."

4. See for example, M. Boyd, "Family and Personal Networks in International Migration"; Brettel, "Theorizing Migration in Anthropology"; Kearney, "From the Invisible Hand to Visible Feet"; Portes, "Economic Sociology and the Sociology of Immigration"; and Vertovec and Cohen, "Introduction," *Migration and Transnationalism*.

Those authors understand migration as a multi-directional, dynamic movement; that is, a network-building system facilitated to a great extent by information and communication technologies (ICTs). Monica Boyd states, "Studying networks, particularly those linked to family and households, permits understanding migration as a social product—not as the sole result of individual decisions made by individual actors, not as the sole result of economic or political parameters, but rather as an outcome of all these factors in interaction."[5] Charles Tilly strongly asserts that it is not people who migrate, but networks, while Barry Wellman argues that "the world is composed of networks, not groups."[6]

ICTs facilitate the flow of people between regions, countries, and continents as well as diaspora formation, growth, and maintenance. They allow migrants to create and maintain social migration networks.[7] In particular, the personal computer and access to the Internet have become routine resources among migrants and their descendants to develop, maintain, and recreate those networks.[8]

In an early study, Andoni Alonso and myself defined digital diasporas as "the distinct online networks that diasporic people use to re-create identities, share opportunities, spread their culture, influence homeland and host-land policy, or create debate about common-interest issues by means of electronic devices."[9] In this regard, diasporas and their online identities constitute digital social networks. As a case-study of migrant communities and their descendants and the use of ICTs, the Basque diaspora is a transnational network of emigrant communities comparable to nodes such as individuals, groups, or organizations in a social network connected by a set of common affiliations, interests, and affinities, and not by space and time.[10] As of 2005, the majority of Basque diaspora webmasters throughout the world argue that the Internet has the potential to help maintain Basque identity abroad, while reconnecting individuals with their identity and with a larger global Basque community—homeland and diaspora.[11]

The creation and development of informal and formal transnational migrant networks among individuals, groups, and organizations from the country of origin and the country of settlement constitute webs of exchange of information and transfers of knowledge in the physical world as well as in the digital world. These networks lead to chain migration, which, in turn, helps to perpetuate migration flows between specific sending and receiving areas and among consecutive generations of immigrants.[12] In other words,

---

5. M. Boyd, "Family and Personal Networks in International Migration," 642.

6. Tilly, "Transplanted Networks"; Wellman, "Structural Analysis," 37.

7. See Castells, *The Rise of the Network Society*; Cohen, "Diaspora , the Nation-state, and Globalization"; and Cohen, *Global Diasporas*.

8. See Hiller and Franz, "New Ties, Old Ties , and Lost Ties"; Alonso and Oiarzabal, eds, *Diasporas in the New Media Age*.

9. Alonso and Oiarzabal, *Diasporas in the New Media Age*, 11.

10. Licklider and Taylor, "The Computer as a Communication Device."

11. Oiarzabal, "The Basque Diaspora Webscape."

12. See Glick Schiller, Basch, and Blanc Szanton, "Transnationalism"; Vertovec and Cohen, eds., *Migration and Transnationalism*.

as Thomas Faist argues, "Information plays an important role for migration decision-making. It is one element that helps us to pay more attention to the bonds between movers and stayers, pioneer migrants, migration brokers, and followers. Depending on the availability of info on transportation and opportunities for jobs and housing potential migrants can optimize their benefits. Such information may flow along various communication channels, such as mass media and friends who migrated before, but also pioneer migrants outside the inner circle of relatives and friends."[13]

Methodology

This chapter presents a preliminary analysis of a longitudinal study that began in 2005 on the presence of the Basque institutional diaspora on the World Wide Web (Web). Due to the ephemeral nature of the Web, the goal of this research was to track changes of such a presence over time in order to study its online evolution. Consequently, between 2005 and March 2009 I studied the usage of different digital platforms by the Basque diaspora and their potential impact on maintaining Basque identity abroad. What difference do "new" online applications such as social network sites (e.g., MySpace, Facebook), weblogs (e.g., Blogger), or podcasting (e.g., YouTube) make for diaspora associations? Are these associations truly facilitating the creation of online communities of "friends" based primordially on a common ethnicity? And why are they building new social networks of informal knowledge online?

The study presented here draws on much larger quantitative, qualitative, and comparative research that took place between 2002 and 2006, and which focused on the online and offline dimensions of the Basque institutional diaspora presence in cyberspace.[14] The research analyzed the formation of a new online landscape created by the Basque diaspora institutional websites, which I defined as the Basque diaspora webscape. At the time, a total of 141 people and ninety-eight Basque diaspora associations from twenty countries participated in the research. This included the participation of 66 percent (fifty-eight) of the total Basque diaspora webmasters from eleven countries in a Web-based survey. I also applied a discursive and rhetorical analysis to ninety sites from sixteen countries as of July–August 2005, which I complemented by studying new websites that had been created since that time up to June 2007 and once again up to March 2009 (see appendix).

My database combines my research findings (e.g., Web search engines) and the Basque Autonomous Community's (hereafter Basque government) registry or database of institutions abroad, which was used to draw the sample of my population.[15] In

---

13. Faist, *The Volume and Dynamics of International Migration and Transnational Social Spaces*, 40.

14. For more information see Oiarzabal, "The Basque Diaspora Webscape."

15. In 1994 the Autonomous Community of the Basque Country established a registry of Basque clubs abroad (meaning outside the BAC's administrative limits) as a legal requirement under Law 8/94 that regulates the relationship between the BAC public institutions and the Basque institutional diaspora. For example, Basque associations abroad need

addition, I used Alexa's index on Web trafficking to find which were the most "popular" (world trafficked) hosting sites and platforms on the Internet, as those could most likely be utilized by Basque diaspora associations.[16] That is to say, there could be more chances to find diaspora associations on the most popular hosting sites than on less popular sites. Once I selected the sites that could potentially host Basque diaspora groups, I searched keywords such as "Basque club," "Basque diaspora," and "Basques" in the Basque, English, French, and Spanish languages in order to find them.

Introducing the Basque Institutional Diaspora

Before the widespread use of electronic mail, the Internet, and the Web, Basques began slowly to "colonize" cyberspace, depicted by technologists and media critics as "the last frontier."[17] Cyberspace as a constructed and shared electronic social and cultural space is the new deterritorialized country of the Basques.[18] In fact, the first identified solid attempts to do so by Basques, individually or collectively, took place in the diaspora. By 1994, the Internet became generally available to the public, and in that same year the first Basque website, www.buber.net, was created in the diaspora by Blas Uberuaga, who grew up in the Basque-American community of Boise, Idaho (US). In the homeland, the Basque government established its first website in October 1996. Prior to this, the Basque presence on the Internet was related to two Usenet groups (online bulletin boards or discussion forums now hosted by Google Groups): Basque-L (established in December 1993) and soc.culture.basque (established in July 1996).[19] Since then, there has been a rapidly increasing access to the Internet through not only computer-based technologies but also through mobile technologies at work, home, and leisure spaces.

By November 1997, there were already sixty-one Basque diaspora institutions registered with the Basque government, but there was only one diaspora association online—the political site from the Caracas, Venezuela Association of Friends of the Basque Country (AVAEH in its Spanish acronym)—which was created in 1996.[20] Following AVAEH, the earliest pioneering diaspora organizations to claim a corner on the Web

---

to be registered with the government in order to receive any financial assistance. For a full account of Basque diaspora institutions online see my database on http://euskaldiaspora.com.

16. Alexa (www.alexa.com).

17. The reader should notice that ephemerality is an intrinsic nature of the Web, and despite the effort made to update the URLs of many of the websites mentioned throughout the chapter, some might have disappeared by the time of its publication.

18. The Basque Country is a region situated at the Spanish-Franco border of the western Pyrenees. The historical Basque territories are divided into three main political administrative areas—the Basque Autonomous Community (BAC) or Euskadi; the Foral Community of Navarre or Nafarroa in the Spanish state; and three Basque provinces or Iparralde in the French state—with a total combined population of nearly 3 million people.

19. Basque-L (http://groups.google.com/group/bit.listserv.basque-l) and soc.culture.basque (http://groups.google.com/group/soc.culture.basque).

20. Venezuelan Association of Friends of the Basque Country (*Asociación Venezolana de Amigos de Euskal Herria*; http://earth.prohosting.com/avaeh).

were the political association Basque Diaspora Association, from Santa Rosa, Argentina; the educational organization based in Buenos Aires Juan de Garay Basque-Argentinean Foundation; and the Basque social club from Seattle, Washington, US, all of which established their respective websites in 1997.[21] The Seattle club or *euskal etxea* became the first Basque diaspora club ever to construct an online presence.

Seattle was soon followed by other clubs such as the Utah Basque Club from Salt Lake City, United States; the Basque Center Euzko Etxea from La Plata, Argentina; the Basque Center of Caracas, Venezuela; and the North American Basque Organizations (NABO) in 1998. NABO became the first diaspora federation to organize in cyberspace. Its Argentinean counterpart, the Federation of Basque Argentinean Entities (FEVA in its Spanish acronym), joined NABO's digital print at the end of 2005. In 1999, the Basque Museum and Cultural Center of Boise, Idaho, the Reno Basque Club Zazpiak Bat, Nevada, and the Calgary Euskal Etxea from Canada also established their own websites.[22]

Nearly 90 percent of the institutional websites (i.e., official sites of diaspora institutions) that comprise the Basque digital diaspora have been established in the new millennium. As of December 2005, the Basque diaspora had engendered 189 associations—federations of clubs, *euskal etxeak* (community-based social clubs), and cultural, educational, political, and business organizations—throughout twenty-two countries.[23] More than half of those associations (ninety-eight, or nearly 52 percent) were online in sixteen countries (or nearly 73 percent) with an institutional presence as of October 2005. By June 2007, the diaspora increased by eight new associations and two new countries—China and Cuba. At that time, 123 diaspora associations, or over 62 percent, had a presence on the Internet in nineteen countries (or nearly 80 percent of the total). The new associations from Brazil, China—the first Basque diaspora association in Asia—and Colombia finally joined the Basque digital diaspora. As of March 2009, the diaspora had formed 211 associations throughout twenty-four countries, of which 135 (or nearly 64 percent) had a presence in cyberspace in twenty countries (or over 83 percent of the total).[24] The Basque association in Puerto Rico also established its online representation

21. Basque Diaspora Association (*Asociación Diáspora Vasca*; www.diasporavasca.org); Juan de Garay Basque-Argentinean Foundation (*Fundación Vasco Argentina Juan de Garay*; www.juandegaray.org.ar); and the Basque club of Seattle (www.seattleeuskal.org).

22. Utah Basque Club (www.utah-basque.com); Basque Center Euzko Etxea from La Plata (*Centro Vasco Euzko Etxea*; www.centrovasco.com); Basque Center of Caracas (*Centro Vasco de Caracas*; www.euskoetxeacaracas.blogspot.com); NABO (www.nabasque.org); FEVA (www.fevaonline.org.ar); the Basque Museum and Cultural Center (www.basquemuseum.com); the Reno Basque Club Zazpiak Bat (www.renobasqueclub.org); and the Calgary Euskal Etxea (www.muturzikin.com/euskalgary.htm).

23. Andorra, Argentina, Australia, Brazil, Canada, Chile, Colombia, El Salvador, France, Germany, Italy, Mexico, Paraguay, Peru, Puerto Rico, Spain, Switzerland, the Dominican Republic, the United Kingdom, the United States, Uruguay, and Venezuela.

24. Andorra, Argentina, Australia, Brazil, Canada, Chile, China, Colombia, Cuba, El Salvador, France, Germany, Italy, Mexico, Paraguay, Peru, Puerto Rico, Spain, Switzerland, the Dominican Republic, the United Kingdom, the United States, Uruguay, and Venezuela.

space. The associations from Cuba, the Dominican Republic, El Salvador, and Paraguay have not expanded their presence into cyberspace (see appendix).

At the same time, some diaspora associations have multiplied their online presence by combining different online platforms (forums, websites, and social network sites). Consequently, by March 2009 the institutional or associative diaspora worldwide has organized itself in 157 online platforms, compared to just a few years prior when the number of sites could be counted on one hand. This trend demonstrates a powerful potential for Basque diaspora expression online. Significantly, in November 2008, the Basque government created a specific website, www.euskaletxeak.net, in collaboration with the different diaspora federations from Argentina, Spain, the United States, Uruguay, and Venezuela, with the goal of becoming a virtual meeting space for Basques abroad.

These diaspora associations, self-defined as Basque, materialized with strong group self-awareness, sustained over a considerable period of time. Diasporas such as those of the Basque are composed of emigrants who shared a collective identity in their homeland, and who have been forced by structural socioeconomic or political conditions or have chosen to leave their land of origin to settle in other countries. There, migrants and their descendants collectively maintain and develop cultural, religious, and political expressions of their identity, and consequently they form a collective identity distinct from that of their host societies' dominant culture. They constitute institutions and transnational networks that maintain explicit and implicit personal and institutional ties of a cultural, social, economic, political, and business nature with the homeland and other countries of Basque presence.

The size of the population of the Basque diaspora is nearly impossible to determine, as it depends on the operational definition of "being Basque" as well as a complete statistical database. Nevertheless, the Basque government estimates that the diaspora population consists of 4.5 million people.[25] However, this figure is extremely difficult to corroborate.

Social Web Platforms

As of February 2009, the search engines Google, which hosts Google Groups, and Yahoo! which hosts Yahoo! Groups, were in first and second place, respectively, of Alexa's index of the world's most trafficked websites. In addition, the powerhouses and symbols of the so-called Web 2.0 were in the top ten places on the index: YouTube (third place), Facebook (fifth), Blogger (eighth), and MySpace (ninth). Also, Flickr was in thirty-third place on Alexa's index, while Fotolog ranked 105th. Both Flickr and Fotolog are used by a number of diaspora groups.

As stated earlier, Google Groups host mailing lists or discussion groups as well as the historical Usenet groups.[26] Usenet or User Network was the initial Internet community prior the creation of the Web, and works similarly to Bulletin Boards (BBs). The

---

25. Gobierno Vasco, *Euskaldunak Munduan, Building the Future*, 47.

26. Google Groups (http://groups.google.com).

original BBs were the precursor to websites and online communities and were structured by topics. According to Jose Luis Brea, BBs were created as "an ideal model of participation, attempting to replace the traditional unidirectional and vertical scheme of emitter-receptor with that of a disseminated rhizome of users." However, they "failed as multimedia browsers appeared and the communicative potential of the medium far exceeded the limitations of a mere notice board."[27]

Since the invention of the Web in 1989–90, its evolution and growth have been exponential.[28] For example, in March 1998, Basques from Mallorca (Balearic Islands, Spain) posted an "ad" on Google Groups in order to contact Basque residents in Mallorca with the goal of setting up a club. In 2006 the Euskal Etxea "Artea" of Mallorca was created, and rapidly established a website in January 2007. In December 2008, the Balearic club also created a Facebook group as part of the booming Web 2.0.[29]

Yahoo! Groups, the equivalent of Google Groups, were created in 1998 and also host forums and mailing lists.[30] In November 1999, the London Basque Society created an online group for the members of its club. As of March 2009, it had eighty-four members, but there had been no new messages or posts since December 2008.[31] In September 2007, the London Basque Society had already set up a group on Facebook.[32] In addition, between June 2000 and November 2001, the political group Basque Diaspora Association from Argentina also set up five online groups or *txokos* (Basque fraternities) in order to complement the activities of its website. As of June 2007, the total combined membership of the *txokos* was 520. The groups were not to be found as of March 2009.[33]

---

27. Brea, "Online Communities," 4–6.

28. See Berners-Lee, *Weaving the Web*.

29. Euskal Etxea "Artea" of Mallorca (www.euskaletxeakmallorca.com).

30. Yahoo! Groups (http://groups.yahoo.com).

31. London Basque Society (www.zintzilik.org/london; http://groups.yahoo.com/group/euskaledge).

32. As of March 2009, there were another eight diaspora associations that also created their respective online groups/mailing lists. All of them are hosted at Yahoo! Groups. Only the "Goizeko Izarra," the "CV Chacabuco," and the "Vascos de Castelli" groups have been active since their creation. In Argentina, the *Centro Vasco Lagun Onak de Pergamino* set up the "Goizeko Izarra" group in August 2004 (thirty-three members; http://ar.groups.yahoo.com/ group/goizekoizarra); the Centro Vasco de Chacabuco established the "CV Chacabuco" group in September 2004 (thirteen members; http://ar.groups.yahoo.com/group/CVChacabuco); the Centro Vasco "Euskal Etxea" de Comodoro Rivadavia set up the "Haize Dantzariak" group in November 2004 (one member; http://ar.groups.yahoo.com/group/Haize_Dantzariak); the Centro Vasco Denak bat de Lomas de Zamora, Province of Buenos Aires also set up in November 2004 the "Denak Bat" group (three members; http://ar.groups.yahoo.com/group/denakbat); the Centro Vasco Castelli "Oneratu" established the "Vascos de Castelli" group in May 2006 (six members; http://ar.groups.yahoo.com/group/vascos_de_castelli); and the Centro Vasco Ibai Txori de Concepción del Uruguay, Entre Ríos, created the "Ibai Txori" group in September 2008 (two members; http://ar.groups.yahoo.com/group/ibaitxori). In Venezuela, the Centro Vasco de Caracas established a group in February 2002 (nine members; http://espanol.groups.yahoo.com/group/centrovascodecaracas); and in Spain, the Centro Vasco "Gure Txoko" from Valladolid created a group in February 2006 (two members; http://es.groups.yahoo.com/group/gure_txoko).

33. Those *txokos* were located at http://ar.groups.yahoo.com/group/vascosdiaspora (271 members in June 2007; in the Spanish language), http://groups.yahoo.com/group/diasporavasca-euskera (70 members in June 2007; in the Basque language), http://groups.yahoo.com/group/diasporavasca-english (115 members in June 2007; in the English language), http://groups.yahoo.com/group/diasporavasca-francais (45 members in June 2007; in the French language), and http://groups.yahoo.com/group/diasporavasca-portugues (27 members in June 2007; in the Portuguese language).

As of March 2009, dozens and dozens of diasporas (e.g., Cameroonian, Corsican, Filipino, Jamaican, Kurdish, and Zimbabwean) have created, for instance, Facebook profiles, groups, and pages from a personal to an institutional level with hundreds of registered members (e.g., "United Macedonian Diaspora," 946 members; "La Diaspora Corse," 647 members; "Kenya Diaspora Network," 1,093 members). The Basque institutional diaspora is one of those diasporas that is utilizing social network sites (SNSs) in order to advance its goals.[34]

Since my initial research began in 2002, new Basque diaspora associations have opted for having a presence in cyberspace; other associations have renewed their sites and domains; and others have constituted themselves into SNSs or user-generated Web applications, facilitated by the release of software architecture coined as Web 2.0.[35] This second face or generation of software facilitates the exchange of data and the existence of collaborative websites, such as MySpace, Facebook, and Orkut; weblogs (textual blogs, photoblogs, and audio blogs; e.g., Blogger and WordPress); micro-blogs (e.g., Twitter); podcasting (e.g., YouTube); and wikis (e.g., Wikipedia). Common to all SNSs is the implicit assumption or belief that people want to share information. That is to say, this new technology allows users to provide content to the Web as well as to share it in an unprecedented manner.

Manuel Castells defines Web 2.0 as a "cluster of technologies, devices, and applications that support the proliferation of social spaces on the Internet."[36] According to danah boyd and Nicole Ellison, SNSs are "web-based services that allow individuals to (1) construct a public or semi-public profile with a bounded system, (2) articulate a list of other users with whom they share a connection, and (3) view and traverse their list of connections and those made by others within the system." The scholars argue that, "What makes social network sites is not that they allow individuals to meet strangers, but rather that they enable users to articulate and make visible their social networks . . . Participants are not necessarily 'networking' or looking to meet new people, instead, they are primarily communicating with people who are already a part of their extended social network."[37]

---

34. See Bustamante, "Tide-like Diasporas in Brazil."

35. Web 2.0, based on XML (eXtensible Markup Language), defines in retrospect the previously known Web as Web 1.0, which is based mainly on HTML (HyperText Markup Language). In the so-called Web 1.0, the text was organized into (Web) pages, and "hyperlinks" or "links" were created to unite them. By following them, the users could "navigate" the Web. That is to say, the hypertextual nature of the Web text allows for networking and for analyzing the relationship among websites, which represent, in the case of the Basque diaspora, organizations as well as the discourses constructed by its online institutions. The online text provides the opportunity to interconnect the diverse Basque text-sites with specific hyperlinks allowing the reader to move from one text to another. The Hypertext Transfer Protocol (or HTTP) allows files (or sites) written in HTML to link to each other thereby constructing a network of interlinked files or sites, which might contain textual, audio-visual, or graphic content.

36. Castells, *Communication Power*, 65. See also Beer, "Social Network(ing) Sites"; and Fuchs, "Social Software and Web 2.0."

37. boyd and Ellison, "Social Network Sites."

SNSs are commercially based companies but their services are free of charge for their users as part of the so-called knowledge economy.[38] Potential users are required to subscribe in order to take advantage of their services. These sites allow registered users to create profiles or groups and lists of contacts ("Friends," "Members," or "Fans"); upload and share videos and photos; and have the ability to post messages or comments as well as to send private messages to other users, all which, in turn, boost the interconnectivity among those in a shared network. For example, in Facebook there are different levels of access to the groups: open groups are those open to anyone to join (public); closed groups are those where new members need to request administrative approval to join; and secret groups, which are not listed, and new members only join by prior invitation ("Friends" only). Only the Basque associations from Mallorca, Medellin, and Santiago de Chile belong to the category of "closed groups."

As boyd and Ellison suggest, while some websites were launched as SNSs, others such as Fotolog (2002), Flickr (2004), and YouTube (2005) soon implemented some of the aforementioned SNSs' features in order to capitalize on the success of sites such as MySpace (2003).[39] Regarding weblog or diary publishing systems, Blogger was created in 1999, while Fotolog was launched in 2002 as an online photo-blog or photolog. Fotolog has more than twenty-two million registered members in over two hundred countries as of December 2008, and it ranks number one among SNSs in Chile and number two in Argentina as of June 2008.[40]

My research identifies the Colorado Basque Club (US) as the first club to establish a presence on the Basque digital diaspora's blogosphere, which goes back to April 2004. This was followed by the establishment of the blog of the dance group of the Basque club of La Plata, Argentina, in December 2004. However, its online presence was discontinued in May 2005. Formal groups, in particular dance groups, within diaspora clubs in Argentina (e.g., Arrecifes, Chascomús, and Necochea) have been keen on establishing their own online presence by setting up photo-blogs. For other associations (e.g., Chivilcoy and Suipacha in Argentina), the establishment of blogs as their official online homes is their first attempt to have an online representation.

As of June 2007, the Basque Club of Barcelona's official website was also supported by a blog. As stated, in 2004 the Colorado Basque Club's site also created two additional online platforms—the Members Blog, and the Topagunea Blog, which was established to facilitate the exchange of ideas regarding a Basque teaching program between the

---

38. Thrift, *Knowing Capitalism*. For a critical perspective on the cultural industries behind SNSs, see also Scholz, "Market Ideology and the Myths of Web 2.0"; and Van Dijck and Nieborg, "Wikinomics and Its Discontents."

39. boyd and Ellison, "Social Network Sites."

40. "About Us," Fotolog, accessed June 27, 2009, http://info.fotolog.com/aboutus. Blogger (http://blogger.com and http://blogspot.com).

Colorado *euskal etxea* and a Basque-language school in Nafarroa. Both blogs have been inactive since 2005 and 2004 respectively.[41]

In addition, Basque clubs in Argentina (Pergamino and Villa Mercedes), Colombia (Medellin), and Uruguay (El Salto) have replaced their official websites with blogs because they do not require any financial investment compared to websites (e.g., domain name, hosting, design, and maintenance) and are easier to set up and run than websites. In another case, after the replacement of the Basque club of Montpellier, France's (Association des Basques de Montpellier et Languedoc) website by a blog, it opted to go back to its original model. So far, this is a unique case within the Basque digital diaspora. The usual trend is for associations to replace their websites with blogs.

If the first SNSs date back to the late 1990s (e.g., SixDegrees.com was launched in 1997), everything points to the fact that their proliferation and popularization did not happen until the purchase of MySpace by Fox Interactive Media in mid-2005, which appeared on the front page of newspapers worldwide. MySpace, "A Place for Friends," was founded in 2003. In comparison to the then main competitor, Friendster (launched in 2002), MySpace allowed its users to add HTML in order to change the layout of their own profile pages.[42] This revolutionary feature became part of a 2.0 user-generated content culture—a "copy/paste code culture"—according to boyd and Ellison.[43] The authors further assert that MySpace underage users (until then an untargeted market) became an active part of this culture.[44]

The first identified Basque diaspora association to establish a profile on MySpace was the Reno Basque Club Zazpiak Bat (Nevada, US) in 2007, followed by the Utah'ko Triskalariak (Salt Lake Valley, US). The Reno Basque Club became the first Basque diaspora association ever to use MySpace. So far, the aforementioned clubs are the only diaspora associations using MySpace.

Facebook was founded in 2004 as a service first to Harvard University students, then to other American college students, American high school students, and later on to corporate professionals. Finally, in 2006 Facebook was opened to everyone. Facebook defines itself as "a social utility that helps people communicate more efficiently with their friends, family and coworkers. The company develops technologies that facilitate the sharing of information through the social graph, the digital mapping of people's real-world social connections." According to Facebook, as of February 2009 it has 200 million active users worldwide. It is available in seventy languages, including Basque, which is offered in Beta version. About 70 percent of those users are outside the United States.[45]

---

41. Basque club of Barcelona (http://blog.euskaletxeak.org); Colorado Basque Club's (http://www.coloradoeuskaletxea.com) Members Blog (http://coloradoeuskaletxea.blogspot.com) and Topagunea Blog (http://topagunea.blogspot.com).

42. MySpace (http://www.myspace.com).

43. boyd and Ellison, "Social Network Sites."

44. Ibid.

45. Facebook, "Factsheet," (June 2009) www.facebook.com/press/info.php?factsheet (accessed June 21, 2009); Facebook, "Statistics" (June 2009) www.facebook.com/press/info.php?statistics (accessed June 21, 2009); and Facebook,

In comparison to other SNSs, Facebook allows the implementation of "applications" developed by third parties for users to modify their profile pages. As of December 2009, there were more than five hundred thousand active applications available on Facebook. "Basques in DC (Euskaldunak Washington, DC-n)" of the Washington, D.C. Basque Club and "Euskaldunak Londresn" (Basques in London) of the London Basque Society are the oldest identified Facebook groups set up by Basque diaspora associations. They were established in August 2007 and September 2007 respectively.

Regarding photo and video-sharing and hosting websites, Flickr was launched in 2004. Users can view, upload, and share photos and videos. As of March 2009, the Shanghai club is the only Basque diaspora association that regularly uses Flickr. YouTube is Flickr's counterpart. It was launched in 2005 under the slogan of "Broadcast Yourself." In addition to Flickr's features, YouTube users are also able to embed videos posted to YouTube in other sites. Also, users registered with YouTube are able to join groups called "Channel Types." The Basque clubs of Shanghai and London as well as the cultural group Akelarre from Concordia, Argentina have created their own "channels." Similar to other SNSs such as Facebook (with 65 million active users currently accessing Facebook through their mobile devices as of December 2009) and MySpace that went mobile, You-Tube Mobile was launched in June 2007, and some cell phones are capable of accessing the content of the site. By 2009, YouTube was available in fourteen languages.[46]

The Basque Diaspora Social Blogosphere and Networkscape

From 2005 to 2009, fifty-five Basque diaspora associations from ten countries (Argentina, Brazil, China, Colombia, France, Mexico, Puerto Rico, Spain, the United States, and Uruguay) went online for first time. During the same period of time, eighteen online associations disappeared. Though the study began in 2005, some earlier websites (e.g., the first identified blog dates back to 2004) were not identified until much later but were included in the study.[47]

A slim majority of the aforementioned associations (thirty-one, or 56.36 percent) chose to establish websites, while the rest chose to set up SNSs: eighteen, or 32.72 percent, were blogs and six, or 10.9 percent, were pages hosted on Facebook and MySpace. In relation to the thirty-one websites, 61.3 percent were created by *euskal etxeak*; 16 percent by cultural associations; and 13 percent by educational groups. Over 29 percent of those websites were established by associations from Argentina, followed by those from

"Statistics" (December 2009) www.facebook.com/press/info.php?statistics (accessed January 8, 2010).

46. Flickr (http://flickr.com) and YouTube (http://youtube.com).

47. Similarly, three Basque diaspora associations on Facebook were only identified after the study had been closed. However, they were not included in the present research. Those were: "Denak Bat" (Centro Vasco Euzko Etxea; La Plata, Argentina), "Eusko Hazi" (Centro Vasco Zingirako Euskaldunak; Chascomús, Argentina), and "Euskal Etxea" (Centre Cultural Barcelona, Spain). "Denak Bat" was established in August 2008, and "Eusko Hazi" and "Euskal Etxea" were created in January 2009. "Denak Bat" and "Eusko Hazi" are both dance groups with photo-blogs, while the Basque club of Barcelona has a multiple presence online through a blog and website.

the United States (25.8 percent) and Colombia (9.7 percent). Of those six identified as hosted on Facebook and MySpace pages, the oldest only goes back to 2008. Five out of six associations preferred Facebook over MySpace as their first online home. Fifty percent were created by *euskal etxeak* and 50 percent by cultural associations, from Argentina, Spain, and the United States.

Regarding the Basque diaspora blogosphere, seventeen out of eighteen blogs were established by associations from Argentina, while the remaining one was set up by a dance group from the United States. Fifteen, or 83.3 percent, were created by cultural groups (fourteen were dance groups); two by *euskal etxeak*; and one by a political association. In this regard, the preference for the hosting site Fotolog among Basque-Argentinean dance groups is phenomenal. The involvement of dance groups in establishing their own photo-blogs is quite relevant as they are constituted by teenagers and youngsters, theoretically the most proactive in adopting new technologies and vital elements within their organizations. Only seven blogs (five *euskal etxeak* and two cultural; two from the United States, and five from Argentina) out of twenty-nine were inactive as of May 2009. Not surprisingly, the blogs set up by dance groups were the most active regarding the number of posts and their frequency. That is to say, dance groups are central for diaspora organizations in both offline and online worlds.[48]

In addition, another twenty-six associations created additional or complementary online platforms to their previously established cyber-headquarters: nineteen Facebook profiles, one MySpace site, and six blogs. Also, five online associations migrated from websites to blogs. The total combined number of MySpace sites (two), Facebook sites (twenty-four), and blogs (twenty-nine) established between 2004 and 2009 is fifty-five.[49] In particular, the majority of SNSs have been developed since 2007. For example, 62 percent of the twenty-one new online platforms created between June 2007 and March 2009 were SNSs. In fact, fifteen out of the then nineteen Facebook profiles (including new sites as well as additional platforms) were set up in just four months, between November 2008 and February 2009.[50] All this points out a preference to choose SNSs among those that establish a presence online for the first time, and particularly among those that seek to reinforce their presence in cyberspace by setting up a secondary or tertiary online home. SNSs constitute a new digital landscape, a networkscape, which is increasingly occupying ground in cyberspace (see chapter appendix).

The Internet (a global collaborative and creative collective platform) is by nature about sharing knowledge regardless of time and space. It is also a community-forming

---

48. For further analysis of dance as one of the key elements of Basque identity abroad, see Corcostegui, "Moving Emblems."

49. This combined number includes those associations that chose to migrate from websites to blogs; those that chose to establish SNSs as their first online home; and those that chose to set up additional platforms to their primary online homes.

50. The date of establishment of two Facebook pages is unknown.

device, where users meet and interact, thereby constituting social networks and online communities—placeless, deterritorialized, and without face-to-face interaction.[51] SNSs are designed to provide opportunities for individuals and groups to boost pre-existing offline world relationships, networks, and partnerships for horizontal knowledge creation and sharing.[52] They also allow for the creation of new relationships and networks by bringing together diaspora associations' members and nonmembers in a common space. In addition, SNSs have increasingly facilitated the exchange of information and knowledge as well as ideas, debate, and discussion among users. For example, diasporans can upload files on any format and share what they know with others.

For boyd and Ellison, "While websites dedicated to communities of interest still exist and prosper, SNSs are primarily organized around people, not interests . . . with the individual at the center of their own community."[53] However, within the particular case of the Basque diaspora, evidence shows that many diaspora associations use Fotolog, Blogger, Facebook, and MySpace to build communities based on a common identity, heritage, culture, political orientation, language, activities, and interests. SNSs facilitate the creation of spaces for individuals as well as for informal and formal diaspora groups that share similar interests and goals within and outside their offline communities and across their immediate geographies.[54] They allow for group cohesion, individual integration, collective identification, and self-expression, as well as socialization. If initially individuals were behind the widespread establishment and use of personal websites and blogs, understood as online diaries for self-expression and self-representation,[55] webs and blogs have also become tools for groups' (such as diasporas) collective expression, identification, and belonging. But, at the same time, Basque diaspora associations seek the implementation of innovative features provided by SNSs, which facilitate communication and interaction among individuals of their immediate clubs and communities and among co-diasporans and institutions. In sum, the online networks of the diaspora mimic to a certain extent those of the offline world—that is, a cyberexpansion of (the diaspora) itself in the online world.

As of March 2009, the total combining "membership" (in terms of "friends" and "fans") of Basque diaspora Facebook and MySpace groups was 1,931. The groups with the largest memberships were the Centro Vasco Euskal Etxea México (Basque Club of Mexico, D.F.; 289 members), Euzko Etxea de Santiago (Basque Club of Santiago de Chile; 239 members), and Kern County Basque Club (Bakersfield, US; 200 members). The study did not analyze the composition of groups' membership, thereby ignoring

---

51. See Bromberg, "Are MUDs Communities?"; Fox and Roberts, "GPs in Cyberspace"; Miller and Slater, *The Internet*; and Watson, "Why We Argue About Virtual Community".

52. See Ellison, Steinfield, and Lampe, "The Benefits of Facebook 'Friends.'"

53. boyd and Ellison, "Social Network Sites"; Section, Expanding Niche Communities."

54. See Gajjala, "Shifting Frames."

55. See Dominick, "Who Do You Think You Are?"

the percentage of "members" that might belong to two or more groups. However, a clear cross-membership might exist due to the intrinsic nature of SNSs, which favor and encourage multiple affiliations. In general terms, if a person wishes to join any offline diaspora association he/she is required to pay a membership as well as to prove, in the majority of cases, his/her Basque ancestry. In the online world, beside the fact that potential hosting sites' users need to register, the great majority of sites established by diaspora associations are open to all, are free of charge, do not require membership or a proof of Basqueness, or to travel physically to the nearest Basque clubhouse in order to learn about events or socialize with other Basques. Consequently, any potential user might feel free to join or become a fan of a group and become a friend to other (mostly already known) users without any strings attached or sense of duty.

In addition to the Basque diaspora institutional presence on sites such as Facebook, there are other noninstitutional diaspora Facebook groups established by diasporans, breaking any monopoly in terms of representativeness that the former groups might have because of their official status within the community and with hostland and homeland institutions such as the Basque government. In many instances, the noninstitutional groups preexist the institutional ones on Facebook and have successfully gathered a greater number of individuals under specific geographical groupings, including "Vascos de Chile" (Basques of Chile; 744 members), "Vascos en Chile" (Basques in Chile; 698 members), "Vasco-Venezolanos" (Basque-Venezuelans; 605 members, established in May 2008), "Vascos en Mexico" (Basques in Mexico; 268 members), "Jóvenes Vascos" (Basque Youth from Mexico; 395 members, established in December 2007), "Vascos en Uruguay" (Basques in Uruguay; 156 members, established in November 2008), and "Vascos en Argentina" (Basques in Argentina; 287 members, established in September 2008).

In the case of Chile, it is estimated that the population of Basque origin is about 20 percent of the entire country (i.e., 0.26 million), and has successfully established the clubs of Santiago de Chile and Valparaiso, but currently only have 240 and 428 members respectively.[56] The Basque-Chilean clubs' Facebook groups have 239 and ninety-nine members respectively; however, the total combined membership of the noninstitutional Basque-Chilean groups is 1,472. The existence of so many Basque diaspora groups (institutional or not) on hosting sites such as Facebook speaks of a great diversity and density of networks among diasporans, particularly in countries such as Argentina, Chile, and Mexico. In some cases, both institutional and noninstitutional associations share the same online space; however, none of the above noninstitutional groups have an offline presence as formal or informal associations.

---

56. Gobierno Vasco, *Euskaldunak Munduan, Building the Future*, 47.

Hybrid Spaces of Participation and Interaction and Multiple Digital Profiles

Since 2005 there has been a clear evolution of the usage of online platforms by Basque diaspora institutions. As seen, between 2005 and 2007, the Basque digital landscape was dominated by websites, while the 2007–09 period is characterized by the increasing establishment of SNSs (first blogs—mainly hosted in Fotolog and Blogger—and then MySpace and Facebook) to the detriment of websites. The Basque digital diaspora is constructing new digital landscapes—blogosphere and networkscape—but without abandoning its initial webscape. It is promoting a hybrid space by combining different online and offline platforms in order to advance their institutions as well as their sociocultural, recreational, folkloric, linguistic, and political agendas.

Digital Profiles

As of March 2009, the institutional diaspora is characterized by the multiple digital profiles or identities of its associations worldwide. The use of official additional online platforms (e.g., mailing lists, websites, social network sites) and applications (e.g., video and photo hosting sites) by one single association has become a new phenomenon of the Basque digital diaspora. That is, many associations have begun to complement their online communities of interest (traditional sense of websites) with SNSs, allowing the construction of different spaces that may accommodate diverse elements of their respective communities. Basque associations tend to participate in various Web platforms because they use them for different, but complementary, purposes.

In 2005, the webmasters interviewed stated that the goals for creating websites were to provide and exchange current information to and with Basques and non-Basques, to institutional members and nonmembers, both locally and nonlocally, to communicate, and to have an online presence. Furthermore, many webmasters referred to offering current information, feasible and fast communication, access to information, and e-learning as some of the exclusive online services provided on the sites, which were not available at the associations.[57] Similarly, at the present, an increasing number of associations have opted for establishing a variety of different online spaces and tools in part due to the technology available to them. These are renewed attempts to attract a newer and younger generation, new members, and the public in general by displaying and making available to their members a variety of attractive tools, while attempting to achieve a greater participation in their institutions and involvement in the activities that they promote.

For instance, associations in Argentina (Akelarre and Ibai'ko, both in Concordia; Bariloche; and Cordoba), China (Shanghai), Spain (Barcelona), the United Kingdom (London), and the United States (Reno) use a variety of online platforms and applications

57. Oiarzabal, "The Basque Diaspora Webscape."

not as replacements but as complements to their "online headquarters." As of March 2009, the Shanghai club, with a website, a blog, and photo and video hosting sites, has the most diversified online presence of the Basque digital diaspora.

For those associations that have opted to use multiple and simultaneous online platforms and applications this marks a differential point with those other organizations that have a single presence in cyberspace. That is to say, the use of multiple platforms by one single association articulates a more diverse, prolific, inter-linked presence and denser network in cyberspace that goes beyond the mere fact of establishing an online presence, which has characterized the earlier stage of the development of the digital diaspora. In turn, this creates an online overrepresentation and exposure of those associations, while marking the beginning of a more mature stage of the development of some nodes of the Basque digital diaspora network. In other words, the institutional diaspora has consolidated and reinforced its online presence by utilizing the social network technology in order to capitalize on existing offline networks.

However, this online overrepresentation implies higher costs in terms of time, dedication, and investment in terms of human and financial resources as well as a higher commitment from institutions, individuals, and members than in an earlier stage, defined by the presence of one online platform per institution, and which was dominated quasi-exclusively by one individual. As of this writing, the aforementioned Basque Club in Shanghai has voluntarily closed its blog to avoid having two competing spaces on the Internet and to ease their work in order to update content in just one day. "We decided to keep and update the website instead of the blog because through the site we can protect the [domain] name of our Basque club as an association. Lately, we have thought about Facebook but we haven't done anything yet," the webmaster explained.[58]

Participation and Interaction

For years, the diaspora webscape has been characterized by the thematic or encyclopedic nature of its institutional websites as well as their hierarchical and vertical organizational structure. By taking a quick look at any of the diaspora websites, one will encounter large amounts of information about virtually anything related to Basqueness. Every single site attempts to embrace as much content as possible in one single space. These sites offer a sense of completeness that often allows redundancy of ideas and arguments as displayed on 70 percent of the websites and illustrated by the reproduction of similar, if not identical, texts, symbols, pictures, and music.[59]

Back in 2005, most of the webmasters were of Basque ancestry (90.7 percent), members of Basque diaspora associations (98.1 percent), and volunteers (88 percent) within their local Basque associations. Sixty-three percent of the webmasters interviewed were

---

58. E-mail exchanges with Shanghai Basque Club webmaster, August 13 and 17, 2009.

59. Oiarzabal, "The Basque Diaspora Webscape."

responsible for the design of their institutions' sites, while 88.9 percent of the webmasters were also responsible for maintaining and upgrading, and 48.1 percent for selecting and/or authoring the content of the sites, following the goals of their associations and the desires of their board of directors. Division of labor was almost nonexistent in the diaspora online world. Although most of the contents were created according to requests originated within their own associations (board of directors, website committees, and members) and the immediate Basque community, the webmasters' input, as part of the managerial structure of their associations, was obviously considerable. They were not only technicians but also content managers.[60]

The webmaster role has tended to evolve toward a more collaborative participation effort in building online communities and social networks as they originally intended. At the time, in 2005, some webmasters already showed their willingness to make their sites available, technologically speaking, to diverse members in order to increase the level of collaboration. For example, at the heart of the trendy replacement of diaspora associations' websites by blogs lays not only the reduction of costs but also the reduction of the actual work of the webmaster, whose workload is to some degree substituted by the content generated by the users. This delegation of responsibility is not only alleviating the webmaster's work, but it is somehow democratizing the site by bypassing the webmaster as the gatekeeper and main authority, which, in turn, facilitates the expression of diverse opinions and ideas on the site.

Nowadays, the growing number of diaspora SNSs is clearly changing the previous role that webmasters had. These social sites are designed to promote a sort of "participatory Web"[61] where users' ("netizens'") engagement is instrumental in its development.[62] Users (co-members and nonmembers of diaspora associations) have become central in designing and authoring the diaspora blogosphere and networkscape, displacing to a certain extent, but not replacing totally, the traditional role of webmasters, as those are still engaged in the development of those diverse digital landscapes. They are constructing a hybrid model of participation and management of the Basque digital diaspora. A more democratizing, decentralized, and horizontal structure has taken place between the online institution and its users and among the users themselves in terms of communication and interaction.

As of March 2005, 66.7 percent of the websites did not provide any interactive application to users or visitors, because the webmasters "[did] not have enough time" (66.7 percent), "[did] not have enough funding" (44.4 percent), and "there [was] not enough

---

60. Oiarzabal, "The Basque Diaspora Webscape."

61. See Hauben and Hauben, *Netizens*.

62. For a critical account of Web 2.0 as a model of participation see Kylie Jarrett, "Interactivity is Evil! A Critical Investigation of Web 2.0." *First Monday* 13, no. 3 (March 3, 2008), available at http://firstmonday.org/htbin/cgiwrap/bin/ojs/index.php/fm/article/view/2140; and Søren Mørk Petersen, "Loser Generated Content: From Participation to Exploitation." *First Monday* 13, no. 3 (March 3, 2008), available at http://firstmonday.org/htbin/cgiwrap/bin/ojs/index.php/fm/article/view/2141/1948.

interest or demand" (22.2 percent). At the time, the most common interactive tools provided on the websites were e-mail (in 64.8 percent of websites), a guest book (16.7 percent), a forum or chat-room (11.1 percent; meaning interaction in real time), e-commerce (3.7 percent), a blog (1.9 percent), and Intranet (1.9 percent).[63] However, back then, 25 percent of the webmasters were eager to make their websites more interactive, using new software applications in order to increase the social ties and the communication among members and users of the associations and sites. Significantly, as seen, from 2004 to 2009, diaspora associations have set up fifty-five social network sites, which fill the vacuum left by the lack of interactive tools of the main and, most of the time, only online site. There are renewed attempts to retain users and attract new ones by offering them spaces where they can express their points of view and build some sense of community—that is, a place where they can express their individuality by connecting to a collective identity.

Expanding Social Networks: Web 2.0 . . . Web 3.0 . . . Did I Hear 4.0?

As of July 2009, MySpace and Facebook, the two largest SNSs in the world, did not offer a common or inter-linked space for their respective millions of subscribers, leaving their respective users to choose between platforms or having to create profiles and groups on both sites. For example, Facebook users cannot import friends from other sites, and videos and photos uploaded to or made on Facebook cannot be shared on other sites like YouTube. Also, these fragmented and isolated spaces make the work of researchers difficult, as they are forced to explore multiple sites individually.

However, things are progressively changing. In December 2008, both Facebook Connect and Google Friend Connection became available for any third-party website to interact with Facebook and Google users and their data.[64] They are services that allow their users to connect with their friends on other (though affiliated) social and non-social sites and share information. They are in fact opening up SNSs to the rest of the Web. Google Friend Connection was introduced in May 2008, while Facebook Connect (under the slogan, "Making the world more social") was introduced in July 2008 and made available to users in December 2008. It was on limited Beta mode as of July 2009.[65] Facebook directors state that the service will allow the connection of different sites with Facebook in order to "interact with your friends on those sites and to share on Facebook through your Wall and friends' News Feeds. Those sites will also be able to automatically post recent activity back to Facebook."

---

63. Total exceeds 100 percent as the participants were asked to choose more than one option. See Oiarzabal, "The Basque Diaspora Webscape."

64. Facebook Connect (http://developers.facebook.com/connect.php) and Google Friend Connection (www.google.com/friendconnect).

65. Later on, Facebook also introduced Facebook Connect Wizard and Playground to help users with little to no coding experience to set up Facebook Connect on their respective sites. According to Facebook's 2009 statistical data "More than 60 million Facebook users engage with Facebook Connect on external websites every month."

There are also an increasing number of applications that attempt to dilute boundaries among the different SNSs. FriendFeed is a life-streaming application, which aggregates information (news feeds) of friends across all the social network sites of which they are members, into one social space (into one stream). Not surprisingly, FriendFeed was bought by Facebook in August 2009. eBuddy is a free, mobile, web-based messenger application that enables users to chat with others using instant messaging services such as Facebook Chat, MySpace, Windows Live Messenger, and Google Talk, in one aggregated interface.[66]

Moreover, the excessive fragmentation of Web 2.0 into parallel SNSs or closed environments might also be overcome by the implementation of a new software framework, the so-called Semantic Web (Web 3.0?). The Semantic Web was first coined as such by Tim Berners-Lee, James Handler, and Ora Lassila in 2001. They described it as a "web of data," which "provides a common framework that allows data to be shared and reused across applications, enterprises, and community boundaries."[67] According to Berners-Lee, director of the World Wide Web Consortium (W3C), the goal of the Semantic Web is "to organize info so users can capture what things are and how they are related . . . What's needed now is . . . the emergence of a single unified view of our info-universe where related objects are freely connected in meaningful webs."[68] In other words, the Semantic Web would imply that search results will provide meaning.

The implementation of the Semantic Web has, for instance, facilitated the creation of Friend of a Friend (FOAF), a "decentralized, semantic social network," where users create a personal profile that best describes them and their interests and then post it in order to find commonalities among other users. In addition, FOAF can integrate information from MySpace and Facebook. According to Lee Feigenbaum et al., by the end of 2007, one million people had already interlinked their FOAF files, including users of weblogs such as LiveJournal (launched in 1999).[69]

Conclusion

Since the early 1990s, the Basque institutional diaspora has progressively established firm ground in cyberspace and has adequately consolidated its efforts to constantly renew its presence according to continuous change and social and technological innovation. Throughout the years, diaspora associations have taken up the challenge to mainstream the issue of ICTs into their agendas, as these facilitate access to information and knowledge in an unprecedented manner. Consequently, they have opted for using technologies that favor their institutional goals, strategic plans, and activities. Evidence shows that

---

66. FriendFeed (http://friendfeed.com) and eBuddy (www.ebuddy.com).

67. Berners-Lee, Handler, and Lassila, "The Semantic Web."

68. Tim Berners-Lee, "W3C Semantic Activity."

69. Feigenbaum et al., "The Semantic Web in Action."

there is a fast and dynamic adaptability and adoption of diaspora institutions to new Web technologies and software applications that meet social needs or have a social purpose such as, for instance, maintaining and promoting communication, interaction, and networks.

The online presence of the Basque diaspora is neither trendy nor temporary. Those technologies make a real difference for institutions and their respective membership. Their impact on migrants and their descendants' lives, heritage, and cultural preservation is unquestionable. Without those digital technologies, some diaspora institutions would become handicapped in their organizational capacity as well as in their capacity to reach their goals.

Since 2007, there has been an increasing tendency for the diaspora to articulate an online presence in the form of computer and mobile-based social network sites. More affordable, faster, and easier accessibility to the Internet and to an increasing array of free software, programs, services, and tools would surely multiply the use of SNSs in the near future.

Taking into account the issue of the so-called digital divide, and the limited access to the Internet and limited use of ICTs by certain communities within the Basque diaspora, the impact of the Internet is uneven and asymmetric. As of March 2009, 36 percent of diaspora institutions had no presence on the Web. In addition, some institutions are still anchored to the Web 1.0 paradigm, while others have fast-forwarded themselves into Web 2.0, or more precisely into what the future might offer them in technological terms. The Basque institutional digital diaspora is found halfway between Web 1.0 and Web 2.0, constructing a hybrid space where elements of both software architectures coalesce. This space is the result of the failures and accomplishments of the implementation of Web 1.0 as well as the establishment of other more modern and better aspirations of Web 2.0.

This digital space takes form in the fact that diaspora associations have begun to move away from static and encyclopedic sites, which had traditionally dominated their online presence, to more dynamic and collaborative ones. That is to say, certain associations are increasingly constructing online communities of relationships, by interacting with people who share similar identities and interests, to the detriment of communities of identity, interest, and self-representation. The focus has shifted from displaying information to producing information and transferring informal knowledge by way of sharing it in a constructive manner. The Internet does not only mean that users can influence each other's lives in any part of the globe, but they can learn from each other as well as collaborate with each other. The diaspora has accelerated its presence across cyberspace in quantitative (e.g., additional platforms) and qualitative (e.g., diversity of platforms) terms by increasingly constructing more diverse, denser, and overlapping and interlinked networks limited by neither time nor space.

The present work opens new venues for future multi- and interdisciplinary analysis that could clearly be of interest to researchers, scholars, and students of migration and ICTs. For instance, longitudinal studies on the long-term implication of SNSs for diasporas such as the Basque one, as well as comparative studies in quantitative and qualitative terms of similar groups' usage of those type of online platforms, would be welcome. The question dealing with the impact of sites such as Facebook on its users, and the potential and active role that those users might have outside the online world—that is, on their local communities and institutions—would depend on an extensive study of those networks in both online and offline realities. Further research is needed in order to establish the users' role and degree of involvement on Facebook or MySpace sites, that is, whether or not their presence in different groups is merely testimonial. In addition, further studies should focus on social network analysis to reveal social structures among online sites in order to infer the social structure among individuals, groups, and institutions that have established those sites. Finally, studies regarding how identity is shaped and enacted in SNSs would also be of interest.

Addendum

As of this writing, from March to December 2009, another twenty-eight Basque diaspora institutions from eight countries (Argentina, Australia, Canada, Chile, Spain, United States, Uruguay, and Venezuela) have established a presence on Facebook. Seventeen out of the twenty-six associations established Facebook groups as additional online platforms to their websites. Six associations chose Facebook as their first online platform, while six associations were subgroups (five dance groups and a choir) of Basque clubs. In addition, during the same period of time three associations from Argentina created blogs as their first online home. Two of them also set up their own Facebook groups. Only four associations (from Argentina and Japan, the first in the Basque diaspora ever) established websites during that time. One of them, the Basque club of Arrecifes in Argentina, had created a Facebook group eleven months earlier. All this clearly reinforces the trend initiated in 2007, as well as the popularity of SNSs such as Facebook among diaspora groups. No Basque diaspora association has been documented to have established a presence on MySpace since 2008. As of December 2009, Facebook has more than 350 million active users worldwide.[70]

Bibliography

Alonso, Andoni and Pedro J. Oiarzabal. "The Immigrant Worlds' Digital Harbors: An Introduction." In *Diasporas in the New Media Age: Identity, Politics and Community,* edited by Andoni Alonso and Pedro J. Oiarzabal. Reno: University of Nevada Press, 2010.

Alonso, Andoni and Pedro J. Oiarzabal, eds. *Diasporas in the New Media Age: Identity, Politics and Community.* Reno: University of Nevada Press, 2010.

---

70. Facebook, "Statistics," for December 2009. See www.facebook.com/press/info.php?statistics.

Beer, David. "Social Network(ing) Sites . . . Revisiting the Story So Far: A Response to danah boyd & Nicole Ellison." *Journal of Computer-Mediated Communication* 13, issue 2 (2008): 516–29.

Berners-Lee, Tim, "W3C Semantic Activity." Available at the W3C's website, www.w3.org/2001/sw (accessed July 16, 2009).

———. *Weaving the Web.* San Francisco, CA: Harper Collins, 1999.

Berners-Lee, Tim, James Handler, and Ora Lassila. "The Semantic Web." *Scientific American,* May 2001. http://www.sciam.com/article.cfm?id=the-semantic-web.

Boase, Jeffrey, John B. Horrigan, Barry Wellman, and Lee Rainie. "The Strength of Internet Ties: The Internet and Email Aid Users in Maintaining Their Social Networks and Provide Pathways to Help When People Face Big Decisions." *Pew Internet & American Life Project,* January 2006. www.pewinternet.org/pdfs/PIP_Internet_ties.pdf (accessed July 16, 2009).

boyd, danah and Nicole B. Ellison. "Social Network Sites: Definition, History, and Scholarship." *Journal of Computer-Mediated Communication* 13, issue 1 (2007). http://jcmc.indiana.edu/vol13/issue1/boyd.ellison.html.

Boyd, Monica. "Family and Personal Networks in International Migration. Recent Developments and New Agendas." *International Migration Review* 23, no. 3 (1989): 638–70.

Brea, Jose Luis. "Online Communities: Experimental Communication in the Virtual Diaspora." 2003. http://www.joseluisbrea.net/articulos/onlinecommunities.pdf.

Brettel, Caroline B. "Theorizing Migration in Anthropology: The Social Construction of Networks, Identities, Communities, and Globalscapes." In *Migration Theory: Talking Across Disciplines,* edited by Caroline B. Brettel and James F. Hollifield. London: Routledge, 2000.

Bromberg, Heather. "Are MUDs Communities? Identity, Belonging and Consciousness in Virtual Worlds." In *Cultures of Internet,* edited by Rob Shields. London: Sage Publications, 1996.

Bustamante, Javier. "Tide-like Diasporas in Brazil: From Slavery to Orkut." In *Diasporas in the New Media Age: Identity, Politics and Community,* edited by Andoni Alonso and Pedro J. Oiarzabal. Reno: University of Nevada Press, 2010.

Castells, Manuel. *Communication Power.* Oxford: Oxford University Press, 2009.

———. *The Rise of the Network Society.* Malden, MA: Blackwell Publishers, 1996.

Cohen, Robin. "Diaspora, the Nation-state, and Globalization." In *Global History and Migrations,* edited by Wang Gungwu. Boulder, CO: Westview Press, 1997.

———. *Global Diasporas: An Introduction.* Seattle: University of Washington Press, 1997.

Corcostegui, Lisa M. "Moving Emblems: Basque Dance and Symbolic Ethnicity." In *The Basque Diaspora/La Diáspora Vasca,* edited by William A. Douglass et al. Basque

Studies Program Occasional Papers No. 7. Reno: Basque Studies Program, University of Nevada, Reno, 1999.

Dominick, Joseph R. "Who Do You Think You Are? Personal Home Pages and Self-representation on the World Wide Web." *Journalism and Mass Communication Quarterly* 76, no. 4 (1999): 648–54.

Ellison, Nicole B., Charles Steinfield, and Cliff Lampe. "The Benefits of Facebook 'Friends': Exploring the Relationship between College Students' Use of Online Social Networks and Social Capital." *Journal of Computer-Mediated Communication* 12, issue 3 (2007). http://jcmc.indiana.edu/vol12/issue4/ellison.html.

Faist, Thomas. *The Volume and Dynamics of International Migration and Transnational Social Spaces.* New York: Oxford University Press, 2000.

Feigenbaum, Lee, Ivan Herman, Tonya Hongsermeier, Eric Neumann, and Susie Stephens. "The Semantic Web in Action." *Scientific American* 297 (December 2007): 90–97. http://www.thefigtrees.net/lee/sw/sciam/semantic-web-in-action.

Fox, Nick and Chris Roberts. "GPs in Cyberspace: The Sociology of a 'Virtual Community'." *Sociological Review* 47, no. 4 (November 1999): 643–72.

Fuchs, Christian. "Social Software and Web 2.0: Their Sociological Foundations and Implications." In *Handbook of Research on Web 2.0, 3.0, and X.0: Technologies, Business and Social Applications,* edited by San Murugesa. Hershey, PA: IGI-Global, 2009.

Gajjala, Radhika. "Shifting Frames: Race, Ethnicity, and Intercultural Communication in Online Social Networking and Virtual Work." In *The Role of Communication in Business Transactions and Relationships,* edited by M. B. Hinner. New York: Peter Lang, 2007.

Garton, Laura, Caroline Haythornthwaite, and Barry Wellman. "Studying Online Social Networks." *Journal of Computer-Mediated Communication* 3, no. 1 (1997). http://jcmc.indiana.edu/vol3/issue1/garton.html.

Glick Schiller, Nina, Linda Basch, and Cristina Blanc Szanton. "Transnationalism: A New Analysis Framework for Understanding Migration." *Annals of the New York Academy of Sciences,* 645 (1992): 1–24.

Gobierno Vasco. *Euskaldunak Munduan, Building the Future.* Vitoria-Gasteiz: Servicio Editorial de Publicaciones del Gobierno Vasco, 1996.

Hauben, Michael and Ronda Hauben. *Netizens: On the History and Impact of Usenet and the Internet.* Los Alamitos, CA: IEEE, 1997.

Haythornthwaite, Caroline. "Social Networks and Online Community." In *Oxford Handbook of Internet Psychology,* edited by Adam Joinson, Katelyn McKenna, Ulf-Dietrich Reips, and Tom Postmes. Oxford: Oxford University Press, 2007.

Hiller, Harry H. and Tara M. Franz. "New Ties, Old Ties, and Lost Ties: The Use of the Internet in Diaspora." *New Media & Society* 6, no. 6 (2004): 731–52.

Kearney, Michael. "From the Invisible Hand to Visible Feet: Anthropological Studies of Migration and Development." *Annual Review of Anthropology* 15 (1986): 331–61.

Licklider, Joseph C. R. and Robert Taylor. "The Computer as a Communication Device." *Science and Technology: For the Men in Management*, no. 76 (April 1968): 21–31.

Miller, Daniel, and Don Slater. *The Internet: An Ethnographic Approach*. Oxford: Berg Publishers, 2001.

Oiarzabal, Pedro J. "The Basque Diaspora Webscape: Online Discourses of Basque Diaspora Identity, Nationhood, and Homeland." PhD dissertation, University of Nevada, Reno (2006).

Portes, Alejandro. "Economic Sociology and the Sociology of Immigration: A Conceptual Overview." In *The Economic Sociology of Immigration,* edited by Alejandro Portes. New York: Russell Sage Foundation, 1995.

Scholz, Trebor. "Market Ideology and the Myths of Web 2.0." *First Monday* [Online] 13, no. 3 (March 3, 2008). http://firstmonday.org/htbin/cgiwrap/bin/ojs/index.php/fm/article/view/ 2138/1945.

Thrift, Nigel. *Knowing Capitalism*. London: Sage, 2005.

Tilly, Charles. "Transplanted Networks." In *Immigration Reconsidered: History, Sociology, and Politics,* edited by Virginia Yans-McLaughlin. New York: Oxford University Press, 1990.

Van Dijck, José, and David Nieborg. "Wikinomics and Its Discontents: A Critical Analysis of Web 2.0 Business Manifestos." *New Media & Society* 11, no. 4 (2009): 855–74.

Vertovec, Steven, and Robin Cohen. Introduction to *Migration and Transnationalism,* edited by Steven Vertovec and Robin Cohen. Aldershot: Edward Elgar, 1999.

——, eds. *Migration and Transnationalism*. Aldershot: Edward Elgar, 1999.

Watson, Nessim. "Why We Argue About Virtual Community: A Case Study of the Phish.net Fan Community." In *Virtual Culture: Identity and Communication in Cybersociety,* edited by Steven G. Jones. London: Sage, 1997.

Wellman, Barry. "Structural Analysis: From Method and Metaphor to Theory and Substance." In *Social Structures: A Network Approach*, edited by Barry Wellman and S. D. Berkowitz. Cambridge, Cambridge University Press, 1988.

Wellman, Barry and S. D. Berkowitz, eds. *Social Structures: A Network Approach*. Cambridge, Cambridge University Press, 1988.

Appendix

The Basque Institutional Diaspora Blogosphere between April 2004 and June 2007.

Argentina	Type of Association	URL	Date Established
"Denak Bat" (Centro Vasco Euzko Etxea), La Plata	Cultural (*)	http://fotolog.terra.cl/centrovasco (old) http://www.fotolog.com/denakbat (current)	Dec. 2004– May 2005 Feb. 2007
"Ugarritzak" (Euskaldunak Denak Bat), Arrecifes	Cultural (*)	http://fotolog.terra.com/dantzaris (old) http://www.fotolog.com/edb_ugarritzak (current)	Jan.–July 2005 Jan. 2007
"Eusko Hazi" (Centro Vasco Zingirako Euskaldunak), Chascomús	Cultural (*)	http://fotolog.terra.cl/cvchascomus (old) http://www.fotolog.com/eusko_hazi (current)	Jan.–June 2005 April 2007
"Gazte Alai" (Eusko Etxea), Necochea	Cultural (*)	http://www.fotolog.com/gazte_alai	Sept. 2005
Centro Vasco Gure Txokoa, Suipacha	Euskal Etxea	http://vascosdesuipacha.blogspot.com	Nov. 2005
"Urrundik" (Asociación Vasco-Argentina Urrundik), Paraná	Cultural (*)	http://www.fotolog.com/urrundik	Nov. 2005
"Beti Alai" (Centro Vasco Denak Bat), Mar del Plata	Cultural (*)	http://www.fotolog.com/beti_alai	July 2006
"Denori Alai" (Asociación Vasca Denak Bat), Cañuelas	Cultural (*)	http://www.fotolog.com/denori_alai	July 2006
"Badia Txuria Dantzariak" (Centro Vasco), Bahía Blanca	Cultural (*)	http://www.fotolog.com/badia_txuria	Feb. 2007
"Emakume Abertzale Batza Dantzariak" (Emakume Abertzale Batza), Buenos Aires	Cultural (*)	http://www.fotolog.com/dantzaris_baires	May 2007
Centro Vasco Beti Aurrera, Chivilcoy	Euskal Etxea	http://centrovascochivilcoy.blogspot.com	May 2007
France			
Association des Basques de Montpellier et Languedoc, Montpellier	Euskal Etxea	http://eskualdunak.midiblogs.com (**) (old) http://www.eskualdunak.jimbo.com (current)	2007 Oct. 2008
Spain			
Centre Cultural Euskal Etxea, Barcelona	Euskal Etxea	http://blog.euskaletxeak.org (***)	Jan. 2006

U.S.	Type of Association	URL	Date Established
"Members" Colorado Euskal Etxea, Denver	Euskal Etxea	http://coloradoeuskaletxea.blogspot.com (***) (old) http://ceemember.blogspot.com (current)	April–June 2004 June 2004
"Topagunea" Colorado Euskal Etxea, Denver	Euskal Etxea	http://topagunea.blogspot.com (***)	Oct. 2004
Venezuela			
Centro Vasco de Caracas	Euskal Etxea	http://euskoetxeacaracas.blogspot.com (**)	August 2006

(*) Formal group within a larger association; (**) Replaced website; (***) Additional platform.

The Basque Institutional Diaspora Blogosphere between June 2007 and March 2009.

Argentina	Type of Association	URL	Date Established
"Mendi'ko Dantzariak" (Euzko Etxea), Bariloche, Río Negro	Cultural (*)	http://www.fotolog.com/dantzariak (***)	July 2007
"Goizeko Izarra" (Centro Vasco Lagun Onak), Pergamino	Cultural (*)	http://fotolog.terra.com.ar/cv_pergamino	August 2007
"Dantzariak" (Centro Vasco Gure Ametza), Río Cuarto, Córdoba	Cultural (*)	http://www.fotolog.com/gure_ametza	Nov. 2007
"Euskara Taldea" (Centro Vasco Argentino Gure Txokoa), Córdoba	Cultural (*)	http://euskaraz.blogspot.com	Feb. 2008
Foro de Debate Diáspora Vasca en Argentina	Political	http://forodebatediasporavasca.blogspot.com	March 2008
"Toki Eder Dantzaris" (Centro Vasco Toki Eder), José Paz	Cultural (*)	http://dantzarisdetokieder.blogspot.com	April 2008
Akelarre Eusko-Argentinar Kultur Taldea, Concordia	Cultural	http://akelarreconcordia.blogspot.com	June 2008
Centro Vasco Euskal Etxea, Villa Mercedes	Euskal Etxea	http://centro-vasco.blogspot.com (**)	July 2008
Centro Vasco Ibai'ko Izarra, Concordia	Euskal Etxea	http://vascosconcordia.blogspot.com (***)	Nov. 2008

Colombia	Type of Association	URL	Date Established
Centro de Estudios Vascos en Antioquia (Universidad de Antioquia; also known as Centro de Estudios Vascos de Medellín, Antioquia), Medellín	Educational	http://centroestudiovascoantioquia.blogspot.com (**)	Nov. 2008 July 2009
China			
Euskal Etxea Shanghai	Euskal Etxea	http://www.blog.chinaeuskaletxea.info (***)	Dec. 2007
U.S.			
"Gazteak Dance and Pelota Goma Group" (San Francisco Basque Cultural Center), San Francisco	Cultural (*)	http://etcharren.blogspot.com	Jan. 2009
Uruguay			
Vascos en Salto	Euskal Etxea	http://saltokoeuskaldunentaldea.blogspot.com (**)	July 2008

(*) Formal group within a larger association; (**) Replaced website; (***) Additional platform.

The Basque Institutional Diaspora Social Networkscape between 2007 and 2009.

Argentina	Type of Association	URL	Date Established
"Eusko Etxea La Plata" (Eusko Etxea La Plata), La Plata	Euskal Etxea	http://www.facebook.com/group.php?gid=38128548679 (***) (61 members)	Dec. 2008
"Centro Vasco Loretako Euskaldunak" (Centro Vasco Loretako Euskaldunak), Las Flores	Euskal Etxea	http://www.facebook.com/group.php?gid=46552179069 (126 members)	Jan. 2009
"Centro Vasco de Arrecifes- Euskaldunak Denak Bat" (Centro Vasco de Arrecifes- Euskaldunak Denak Bat), Arrecifes	Euskal Etxea	http://www.facebook.com/group.php?gid=57918159400 (26 members)	Jan. 2009
"Centro Vasco de Córdoba" (Centro Vasco Argentino Gure Txokoa), Córdoba	Euskal Etxea	http://www.facebook.com/group.php?gid=49258940185 (***) (84 members)	Jan. 2009
"Centro Vasco Ibai Guren de Paraná" (Centro Vasco Ibai Guren, Paraná), Paraná	Euskal Etxea	http://www.facebook.com/group.php?gid=49790508674 (***) (18 members)	Feb. 2009

Argentina	**Type of Association**	**URL**	**Date Established**
"Centro Vasco de Mar del Plata" (Centro Vasco Denak Bat), Mar del Plata	Euskal Etxea	http://www.facebook.com/group.php?gid=33137314615 (***) (37 members)	(unknown)
Chile			
"Eusko Etxea Viña-Valparaíso" (Eusko Etxea Valparaíso), Valparaíso	Euskal Etxea	http://www.facebook.com/group.php?gid=22260998653 (***) (99 members)	June 2008
"Euzko Etxea de Santiago" (Euzko Etxea de Santiago), Santiago de Chile	Euskal Etxea	http://www.facebook.com/group.php?gid=49075146984 (***) (239 members: closed group)	Nov. 2008
Colombia			
"Centro Vasco Colombia-Euskal Etxea" (Centro Vasco Colombia), Bogotá	Euskal Etxea	http://www.facebook.com/group.php?gid=5521924286 (***) (45 members: closed group)	(unknown)
Mexico			
"Vascos Jóvenes de México!!" (Vascos de México), Mexico D.F.	Cultural	http://www.facebook.com/group.php?gid=44553586227 (***) (69 members)	Nov. 2008
"Centro Vasco Euskal Etxea México" (Centro Vasco Euskal Etxea México), Mexico D.F.	Euskal Etxea	http://www.facebook.com/group.php?gid=45451673662 (***) (289 members)	Jan. 2009
Spain			
"Euskal Etxea de Mallorca Artea" (Euskal Etxea Artea), Mallorca	Euskal Etxea	http://www.facebook.com/group.php?gid=38368159365 (***) (3 members: closed group)	Dec. 2008
"Equipo de futbol Euskal Etxea Madrid" (Euskal Etxea Madrid), Madrid	Cultural (*)	http://www.facebook.com/group.php?gid=45097841733 (22 members)	Jan. 2009
"Euskaltegi de la Euskal Etxea Madrid/ Madrilgo Euskal Etxeko Euskaltegia" (Euskal Etxea Madrid), Madrid	Cultural (*)	http://www.facebook.com/group.php?gid=50298130871 (14 members)	Jan. 2009
U.K.			
"Euskaldunak Londresen" (London Basque Society), London	Euskal Etxea	http://www.facebook.com/group.php?id=18497354928 (***) (24 members)	Sept. 2007

U.S.	Type of Association	URL	Date Established
"Reno Basque Club" (Reno Basque Club Zazpiak Bat), Reno	Euskal Etxea	http://www.myspace.com/renobasqueclub (***) (160 "friends")	2007
"Basques in DC (Euskaldunak Washington, DC-n)" (Euskal Etxea Washington DC), Washington DC	Euskal Etxea	http://www.facebook.com/group.php?gid=6573709009 (***) (18 members)	August 2007
"Utah'ko Triskalariak" (Basque Club of Utah), Salt Lake City	Cultural (*)	http://www.myspace.com/utahbasco (25 "friends")	2008
"Utah Basque Club" (Utah Basque Club), Salt Lake City	Euskal Etxea	http://www.facebook.com/group.php?gid=52592605867 (***) (39 members)	Nov. 2008
"New Mexico Euskal Etxea" (New Mexico Euskal Etxea), New Mexico	Euskal Etxea	http://www.facebook.com/group.php?gid=32343412968 (***) (20 members)	June 2008
"Oinkari Dantza Taldea" (Oinkari Basque Dancers), Boise	Cultural	http://www.facebook.com/group.php?gid=50210503274 (***) (87 members)	Dec. 2008
"Basques in NY" (New York Basque Club), New York	Euskal Etxea	http://www.facebook.com/group.php?gid=49725110958 (***) (36 members)	Feb. 2009
"Basque Museum & Cultural Center" (Basque Museum & Cultural Center), Boise	Educational	http://www.facebook.com/pages/Boise-ID/Basque-Museum-Cultural-Center/64885564760?ref=s (***) (50 "fans")	Feb. 2009
"Kern County Basque Club" (Kern County Basque Club), Bakersfield	Euskal Etxea	http://www.facebook.com/pages/Bakersfield-CA/Kern-County-Basque-Club/29801739976?ref=mf (***) (200 "fans")	Feb. 2009
"Los Banos Basque Club" (Los Banos Basque Club), Los Banos	Euskal Etxea	http://www.facebook.com/group.php?gid=12743112167 (3 members)	(unknown)
Venezuela			
"Centro Vasco Venezolano de Carabobo" (Centro Vasco de Valencia), Carabobo	Euskal Etxea	http://www.facebook.com/group.php?gid=46853268985 (***) (137 members)	Nov. 2008

(*) Formal group within a larger association; (***) Additional platform.

Basque Institutional Diaspora Video and Photo Hosting Sites between 2007 and 2009.

China	Type of Association	URL/Channel	Date Established
Euskal Etxea Shanghai	Euskal Etxea	http://www.youtube.com/chinaeuskaletxea (number of members unknown) (****) http://www.flickr.com/photos/chinaeuskaletxea (****)	June 2007 July 2008
U.K.			
London Basque Society	Euskal Etxea	http://www.youtube.com/euskaledge (number of members unknown) (****)	August 2007
Argentina			
Akelarre Eusko-Argentinar Kultur Taldea, Concordia	Cultural	http://www.youtube.com/user/AkelarreTV (38 members) (****)	Dec. 2008

(****) Additional applications.

Number and Year of Establishment of New Blogs, New Social Sites, and Additional Platforms between 2004 and 2009.

	2004	2005	2006	2007	2008	2009	TOTAL
New Blogs	1	5	2	5	4	1	18 (36%)
New Social Sites[1]	0	0	0	0	1 (MySpace)	4 (Facebook)	6 (12%) (1 MySpace; 5 Facebook)
Additional Platforms[2]	2 (Blogs)	0	1 (Blog)	5 (2 Blogs; 1 MySpace; 2 Facebook)	10 (1 Blog; 9 Facebook)	6 (Facebook)	26 (52%) (6 Blogs; 1 MySpace; 19 Facebook)
TOTAL	3 (6%) (Blogs)	5 (10%) (Blogs)	3 (6%) (Blogs)	10 (20%) (7 Blogs; 1 MySpace; 2 Facebook)	15 (30%) (5 Blogs; 9 Facebook; 1 MySpace)	11 (22%) (1 Blog; 10 Facebook)	50 (100%) (24 Blogs; 24 Facebook; 2 MySpace)

[1] New Social Sites include all social sites besides blogs. The date of creation of one site is unknown.

[2] The date of creation of two Additional Platforms is unknown.

Basque Institutional Diaspora Offline and Online as of December 2005, June 2007, and March 2009.

	December 2005	June 2007	March 2009
BASQUE INSTITUTIONAL DIASPORA	**Total Associations:** 189 (100%) **Total Countries:** 22 (100%)	**Total Associations:** 198 (100%) **Total Countries:** 24 (100%)	**Total Associations:** 211 (100%) **Total Countries:** 24 (100%)
Associations: • Online o Registered o Unregistered • Offline Registered	**98 (51.85%)** 63 (33.3%) 35 (18.51%) **91 (48.14%)**	**123 (62.12%)** 86 (43.43%) 37 (18.27%) **75 (37.87%)**	**135 (63.98%)** 89 (41.18%) 46 (21.8%) **76 (36.01%)**
Additional Online Platforms:	0	4	22
TOTAL ONLINE PLATFORMS:	98	127	157
Countries: • Online o Registered o Unregistered • Offline Registered	**16 (72.72%)** 14 (63.63%) 2 (9.09%)[1] 6 (27.27%)[2]	**19 (79.1%)** 16 (66.66%) 3 (12.5%)[3] 5 (20.83%)[4]	**20 (83.3%)** 18 (75%) 2 (8.3%)[5] 4 (16.6%)[6]
TOTAL ONLINE COUNTRIES:	16	19	20

[1] Two associations from Germany and Switzerland with a presence on the Web were not registered with the Basque government.

[2] Basque diaspora associations from Brazil, Colombia, El Salvador, Paraguay, Puerto Rico, and the Dominican Republic, registered with the Basque government, did not have an institutional presence online.

[3] Three associations from China, Germany, and Switzerland with a presence on the Web were not registered with the Basque government.

[4] Basque diaspora associations from Cuba, El Salvador, Paraguay, Puerto Rico, and the Dominican Republic, registered with the Basque government, did not have an institutional presence online.

[5] Three associations from China, Germany, and Switzerland with a presence on the Web were not registered with the Basque government.

[6] Basque diaspora associations from Cuba, El Salvador, Paraguay, and the Dominican Republic, registered with the Basque government, did not have an institutional presence online.

Index

Contributors

Andoni Alonso is an Associate Professor at the University of Extremadura, Campus of Cáceres, Spain. He has earned philosophy degrees from the University of the Basque Country (PhD) and from the University of Navarre, Spain (BA). He was a Research Fellow at Penn State University from 1996 to 1998, where he worked closely with Carl Mitcham and Ivan Illich, as well as a Visiting Scholar at the University of Nevada, Reno, from 2003–04. Alonso's main interests include philosophy of technology, with particular emphasis on new technologies of information and communication. Currently, his research focuses on free software and knowledge and how these topics relate to political and communitarian movements that utilize the Internet. Alonso has published papers in the journals *Technology and Culture, Argumentos de razón técnica, Isis,* and *Isegoría.* His most recent publications include *Basque Cyberculture: From Digital Euskadi to CyberEuskalherria* (with Iñaki Arzoz; Center for Basque Studies, University of Nevada, Reno, 2001), *La nueva ciudad de dios* (Siruela, 2002), *Carta al homo ciberneticus* (with Iñaki Arzoz; Edaf, 2003), *La quinta columna digital* (with Iñaki Arzoz; Gedisa, 2005. They received the 2004 Epson Foundation Award for this book), and *Diasporas in the New Media Age: Identity, Politics, and Community* (with Pedro J. Oiarzabal; University of Nevada Press, Reno, Nevada, 2010).

Javier Echeverría is the "Ikerbasque" (Basque Foundation for Science) Research Professor at the University of the Basque Country, Bilbao, Spain, and in 2008–09 was the William A. Douglass Distinguished Visiting Scholar at the Center for Basque Studies, University of Nevada, Reno. In addition, he leads a research project at the Institute of Philosophy, Spanish National Scientific Research Council (CSIC, Madrid, Spain). He holds degrees in philosophy and mathematics as well as a PhD in philosophy (1975) from the Universidad Complutense, Madrid. In 1980, he obtained the title of Docteur d'Etat-ès Lettres et Sciences Humaines from the Université Paris I (Panthéon-Sorbonne, Paris, France). Echeverría has conducted research in academic centers in Paris, Brussels, Hannover (Germany), and Urbana-Champaign, Illinois. He has been a Professor at the University of the Basque Country and a Research Professor of Science, Technology and Society at the Philosophy Institute, CSIC. Echeverría has served as Vice-President of the Spanish Society of the History of Sciences (1983–85), President of the Basque Association of Semiotics (1989–92), President of the Society of Logic, Methodology and Philosophy of Science, in Spain (1993–2000), and member of the Executive Council of the Spanish Foundation of Science and Technology (FECYT, 2002–05). He is also a member of the

International Academy of the Philosophy of Science. He won the 1997 Euskadi Research Prize in the area of Humanities and Social Sciences, awarded by the Basque Government for lifelong research work. He also obtained the Spanish prizes Premio Anagrama de Ensayo in 1995 for the essay *Cosmopolitas domésticos* and the Premio Nacional de Ensayo in 2000, which was granted by the Spanish Ministry of Culture for the essay *Los señores del aire*. Major research areas of interest include philosophy of science and technology, axiology of science, science, technology and society studies, new technologies of information and communication, and Leibniz. Among his publications are *Telépolis* (Destino, 1994), *Cosmopolitas Domésticos* (Anagrama, 1995), *Los señores del aire: Telépolis y el tercer entorno* (Destino, 1999), *Introducción a la metodología de la ciencia: la filosofía de la ciencia en el siglo XX* (Cátedra, 1999), *Ciencia y valores* (Destino, 2002), *La revolución tecnocientífica* (Fondo de Cultura Económica, 2003), and *Ciencia del bien y el mal* (Herder, 2007). Echeverría has also edited the book *Gobernar los riesgos: ciencia y valores en la sociedad del riesgo* (with J. L. Luján; OEI-Biblioteca Nueva, 2004).

Ibon Galarraga is a Researcher at the Basque Center for Climate Change. He holds a PhD in economics (environmental economics) from the University of Bath, UK, an MA in economics from the University of Essex, UK, and a BA in economics (international economics and development) from the University of the Basque Country. He has worked as an environmental consultant for many years for both public and private institutions such as the World Bank, the Department for International Development of the British Government, and the Basque Government. More specifically, from July 2005 to May 2009, Galarraga was the Deputy Minister of the Environment of the Basque Government, where he was in charge of the preparation of the Environmental Framework Program 2007–10, the Basque Plan to Combat Climate Change 2008–12, and the Contaminated Soil Plan 2007–12. In addition, between 2005 and 2008 he was Deputy Co-Chair of the Network of Regional Governments on Sustainable Development (nrg4sd) and has actively participated in the Conference of the Parties 11, 12, 13, and 14. Finally, he taught microeconomics and macroeconomics at the University of Bath and economic policy at the University of Deusto. He has several publications in the field of environmental economics in journals such as *European Environment, Fiscal Studies, Economía Agraria y Recursos Naturales*, and *Papeles de Economía Española*.

Mari Carmen Gallastegui is a Professor of Economic Theory at the Department of Economic Analysis I in the Faculty of Economics and Business Administration of the University of the Basque Country. She is in charge of the Environmental Economics Unit at the Institute of Public Economics, University of the Basque Country. She earned degrees in economy from Brown University, US (PhD), London School of Economics, UK (MSc), and the University of Valladolid, Spain (BA). She served as Minister of Economy and Planning in the Basque Government (1991), Vice-Chancellor of the University of the Basque Country (1987), and Director of the Department of Economic Theory as well as of the Institute of Public Economics. She has worked in the area of environmental and natural resource economics and has been involved in research projects financed by the Ministry of Technology and Science of Spain, the Department of Education and Research of the Basque Government, the University of the Basque Country, and the European Union. Her research has also focused on public economics. She holds the National Award on Economy and Environment (2005) from the Ministry of the Environment (Spain), and the Euskadi Research Prize, awarded by the Basque Government (2006). Gallastegui is the author of over fifty publications. Major publications include "Case Study Presentation: Pontevedra Economic Presentation, PECHDEV. Case Study Presentation N. 3," in P. Failler et al. (eds.) *Assessment Method Reviews* (2003)*; Economics, Ecology and Biological Frameworks, Regional expectancies, Case study Presentations, PECHDEV REPORT N. 1.* Project funded by the European Union (EU QLRT-2000-002277), CEMARE, University of Porsthmouth, UK (with J. Fernández, P. González, and A. Murillas); "Una revisión de la política ambiental: Perspectiva económica," *Economistas* (2003)*;* "Bankruptcy of Fishing Resources: The Northern European Anglerfish Fishery," *Marine Resource Economics* (with Elena Iñarra and Raúl Prellezo, 2003), and "La economía vasca: Una panorámica sectorial y temporal," *Hrvatska Revijá* (2002).

Anna María Guasch is a Professor of Art History and Art Criticism at the University of Barcelona (Spain). She holds a PhD in contemporary art history from the University Hispalense of Seville (Spain), and a BA in geography and history (specialty in art history) from the University of Barcelona. She is the editor of the contemporary art series *Akal/arte contemporáneo* (Madrid). Among her recent publications are *El arte del siglo XX en sus exposiciones: 1945–1995* (Serbal, 1997), *El arte último del siglo XX. Del postminimalismo a lo multicultural: 1968–1995* (Alianza, 2000), *Arte y globalización* (Universidad Nacional de Colombia, 2004), and *Autobiografías visuales: Del archivo al índice* (Siruela, 2009). She is editor of *Los manifiestos del arte posmoderno. Textos de exposiciones 1980–1995* (Akal, 2000), *Learning from the Bilbao Guggenheim* (with Joseba Zulaika; Center for Basque Studies, UNR, 2005), and *La crítica dialogada. Entrevistas de arte y pensamiento* (Fundacio ESPAIS, 2007) as well as co-author of *Crítica de arte: Historia, teoría y praxis* (Serbal, 2003). She has been awarded the Espais Prize for Art Criticism (1998, 2007) and the ACCA Prize for Art Criticism (2001). She has also received a research grant by the Getty Research Institute, Los Angeles (2003).

Ander Gurrutxaga is a Professor at the Department of Sociology II, University of the Basque Country, Campus of Leioa (Spain). He has held various administrative positions in the University of the Basque Country as well as in the Ministry of Education of the Basque Government. Currently, he is a member of the University of the Basque Country's Commission of Experts on the Reform of Bologna. Gurrutxaga is also a member of the editorial boards of four scientific journals, and is responsible for the Social Sciences Series of the University of the Basque Country Press. For the last ten years, he has lead fifteen research projects dealing with the following three main areas: the sociology of innovation; government and new forms of government and social change; and complexity and innovation. Additionally, for the last five years he has organized two international symposia on Social Change, and Government and Innovation in the Knowledge Society. Gurrutxaga has been a Professor and Visiting Research Scholar at the American universities of Berkeley, Santa Barbara, and San Diego in California, and in Reno, Nevada, as well as the University of Tel Aviv and Hebrew University in Jerusalem. He has published twelve books, over fifty articles, and has co-authored another fifteen manuscripts. His latest publications include *El presente del estado-nación* (UPV, 2004), *Retratos del presente* (UPV, 2006), *La responsabilidad social corporativa en el País Vasco* (Paradox, 2005), *La conciencia del nosotros* (Vitoria, 2005), *Crisis de occidente y modernizaciones posibles* (Abada, 2006), and *¿Es posible innovar?* (San Sebastián, 2006).

Caroline Haythornthwaite is a Professor at the Graduate School of Library and Information Science, University of Illinois at Urbana-Champaign, and in 2009–10 was Leverhulme Trust Visiting Professor at the Institute of Education, University of London. She has an international reputation in Internet research and e-learning, with particular emphasis on how information and knowledge are shared through social networks, and the impact of computer media and the Internet on work, learning, and social interaction. Empirical and theoretical work has addressed social networks of work and media use, the development and nature of community online, distributed knowledge processes, interdisciplinary collaboration, the transformative effects of the Internet on learning and collaborative practices, and automated approaches to evaluation of online communication. Major publications include *The Internet in Everyday Life* (with Barry Wellman; Blackwell, 2002), *Learning, Culture and Community in Online Education: Research and Practice* (with Michelle M. Kazmer; Peter Lang, 2004), *The Handbook of E-learning Research* (with Richard Andrews; Sage, 2007), and *E-learning Theory and Practice* (with Richard Andrews; Sage, 2011).

Christopher Kelty is an Associate Professor at the University of California, Los Angeles and has a joint appointment in the Center for Society and Genetics and in the Department of Information Studies. His research focuses on the cultural significance of information technology, especially in science and engineering. He is the author most recently of *Two Bits: The Cultural Significance of Free Software* (Duke University Press, 2008), as well as numerous articles on open source and free software (including its impact on education), nanotechnology, the life sciences, and issues of peer review and research process in the sciences and in the humanities. He is trained in science studies (history and anthropology) and has also written about methodological issues facing anthropology today. Current projects include an ethnographic study of research in nanotechnology, which focuses on new formulations of responsibility in the study of the environmental and biological implications of new materials; an ongoing historical/media theoretical investigation of the development of computer science, and in particular the development of "logical instruments" such as regular expressions and l-systems; a project on the history of "grey literature" in the life sciences, in particular newsletters and forms of cooperation/coordination around model organisms like the Drosophila Information Service; and sporadic attempts to help facilitate "radical public engagement" in science through exploring how the ideas of free and open Source software are taken up in biology, nanotechnology, and design.

Antonio Lafuente holds a PhD in physics from the University of Barcelona (Spain) and is a Scientific Researcher at the Institute of History, Spanish National Scientific Research Council (CSIC, Madrid, Spain) since 1987. He was a Visiting Scholar at the University of California, Berkeley, from 1989 to 1990. Lafuente has worked on the expansion of science during the Hispanic Colonial era and on the relation of science to the public and laymen's knowledge. His most recent research is about the relationship between technology and the commons, as well as the links between old and new heritage. His interest in the commons led him to the study of problems related to the expansion of intellectual property rights in science, in addition to the analysis of the implications of the concepts of governance, open knowledge, participation, technical democracy, biz science, and scientific culture. Some of his latest papers have been published in the journals *Osiris, Social Studies of Science, Claves de razón práctica, Revista de libros,* and *Archipiélago.* Major publications include *Los públicos de la ciencia en España, siglos XVIII a XX* (with Tiago Saraiva; FECYT, 2002), *Los mundos de la ciencia en la ilustración española* (with Nuria Valverde; FECYT, 2003), and *El carnaval de la tecnociencia* (Gadir, 2007).

Álvaro Luna holds a BA in sociology, a Diploma in advanced studies, and a Master's degree in innovation and knowledge management from the University of the Basque Country. He is currently conducting his PhD dissertation on social innovation and social change under the supervision of Ander Gurrutxaga at the University of the Basque Country. He has participated in the research project "Risk and Climate Change in the Basque Society," and collaborates on other projects with the University of the Basque Country's research group "Change, Complexity and Innovation."

Marcelino Masa is a Researcher at the Department of Sociology II, Faculty of Social Sciences and Communication, University of the Basque Country, Campus of Leioa (Spain), and Coordinator of the Master's in Innovation and Knowledge Management at the University of the Basque Country. He holds a PhD in political science and sociology from the University of the Basque Country. For the last ten years, he has been a Project Manager in a sociological and market studies company. His research deals with education, corporate social responsibility, public/private dichotomy, sociology of consumption, employment, conciliation of work and family life, and social innovation. Among his recent publications are *Space and Sociality: An Analysis on Sub-metropolitan Kitchen Gardens in the Bilbao Suburb of Bolueta* (1996), *From A Private/Public Arrhythmia: Housing, Family and Young*

Generations (1997), *Families and Social Policies* (2000), *Before Politics: The Structuring of Daily Life in the Basque Country* (2000), *Diagnosis of the Basque Public University System* (2001), *Violence Against Women in Domestic Settings: Results of an Investigation Carried Out in Bizkaia* (2006), and *The Consequences of Care. Strategies of Conciliation in Daily Life between Men and Women in the Basque Country* (2007).

Carl Mitcham is a Professor of Liberal Arts and International Studies, Colorado School of Mines, Golden, Colorado. Additionally, he is a Faculty Affiliate of the Center for Science and Technology Policy Research, University of Colorado, Boulder, and Adjunct Professor at the European Graduate School, Saas Fee, Switzerland. He earned degrees from the University of Colorado (BA, MA) and Fordham University (PhD) and has held faculty appointments previously at Berea College (Kentucky), St. Catharine College (Kentucky), Brooklyn Polytechnic University, and Pennsylvania State University. He has also served in visiting positions at the Universidad de Puerto Rico, Mayagüez (1988), University of Oviedo, Spain (1993), the Universities of Tilburg and Twente, Netherlands (1998), and as Fulbright Professor at the University of the Basque Country, Spain (2003–04). Mitcham has worked to promote ethical reflection on technology in positions at Brooklyn Polytechnic University (1982–90), Pennsylvania State University (1989–99), and Colorado School of Mines (1999–present). Among his recent publications is a four-volume *Encyclopedia of Science, Technology, and Ethics* (Macmillan Reference, 2005), for which he served as editor-in-chief. He is awaiting the publication of *Technology and Religion: Oppositions, Sympathies, Transformations* (Greenwood Press), and *Science, Technology, and Ethics: An Introduction* (Cambridge University Press).

Pedro J. Oiarzabal is a Research Scholar at the International Migration Research Unit, University of Deusto, Bilbao. He was a Visiting Research Scholar at the University of Nevada, Reno, between 2007 and 2009. He holds a PhD in Basque Studies-Political Science from the University of Nevada, Reno, a MPhil in Economics and Social Sciences from Queen's University of Belfast (N. Ireland), and BA in History from the University of Deusto. His research examines diaspora creation and diaspora interaction with information and communication technologies as well as the meaning of identity in both homeland and diaspora realities, with a particular emphasis on the Basque case. Among his publications are *La identidad vasca en el mundo* (with Agustín M. Oiarzabal; Erroteta, 2005), *A Candle in the Night: Basque Studies at the University of Nevada, 1967–2007* (UNOHP, 2007), *Gardeners of Identity: Basques in the San Francisco Bay Area* (Basque Government, 1st edition, 2009; Center for Basque Studies, UNR, 2nd Edition, 2009), and *Diasporas in the New Media Age: Identity, Politics, and Community* (with Andoni Alonso; University of Nevada Press, Reno, Nevada, 2010).

Natxo Rodríguez holds a PhD in fine arts and is a Professor at the University of the Basque Country since 2000. Since 1994 he has participated in the Rodríguez Foundation

Art Collective, which has organized and coordinated several projects, mainly related to contemporary culture and new media, understood as an extension of his artistic work, through experimental projects such as "TV Interventions" (1999–2010), "Art and Electricity" (2000–04), "Web-Side 1.0" (2003–04), "TESTER" (2004–06), and "Structures, Networks and Collectives. A Connective Segment" (2007). Some of Rodríguez's work has been published on DVDs, CD-ROMs, the Web, and in books such as *TESTER, Nodes at Work* (2006), *Structures, Networks and Collectives. A Connective Segment* (2007), and *Control Panel, Critical Switches for a Surveillance Society* (2007). The Rodríguez Foundation has presented its work in international forums in Bilbao, Beijing, Barcelona, Graz, Helsinki, Lima, Madrid, Mexico D.F., Nagoya, Rio de Janeiro, Salamanca, San Sebastián, Seville, Shanghai, Stockholm, and Tallinn. Rodríguez was a member of SEAC (Selection of Basque Conceptual Art) from 1994 to its dissolution in 1998. Until 2008 he was a member of the editorial board of Arteleku.net and the weblog "Laburrak," on digital culture. He has been a member of the organizing committee of the "Copyleft Conference" (Arteleku, San Sebastián, 2005) and administrator of the discussion list "Art/Copyleft." He has also been a member of various organizing committees of conferences and seminars at the Faculty of Fine Arts, University of the Basque Country, Leioa: "AKME. Arte, kultura eta medio berriak" (2006), "Punk 77+30. Relations between Punk and Art" (2007), "Freeweek. Seminars on Free Culture" (2007, 2008), and "AKME 2008. Trash Culture" (2008).

Peter Selz is a Professor Emeritus of Art History at the University of California, Berkeley, where he taught for over two decades. He earned a PhD degree from the University of Chicago in 1954 with a dissertation on German Expressionism. He taught at the Institute of Design in Chicago, and at Pomona College in Claremont. Selz was appointed Chief Curator of Painting and Sculpture at the Museum of Modern Art, New York, in 1958, where he sponsored Jean Tinguely, "Homage to New York" in 1960. He was also a Founding Director of the University of California, Berkeley Art Museum between 1965 and 1973, where he curated the pioneering exhibition, "Directions of Kinetic Sculpture" in 1966. Selz has authored fifteen books, from *German Expressionist Painting* (University of California Press, 1957) to *The Art of Engagement: Visual Politics in California and Beyond* (University of California Press, 2006), and numerous reviews and articles on twentieth-century art.

Alfonso Unceta holds a PhD degree in political science and sociology from the University of the Basque Country. Currently, he is the Dean of the Faculty of Social Sciences and Communication at the University of the Basque Country, Campus of Leioa, and Director of the Master's degree in Innovation and Knowledge Management at the University of the Basque Country. Earlier, he was Joint Secretary of Education as well as Director of Universities of the Basque Government. He has received the 6th Euskoiker Research Award (Section of Humanities and Social Sciences, 2004), and the Jesús María Leizaola

Research Award (2004). Unceta's research focuses on education, corporate social responsibility, social innovation, social change, and social structure. Among his publications are *The Challenges of Education Facing the Processes of Social, Cultural and Political Transformation at the End of the 20th Century* (2000), *Approximation to Public and Private Dimensions in the Non-university Educational System in the Basque Country* (2001), *Vocational Education and Training in Autonomous Communities. The Peculiarity of the Basque Model* (2003), *Social Corporate Responsibility in the Basque Country* (2005), *Social Corporate Responsibility in Small and Medium-Sized Companies in Bizkaia* (2005), and *Towards a Compared History of Innovation: Change, Complexity and Globalisation* (2006).

Joseba Zulaika is Professor and Co-Director of the Center for Basque Studies at the University of Nevada, Reno. He received his undergraduate degree in philosophy at the University of Deusto, Bilbao (Spain), his Master's in Social Anthropology at Memorial University of Newfoundland, Canada, and earned his PhD in Cultural Anthropology from Princeton University. He has conducted fieldwork and published ethnographies of deep-sea fishermen, farmers, soldiers, terrorists, hunters, and artists. Zulaika's research involves the study of the role of art and museums in urban regeneration and cultural change. He is currently writing an ethnographic study of the city of Bilbao. He has authored and edited over twenty-five books and nearly one hundred articles, including book chapters. Among Zulaika's publications are *Tratado estético-ritual vasco* (Baroja, 1987); *Basque Violence: Metaphor and Sacrament* (University of Nevada Press, 1988), *Terror and Taboo: The Follies, Fables and Faces of Terrorism* (with William A. Douglass; Routledge, 1996), *Crónica de una seducción: El Museo Bilbao-Guggenheim* (Nerea, 1997), *Basque Culture: Anthropological Perspectives* (with William A. Douglass; Center for Basque Studies, UNR, 2007), and *Terrorism: The Self-Fulfilling Prophecy* (Chicago University Press, 2009).